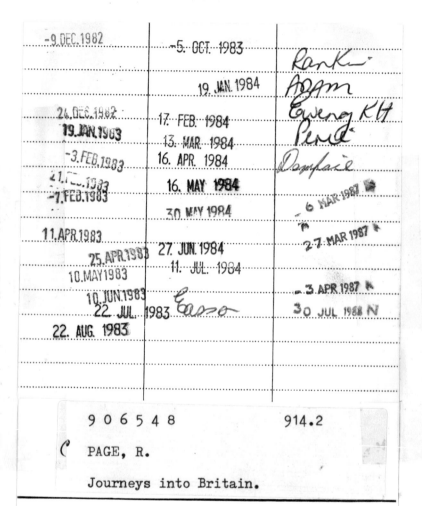

-9. DEC. 1982   -5. OCT. 1983   Rankin

                   19. JAN. 1984   ADAM

24. DEC. 1982   17. FEB. 1984   Eweng KH
19. JAN. 1983   13. MAR. 1984   Pere
-3. FEB. 1983   16. APR. 1984   Dunfaie
-7. FEB. 1983   16. MAY 1984
                   30 MAY 1984   -6 MAR 1987

11. APR. 1983   27. MAR 1987
25. APR. 1983   27. JUN. 1984
10. MAY 1983   11. JUL. 1984
10. JUN. 1983   -3. APR. 1987
22. JUL. 1983   Esso   30 JUL 1988
22. AUG. 1983

This book is due for return on or before the last date indicated
on label or transaction card. Renewals may be obtained on
application. Loss of transaction cards will be charged at 10p. each.

Loss of Reader's tickets will be charged at 25p. for Plastic Type.
10p. for Manilla Type.

Journeys into Britain

Journeys into Britain

Robin Page

Illustrations by Fiona Silver

HODDER AND STOUGHTON
LONDON SYDNEY AUCKLAND TORONTO

7906548

914.2

British Library Cataloguing in Publication Data
Page, Robin
    Journeys into Britain
    1. Country life—Great Britain
    2. Great Britain—Description and travel—1971–
    I. Title
    914.1'04858   DA11
    ISBN 0 340 26327 X

Printed in Great Britain for Hodder and Stoughton Limited, Mill Road, Dunton Green, Sevenoaks, Kent by St Edmundsbury Press, Bury St Edmunds, Suffolk. Photoset by Rowland Phototypesetting Limited, Bury St Edmunds, Suffolk.
Hodder and Stoughton Editorial Office: 47 Bedford Square, London WC1B 3DP.

To "Pack" Odams, although from an earlier generation, for the memory of his friendship, encouragement and humour.

Introduction

In spite of hard trying, man has not yet succeeded in doing his dirt everywhere. The earth is so vast and still so empty that even in the filthy heart of civilisation you find fields where the grass is green instead of grey; perhaps if you looked for them you might even find streams with live fish in them instead of salmon tins.

George Orwell, *The Road to Wigan Pier* (1937)

In conversation with a friend it was suggested that I should retrace the journeys of William Cobbett or Daniel Defoe, on a horse. At first I thought it was an attractive, romantic proposition, conjuring up images of wayside inns, the timelessness of hot summer days and the sheer pleasure of travelling through the countryside on horseback. On reflection, however, would this accurately show the realities of a changing as well as a living countryside in the last quarter of the twentieth century?

It would also have been possible to produce a chronicle of despair showing how in Britain at least, civilisation has succeeded in despoiling or polluting most of the land. Since Orwell's time the erosion of the countryside has accelerated and man has managed to spread his dirt and destruction almost everywhere. But would this have been the whole truth, presented the real dilemmas, or portrayed the genuine beauty that can still be found?

Instead I decided to make a number of modern journeys from my Cambridgeshire village, to describe the areas I saw and the people I met, in the hope that they would show rural Britain as it is, in order to entertain and to inform, as well as to sound a number of warnings. I also decided to use a contemporary form of transport; in 1826 William Cobbett wrote: "There is no pleasure in travelling, except on horseback, or on foot. Carriages take your body from place to place; and if you merely want to be conveyed, they are very good; but they

7

enable you to see and know nothing at all of the country." To a certain extent he is still right, for there is no great joy in travelling by car along miles of featureless motorway. Nevertheless, modern travel has its advantages, for it is fast and simple, and it allows the discerning traveller to gain a more complete view of the country than ever before. In fact that is another aim of the book; to make people more aware of what they can still see and enjoy around them.

The journeys, all of which started from Cambridgeshire, were made over three summers, despite my being hemmed in by work on our small family farm, by visits to Africa, and by other writing. As a result of bad weather or lack of time, some were even accomplished in stages – another advantage of modern travel. At times my paths and experiences crossed those of earlier writers, and in places I have quoted from Cobbett, Defoe, Thomas Bewick, John Clare, Gilbert White and Richard Jefferies, to provide links with the past and to emphasise the threats to the present.

My travels took me to places of wild, remote beauty, as well as to areas of overcrowded urban sprawl, and I met a wide range of people; some showed character and kindness, having managed to resist the conforming pressures from our increasingly organised corporate society; others were "processed", unaware, uncaring and unconcerned.

I travelled as far south as Laughter Hole Farm on Dartmoor, and north to the Shetland Islands, as well as to the east and west coasts. From all the journeys a number of options clearly emerged: we can have wildflowers or prairie farms; birds of prey or poisoned carcasses; marshes and clear-flowing streams, or drainage schemes and industrial waste; sea birds or off-shore oil; less energy or nuclear power; individuality or conditioned urban living; simple aesthetic pleasures or "progress" and material possessions. With care the options can be mixed, but the choices are ours and there is little time left in which to make them.

Contents

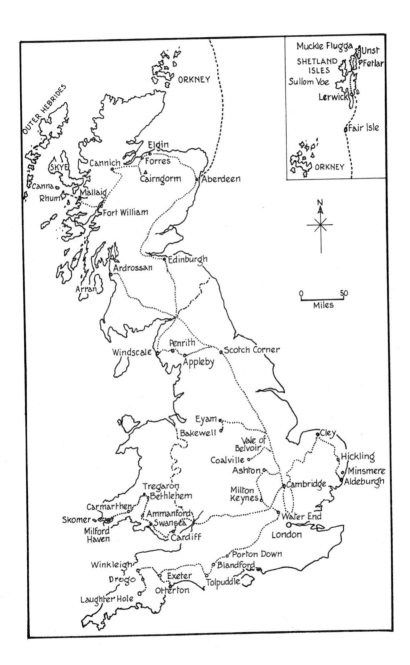

I

Castles and Coalfields

The comparison between scattered farms and villages growing from a patchwork of fields and hedgerows, and sprawling
slag heaps surrounded by housing estates and roads, vividly
reflects the two revolutions that have created the British
landscape: the "agrarian" and the "industrial". A third revolution, the "technological" is now well under way, and by
transforming both industry and agriculture, as well as freeing
people from work, the future changes and pressures on both
man and his environment could soon become greater than
anything that has gone before.

During the Industrial Revolution the demands of industry
sucked rural people away from country areas, leading to
urbanisation and industrialisation that disfigured the land. At
the same time enclosure gave farming a visual pattern that in
many places survives today; the English Midlands is one
region where the two areas still exist side by side. To some it
forms the industrial heartland of Britain; a densely populated
area of development based on mining and manufacturing,
with factories, estates and people. But travelling eastwards
there is a sudden change, with rows of old terraced housing,
and the large new "open plan" estates, giving way to farmland
of fields and villages; it becomes the country of the shires, a
complete contrast to what has gone before.

It is in part of this region that the Vale of Belvoir lies; an area
that, although close to industry, has managed to avoid the
ravages of the Industrial Revolution. By so doing it has
retained the spirit and the traditions of rural life, and change
has been leisurely and linked to agriculture. To the south the
vale is attractive and undulating, with both mixed farming and
arable fields, while to the north it is flat clayland, intensively

The scarp

farmed. The two halves are separated by a steep, meandering escarpment, where the network of hedges, fields and copses can be seen mapped out for many miles. This is famous hunting country, and in the nineteenth century sportsmen used its market town of Melton Mowbray as a centre from which to ride with the Cottesmore, the Quorn, and the Belvoir hunts. To the north, the area is dominated by Belvoir Castle, high up on the escarpment, the seat of the Dukes of Rutland – no wonder the name Belvoir means "beautiful view".

The region is still predominantly rural, with names such as Long Clawson, Waltham on the Wolds and Woolsthorpe emphasising its country character and its past. It is quiet; in places pastoral. Flowers are still allowed to grow on the roadside verges and birdsong can be heard without the background whine of internal combustion. Surprisingly too the Vale is the main area in Britain for the production of Stilton cheese, its fine herds of local Friesian cattle supplying all the milk.

Appearances are deceptive, however, and belated change could overtake and swamp the peace and tranquillity, for beneath the Vale the National Coal Board has found coal. Developed industrial nations need energy, and the ninety-six square miles of the Vale could be the source of an estimated 510 million dormant tons of it. The National Coal Board, with the support of the National Union of Mineworkers, wants to open three mines, at the villages of Asfordby, Hose, and Saltby, yielding about 7.2 millions tons of coal annually. With the political pressure to "create jobs", and some miners demanding immediate action to mine the Vale, a change of government, or attitude, could mean maximum production within fifteen years of any work starting.

At least 2,000 acres would be needed for the mines and the waste tips, with 2.72 million tons of spoil to dispose of each year. The development would require larger roads, the reopening of railway lines, and the use of "roundabout" trains. In addition nearly 4,000 miners would, with their families, increase the Vale's population by at least 12,000, and would demand houses, schools and urban amenities. The Coal Board argues that the proposed development would not destroy the nature of the Vale, and the National Union of Mineworkers claims that the mining community would mix readily and easily into the villages and countryside of East Leicestershire. They both state that, at a time of energy crisis, the coal of the Vale of Belvoir must be mined in the national interest.

Most of the local people disagree. They are proud of their past, content with the present, and consider that the energy requirements of the future should be linked to the technology of the twentieth century and not to the methods and mentalities of a bygone industrial age. It is a confrontation between two vital interests: those who produce food, and those who dig out coal. George Orwell wrote: "In the metabolism of the Western world, the coalminer is second in importance only to the man who ploughs the soil; he is a sort of grimy caryatid upon whose shoulders nearly everything that is not grimy is supported." Since then circumstances have changed; food mountains have developed and the energy crisis has arrived and will not go away. As a result, although most people would find it difficult to eat coal, fried or braised, the miner has replaced the farmworker as the most important producer on whom the rest of society depends, and, what is more, he has the organisation and the industrial strength to prove his point.

On account of the conflicting views and emotions, a public enquiry was arranged to hear the arguments from both sides, and by coincidence, among the protagonists were Lord

Colville for the Coal Board, and Dr. Coleman against. Public enquiries, however, are largely irrelevant, nothing more than expensive and lengthy public relations exercises, aimed at giving ordinary people the feeling of participation, and democracy. In practice, most governments tend to ignore the findings, preferring to make their judgments on purely economic, populist and political grounds; in addition, enquiries tend to deal with facts, figures and hypothetical arguments, rather than the feelings of local people and the character of the places concerned.

During the summer in which the Belvoir Enquiry started, I drove up to the area, to see both the Vale and the nearby South Leicestershire coalfield. After an hour of motorway driving I approached the castle through the villages of Denton and Woolsthorpe. With its towers and turrets it is a most impressive building on a wooded hill, dominating the whole area. Inside, military relics, art treasures, and furnishings of opulence and taste vie with a "Beer Cellar", signposted for eager tourists to follow. It is not, however, a bar selling alcohol, but a genuine cellar where beer was once stored; their disappointment creates much free entertainment. The Duke and Duchess still live in the castle, but because of the financial burdens of owning a stately home, they have to open their doors each summer to 90,000 visitors. As I arrived a rowdy family was playing rounders, shouting and screaming among the statues and rose gardens.

The Duke's estate covers 15,000 acres, fourteen parishes and one-third of the coalfield. It is run from a small, old-fashioned office by a farm manager, whose genuine concern showed through his monotonous public-school accent. He smoked continuously as we spoke, as if he was already preparing himself for the advent of industrial fug. His offices were in old stone buildings to the side of the castle, which once included a brewery, stables, and workers' houses. Nearby, the ancient circular riding school is still used by the Duchess for her Arab horses. The farm manager considered that mining and the accompanying subsidence would create numerous difficulties for all farmers, hence his involvement in the efforts of the Vale of Belvoir Protection Group, the Vale of Belvoir Parish

Councils' Committee and the National Farmers' Union, for a united front to defend the area.

The estate is made up of low-lying clays which are good for cows, wheat and rape, and the escarpment land where "Cotswold farming" takes place, producing barley, roots and sheep. Foresters and gamekeepers are employed by the estate in addition to the farmworkers. One old gamekeeper, happy in his retirement, wanders the fields and breeds prize-winning smooth-coated retrievers. A keeper on the estate for twenty years, he hoped that mining would never reach the Vale: "I like the Duke and would not have worked for anybody else; this set-up's not feudal, he's just a good employer. He looks after me better than the government would. We've got the best shoot in the Midlands and in addition we've got buzzards, several badgers, and the odd fallow deer passes through." He was proud of the area too: "I love Stilton, we eat it as ordinary cheese here. But you should not scoop out the middle and pour in port as people do who don't know any better. They drown the cheese; it's a waste of good cheese and a waste of good port."

Away from the farm buildings mature trees and a large walled garden seemed to reflect more benevolent and contented times. The baying of hounds heralded the arrival of the Belvoir hunt: "fifty-four couple" (108 hounds) that were being exercised around the estate, in preparation for the approaching season. They were a fine sight, with some of the younger puppies linked to more mature dogs, to encourage good behaviour. When the huntsman stopped to pass the time of day the hounds found numerous nasal delights to occupy them in the shade. Nearby, too, were Arab horses of the Duchess's Rutland Stud in magnificent condition, with shiny coats from the good summer grazing. When one of the grooms introduced a stallion to a mare, to confirm that the mare was in season, it also confirmed the immodesty of the horses' mating habits. Paddy the Irish groom was amused: "Do you know, that's what I like about working here. The Duke and Duchess aren't stuck up at all. The other day I said to her: 'Do you know what the Irish family planning pill is made of? Syrup of Figs and Epsom salts – then you can't stay in bed long enough to get your woman into trouble.' She laughed like the rest of us." It was clear that the horses were on a totally different diet.

After leaving the castle and driving slowly through the area, Holwell, with its small steelworks of decaying buildings, showed what could easily come. One village was particularly quiet and attractive, its cottages built from local sandstone. There I met Mrs. Reid-Scott, a former Master of the Belvoir Hunt; I expected an upper-class "horsey" lady, with an accent to match her hyphen – in fact she was a pleasant, affable woman of taste and culture. Her house was surrounded by a walled garden filled with working bees and the traditional flowers of a country cottage. She spent her time gardening, riding, reading, and lamenting the changes she considered inevitable: "It is such a great pity for things will get worse; you only have to see what has happened elsewhere. The noise from the roads and railways will be particularly unpleasant and on a personal note, hunting will be more difficult. It is also true that the new people will not mix very easily." To emphasise the differences she showed me a copy of a newspaper, *The Miner*, that had been delivered to every house in the area. It claimed to be "The Voice of the National Union of Mineworkers", and in large type quoted the Union President saying: "Give us a chance and we'll get along together." The whole issue was designed to convince the local people that the miners should be welcomed with open arms; one miner's wife had written a recipe book; a young man had left farming in Norfolk to drive a £50,000 tunnelling machine in the mines; a "methane drainage pump attendant" had sent some of his hand-made jewelry to the Queen; a column proclaimed the wonders of a Miners' Welfare Centre, and as a final attraction a photograph of a bedraggled miner in ill-fitting riding clothes, complete with his crop stuffed down a boot, showed that even mining and hunting could go hand in hand. Mrs. Reid-Scott was not impressed, convinced, or amused.

Most visitors to the area stay at the Red House Inn, at the small village of Knipton, behind Belvoir itself. The inn is rather a plain red-bricked building in a wooded setting, but it is comfortable. The menu was far from plain, including sea food, grouse out of season, and a wide selection of wines. At the bar, the subject, inevitably, was mines and how the miners "would not fit in". One ex-military gentleman, with the accent of an officer, equated them with "foreigners", and he for one could not get on with "foreigners", particularly Arabs: "I just don't like Arabs, horses or people. They are all dirty and covered with bugs."

A loud, red-faced Australian vacuum cleaner salesman gave us the benefit of his alcoholic antipodean wisdom. He thought the "miner problem" was the same as the Australian Aborigine problem: "The Aborigines are different; it's not colour, they are just useless. They should all be put in a big fenced-off area and told they've got five hundred years to catch up. The big difference between people from the West and Aborigines is what I call the squirrel syndrome. When we work we store up for the winter; they don't do anything like that."

He was in England for several weeks, trying to sell vacuum cleaners to British Rail; ones that fit over the carriage doors and suck the whole compartment clean. The barman had never heard of such a machine before, or such arguments; after the salesman had gone to bed, however, he revealed that he had heard of the thinnest book in the world: "The Australian book of intellectuals." He too was a hunting man, but was gloomy about the future: "Most people are against the mines; but some are for. Their attitude is 'We'll have a coalmine under that castle if it's the last thing we do'."

It was a pleasure to wake up just after dawn to the chattering of housemartins as they fed their young above my window. At six the village streets were deserted; it was a most appealing place with stone cottages and no street lamps. By a farmyard gate, geese and goslings ventured out on to the road, hens scrapped, and horses stamped and rested; a rural scene that in most places vanished thirty years ago. A fine, trimmed hedge of holly kept cattle in one field; ancient "stag's head" oaks and willows towered over a stream; a chiff-chaff called. From a private roadway, as the sun rose, I gained a view of the castle standing above a wide low valley, overlooking fields of wheat, lakes, grazing cows and a stone bridge arching over water.

Beams of early-morning light illuminated the mist, and banks of rosebay willow herb tinged the watery haze with shades of mauve and pink; as the sun's warmth increased, so the colours gradually gained in clarity and texture. The whole parish formed part of a conservation area yet, incredibly, it was on the nearby Knipton cricket pitch that the Coal Board first proposed to site a mine.

At breakfast, the Australian, totally absorbed by cornflakes and vacuum cleaners, was preparing for a visit to Derby. I however drove to the straggling, aptly-named village of Long Clawson. My journey along a recently gritted road, with warnings, "Do not exceed 20 m.p.h.", was interrupted when a police car with a solitary occupant sped by, shooting stones in all directions. No light flashed to mark an emergency.

The manager of Long Clawson Dairies was proud of his Stilton, a cheese that has been produced in the area for over 300 years, now mainly made in and around the Vale of Belvoir, Melton Mowbray, and Dovedale in Derbyshire. It is ironic, that just as any wine made outside the Champagne area of France cannot legally be called "Champagne", so any cheese-maker outside this small area of the Midlands is prevented from using the name Stilton. With bureaucratic logic that defies description, this includes anybody wanting to make "Stilton" in the village of Stilton thirty-five miles away in Cambridgeshire.

Daniel Defoe was familiar both with the village and the cheese. On his journey through the Midlands in the 1720s he wrote: "Coming south from hence we passed Stilton, a town famous for cheese, which is called our English Parmesan, and is brought to table with the mites, or maggots round it, so thick, that they bring a spoon with them for you to eat the mites with, as you do the cheese." At one time it was also known as Lady Beaumont's cheese, after a lady of the same name, who had it made at Quenby Hall, her home. It was made in farmhouses throughout the Belvoir area, and when a local girl moved south, to marry the landlord of the Bell Inn at Stilton, her sister sent cheeses for her to sell. Consequently the Bell Inn, which served travellers on the Old North Road, gained a wide reputation for its special cheese.

The making of farmhouse cheeses gradually went out of fashion before the First World War, and Stilton is now produced in factories. However, it is not mass produced, and many of the traditional techniques are still used. At Long Clawson Dairies the milk is poured into large cheese tubs, in which a secret "starter" and rennet are added. After a curd has formed, twenty-six-pound portions are placed inside stainless-steel cylinders for about six days. The cheeses are then taken out and covered with cloths. They are turned and checked each day, and after a good "coat" has formed, are pricked with steel needles to allow the blue veins of mould to form more easily, before being transferred to the ripening rooms. A really good cheese takes between three and four months to mature and weighs between fourteen to fifteen pounds. Each is made from seventeen gallons of milk.

As we walked around the factory, white-clad men and women went about their work of turning and checking, and I was allowed to sample a large portion of a new cheese. As the people of the area claim, Stilton really is the "King of cheese", and far superior to its many foreign competitors such as Danish Blue and Roquefort.

Like the old gamekeeper, the manager was adamant that it was a crime to scoop out the cheese, or add port, being a sign of ignorance rather than expertise. He considered that port could be drunk, from glasses, to bring out the best of the Stilton after dinner, but the cheese could also be eaten as a meal itself with crusty bread, fresh butter and a glass of beer or milk. In the Vale they have a saying: "Cut high, cut low, cut level" – this method of cutting leaves little wasted. The cheese-making side of the factory, with its dependence on tradition, made a striking contrast to the area dealing with milk bottling. That was completely automated with machines, belts, and platoons of rattling milk bottles; the urban visitor would be excused for thinking that milk production had nothing to do with cows, farms or fields.

Some of the milk for the dairy came from the nearby village of Hose, where the Coal Board wants to develop the largest mine. It was there that I spoke to Allenby Stephenson, his red-bricked farmhouse surrounded by grass meadows and grazing Friesian cattle. He lived with his elderly parents, his attractive wife and two small children, and ran the 600 acres with the help of four farmhands. The farm, which produced milk, wheat, horses and prize-winning Shetland ponies, had been in the family for two hundred years, but the mine would take 400 acres. If it became established Allenby would be left with several scattered pieces of fields, and as he has no wish to do anything else ("For farming is a way of life"), he would have to try to buy a farm elsewhere. It would be foolish to do otherwise or else his likely compensation money could be taxed away.

In his view, if coal is mined in the Vale, it would also mean the establishment of a massive petro-chemical industry on the site: "I try not to get emotionally involved, but the so-called energy problem will create balance of payment problems and we must use our resources to reduce it. I think coal will be needed, the question is when, and what will they use it for? I hope we are not going to lose, but if you take a long-term view they should do what's in the best interest of the country. We can probably delay the Coal Board – I like to think we can stop them."

Mike Nichols, a neighbouring farmer, was much more forthright, his views reinforced by the fact that his original home was Barnsley in Yorkshire: "I've seen what mining brings in its wake; it takes over whole villages, it brings dereliction and disrupts rural life. You are left with an urban mess, fences down and crops trampled, but of course you are not supposed to say all this – you mustn't upset the miners. But if you put people together in large numbers you get problems; even a load of stockbrokers with their pinstripes and ponies would give us troubles; so will miners, with their Miners' Welfare, their pigeons and their whippets. I've got 70,000 hens here; I don't want them disturbed by mining and tipping. And if the miners get here, they'll only go slow to make the coal last longer. Coal is not necessary – we want nuclear.

"We only grow fifty per cent of our own food; that is more important than fuel, but once the Coal Board has restored a field ruined by mining, where you could once grow barley, all you can have is rough grazing. Then of course they say that they are going to make a 'linear country park' along the escarpment. Who wants to walk along a 'linear country park' overlooking tip heaps and pits?

"Some locals want it, but it's just to get at the landowners; if they really want to go down a mine, let them go. Miners don't see anything, just green grass, which doesn't cost anything – according to them. All they want is bigger pubs and Miners' Welfare; the landscape value is unknown. It is a pity, for we have kestrels and barn owls here; it is a good part of the country. I've been here twenty-four years, all my life's work, and I employ seventeen people. I want my three sons to follow me, but by then thirty of my eighty acres will have been ruined.

"There will be about 17,000 people extra, mostly urban riff-raff, and what's the good of compensation when you are covered with industrial estates? Then they'll want to turn coal into petrol and all the rest. They'll win of course; the inspector is appointed by the government and they are paying him. They'll get what they want; you see, it's all over. In coalmining towns you want to see the councillors drinking with the Coal Board officials and the Union men – they run the towns completely." He spoke with a mixture of anger and contempt; but of course the farming community, in an urban-dominated society, could never convert such feelings into effective industrial action.

As the sun began to set, I stopped in a small road at the back of Willow Farm, to walk over the fields towards the escarpment. Along the roadside verges there were poppies, clear blue clumps of meadow-cranesbill, and honeysuckle in a hedge. Over a meadow where cattle grazed, intruding blackthorn had stockproofed a thin belt of old hawthorn; by a ditch, great hairy willow-herb grew, with meadowsweet and patches of birdsfoot trefoil and in adjoining fields the year's crop of hay had been cut and looked good. Tits fed and called in the hedges and two grey-wagtails were on ears of green wheat, flitting after flies as they normally do over water. Flocks of sparrows had already started to eat the swelling grain and, in the distance, a kestrel hovered. The pattern of fields and farms continued along the escarpment, and it seemed right that the small country road should be called Pasture Lane. In a few years' time it could well be renamed Slag Heap Alley.

Although first impressions suggest that miners and country people have little in common, this is not strictly true; in many mining areas a tradition has grown up of greyhounds, whippets and lurchers. The dogs are raced, used for coursing and poaching hares, and are already bringing some members of the two communities together. Because of this, I decided to go to a lurcher show in the Belvoir area near Cottesmore, in what used to be the county of Rutland.

For those who have never encountered one, a lurcher is not a person who tends to stagger or lurch, but a dog, or more accurately a crossbreed not recognised by the Kennel Club, but at the same time not simply another mongrel. It is a planned cross between a coursing dog, a greyhound, whippet, deerhound, or saluki, with a working dog, a labrador, border collie, alsatian, foxhound or terrier. Consequently, among lurchers there is a considerable amount of variety, with possibly the best combination being a cross between a greyhound for speed and a collie for intelligence. The resultant lurcher usually resembles a rather shaggy greyhound, being fast, alert, attractive and affectionate.

Rough-coated lurcher

The word "lurcher" was first recorded in 1668, and over the years has become associated with gypsies and poachers, who have used them for taking hares, rabbits and deer for the cooking pot, as well as for making money. Gangs of poachers still use them illegally, particularly after deer, and they are also used to kill foxes.

I saw my first lurcher several years ago, tied to the caravan of a local gypsy, who, although he had ceased travelling, had the genuine gypsy name of Loveridge. Whenever he had such a dog, the local hare population always plummeted. But although the lurcher has normally been associated with gypsies and the like, it also has admirers among the aristocracy, landowners, racegoers, and military men. Their interest has been mainly sporting, for lurchers are ideal dogs for coursing.

Over recent years, unaccountably, the lurcher's popularity has increased. It has even become fashionable, the fashion extending from those with Range Rovers and town houses, to caravan-dwelling scrap-metal merchants who carry their dogs about in clapped-out Ford Transit trucks. Lurcher shows have been another inevitable development; the first was held in a field at Upper Lambourn, in Berkshire, in 1971, and since then Lambourn has become the Mecca for both lurcher owners and those who like country gatherings. Now shows take place all over the country, raising money for a variety of causes.

The lurcher show I visited, not far from Oakham, Rutland's former county town, was organised by the Cottesmore Hunt Supporters' Club at Burley on the Hill, an old country house built by Daniel Finch, the Second Earl of Nottingham, between 1674 and 1704. As the name suggests, it stands on a hill overlooking Rutland Water, a large man-made reservoir. It is ironic indeed that what was once England's smallest and most rural county should disappear administratively, through a change of name, and physically almost totally beneath water. Perhaps, in the future, what is left could be turned into a coal tip.

The old stately home stands in 2,000 acres of farmland; from a distance on a warm Sunday afternoon, it looked impressive, but on closer inspection was obviously under-occupied, and gave the impression of decay, for the cost of maintaining such a building must be enormous. The gardens, too, had a slightly run-down appearance, and the rose bushes and lawns looked as if they were being maintained by one harried gardener, where once there had been five. The view of the reservoir took in a neglected avenue of trees, and in the other direction, away from the house and outbuildings, large wrought-iron gates, rusting and chained together had once opened on to parkland, but now the fields were all intensively farmed. Belvoir Castle survives with the aid of visitors, but Burley on the Hill seemed to be drifting towards dereliction. Here was a fine example of our architectural past being threatened by a harsh tax system, created by the social and political prejudices of politicians; unfortunately the saving of crumbling country houses brings in few votes.

At its most prosperous, the house was in the possession of the Duke of Buckingham, who on one occasion entertained King Charles I there. During the festivities, according to a local historian, a famous dwarf, Jeffrey Hudson, "the smallest man in the smallest county in England, was served up in a pie at table and presented by the Duchess to Queen Henrietta, who at once took him into her service".

There were no dwarfs at the lurcher show, but a wide range of people, from those with upper-crust accents and affectations, to others with a rural ring to their speech. The cross-section was complete, from dukes to didecoys, commanding officers to coalminers, all assembled to show, or look at, lurchers. Military men with caps and cravats, and landowners with the intonation of the public school and the Conservative Club, mingled with dealers and farmworkers with tattoes, ear-rings, and T-shirts proclaiming the wonders of Carlsberg lager. Did not the several miners from the South Leicestershire Colliery feel embarrassed about mixing with landowners and country gentlemen? "Oh no, we are not snobs, we'll mix with anybody."

Nearly all those present had dogs, or were with friends who owned dogs: some entered them in classes, others went in for the obstacle course, and some were content simply to wander around looking at the varieties of dogs and owners. The owner of the Supreme Champion was a dealer who had travelled from Evesham. He had half-a-dozen dogs and gave the impression that he would have enjoyed his day, even without winning anything. There were many who just watched and talked, and I spoke with several who admitted running their dogs at deer.

The afternoon finished with terrier and lurcher racing, which proved extremely popular. The terriers ran first, chasing a fox's brush on a length of rope, and those that did not stop to fight halfway dived into bales of straw at the end of the course, desperately trying to follow the disappearing tail. The lurchers were more dignified, chasing a stuffed rabbit wound in by a small electric motor. It was a day that would have given no comfort to those people who seek to perpetuate the class war; for those, like me, who regard deer as being among our most sensitive and beautiful creatures, it gave cause for some concern.

It was hardly surprising to meet coalminers from the South Leicestershire Colliery at the lurcher show, for many of them consider the Vale of Belvoir to be within commuting distance, which makes them anxious to work the coal. From Burley I travelled to the coalfield, passing through Oakham, Melton Mowbray, Loughborough and Quorn. Once more, it was attractive countryside, with plenty of hedges, coverts and grass fields, and the lingering influence of hunting on the landscape was easy to see. After the road passed beneath the M1 motorway, the feel and focus of coalmining and urban living became clearer, with conspicuous "headstocks" – the large winding wheels of the "cages" that take the miners underground – and housing estates.

The South Leicestershire Colliery was on the road to Ellistown, near Coalville. The party I was to join for the mine visit assembled at the colliery offices, in an ordinary red-bricked house that looked more suitable for a demolition order. We were a small group; a reporter from *Coal News*, and two extraordinary individuals. One, called Douglas, was quiet, slight and effeminate, wearing denims: "I am a designer and write plays in my spare time. One is probably going on television." I have lost count of the times I have heard such sentiments. The other, Brian, was fat, loud, and resembled Billy Bunter, with spectacles, a cravat, tartan shirt and beret. Two cameras dangled from his neck: "This is exciting," he informed us. "I've only taken pictures of bishops for the *Church Times* before."

Colin, the personnel manager, blinked in disbelief at the combination of playwright and photographer, and quickly guided us to the changing rooms, to exchange our own clothes for grey-brown Coal-Board underpants, overalls, boots and helmets, before taking us to the "cage". On the way we passed a board showing that the proceeds from a raffle were approaching £500. The money was for a twenty-year-old youth who had recently lost his leg underground, severed as he was riding on a conveyor belt meant only for coal. Colin said that a surface job would be found for him: "We look after our own."

Colin, who was about sixty, had been down the mines all his working life since leaving grammar school at the age of sixteen. He was how I imagined an old miner should be, wearing knee pads, and walking with a limp because of arthritis, but he was good-natured, blunt and, because of his background, Labour to the core. He seemed to know all the men and several stopped him to ask advice about various courses and shift work. He enquired about a sick father and a youth greeted him: "Heh Colin, you wicked old boogger. You got the old feller so pissed on Friday night that he had to crawl upstairs on his hands and knees."

He took us to the "cage", directly below the large wheels of the winding gear. Going through the entry door we were met by gale-force winds and my ears popped. It was like transferring into a distant, old-fashioned world, with dirt, dust and the smell of dampness. At the bottom of the shaft the lights showed cables, rails, metal arches and wooden props. Ahead lay darkness, apart from the helmet lamps. The roof became much lower and a group of long-striding men overtook us; underground workers walk many miles in the course of a week, walking between the cages and the coal face. Along one section we had to lie face down on a man-carrying conveyor. Walking once more, the shale in the tunnel walls turned to coal, ebony black and shining, and as we approached the face the smell of cordite hung in the air as if there had been some blasting. A string of Anglo-Saxon and motherless oaths came through the intercom; Colin spoke into a small box on the wall: "The lady didn't really want to hear that, Mick" – silence followed.

At the face were more cables, ramps, motors and several black-faced, sweating men. Douglas could not contain himself any longer: "Oh, aren't these miners big", and Brian appeared to lose control of his clicking fingers. He was taking photographs without a light meter or a flash-gun, in darkness; he looked like an eccentric, over-weight scoutmaster and all his films must have been quite blank. There were knowing nods, winks and nudges from the miners and one whispered to me: "Bloody hell, where did you find them? I hope they don't ask you to look for the soap in the showers."

Colin guided us along the face itself, which was about 200 yards long. The passageway was cramped, three or four feet wide and the same high, with hydraulic chocks that can hold 120 tons, to keep up the roof. Several miners were stationed at intervals along it, as the ranging drum-shearer worked backwards and forwards in front of them. With flailing blades it pulled itself along on a large chain, ripping out the coal as it went, with the driver clambering after it. There was noise, shouting, thick dust, sharp splinters of coal flying through the air, and the cut-out coal fell into a "panza", an armoured face conveyor-belt. Some of the miners wore masks, similar to those worn by farmers on their combine harvesters, and after the cutter had passed, the coal around us creaked and groaned. The chocks were then moved forward a yard and the rock immediately behind crashed down. Ahead, too, some coal fell from the roof, but the men close to it were in no danger, and they considered their job to be reasonably safe. Indeed, surprisingly there are usually more fatalities on farms each year than down mines.

With the shouting and laughing, the camaraderie among the miners was easy to see. In liberal circles it is fashionable to say: "The miners should be paid all they can get; you would never get me down a mine", but such people would usually find the prospect of any form of physical work alarming. In fact there are aspects of mining which some men find attractive. The work is physically demanding, the miners work as a close-knit team, and the element of danger binds men and the pit communities together. It is a closeness that can also be seen among serving soldiers; each is part of a highly-disciplined team, in which the failure or error of any member can lead to the death or injury of a colleague.

As we walked back, Colin talked of his fears: "Nearly 540 men work here, but it is an old mine and there are only plans for another five years as the coal is gradually running out. We mine about 1,600 tons a day – 400,000 tons a year, and about eighty per cent goes to power stations. But if there's a gap between closing down here and starting in the Vale, then we're finished; we have to get the boys straight from school, for if they go into factories first, or some other soft job, then they are lost. Once they've worked in the clean and comfort they'll never come down a mine."

In the showers the atmosphere was warm and steamy as men from a recently-finished shift sluiced themselves down amid laughter and lather. They were as dirty as I get after a day in the harvest field. "This makes you feel good at the end of the shift," Graham was telling me. "I came straight from school and I work at the face now. I wouldn't change, it's great, I've got the rest of the day free."

Clean again, Colin took me to a small room where the colliery canaries were kept, for they are still used in certain conditions to warn of gas: "I can remember ponies being used underground too. We looked after them really well. Their health was cared for more than ours, and if a miner was off ill, then sometimes the pony would refuse to work for anybody else."

After a stodgy meal in the plain canteen an "audience" was arranged with the mine manager; it really was an audience for he sat at his desk like a monarch on a throne, but instead of a crown and sceptre, he wore a helmet and held a bottle of "pop" in his hands. He offered us drinks; beer, tea or coffee, and periodically took a swig from his bottle. On a blackboard he had written "WORK THE VALE" and once various other members of his management team had arrived, including Colin, the performance began.

It was extraordinary. The manager started with details about the mine and the Vale, full of "break-even situations", "at this point in time" and "the need for energy". The delay in mining the Vale was the fault of the farmers: "The enquiry is just to placate the farmers; they are the ones who have delayed mining in the Vale."

"They're just greedy; the richest farmers in the country live in Leicestershire with their Jags and holidays in Majorca."

"That's why they don't want mining in the Vale, because the workers will go to the mines."

"You never see a poor farmer. Even the working farmer is well-off; they just want cheap labour."

"When potatoes went up it was only the farmers after more profit. If it rains everything goes up. If the sun shines it all goes up, and when anything goes up it's always the working class that has to pay."

They also had a series of new and original views about the way in which development actually improved the rural outlook. Far from harming the countryside the "roundabout trains" would become a bonus; "A railway line can be pretty, just think of *The Railway Children*," and, with even more originality: "Motorways have saved British wildlife" – unfortunately badgers, deer and flattened hedgehogs have not yet heard this good news. To prove the point of country co-existing with industry, nearby Charnwood Forest was said to be "the prettiest part of Britain". When I pointed out that the tip heap next to the mine certainly was not the prettiest place in Britain, this was considered most unfair: "That is nothing to do with this mine. That comes from an open-cast mine and is just brought here."

The manager finished on a determined note: "The Vale of Belvoir must be used for the country. Where would the farmers be without the miners? They need us for fertiliser and electricity and our men need the jobs. If the farmers are worried about loss of land, why aren't they reclaiming the Wash? The country needs energy; nuclear power and coal together. Nuclear energy will be a friend, not an enemy."

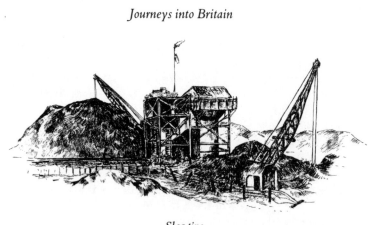

Slag tips

The bizarre proceedings had shown the huge gulf that exists between the urban and rural dweller. Because of the way in which society has developed most country people visit towns regularly, and many work in them. Consequently they see and understand urban life. The average town dweller simply passes through the countryside; to him it is a feudal place of fox-hunting landowners, exploited peasants, and high food prices, to drain the working man of his money. Early on the manager had quoted a short local rhyme:

> Leicestershire born and Leicestershire bred,
> Strong in the arm and weak in the head.

By the time I left his office I agreed with him.

After the visit to the mine I had two hours to kill before visiting a Miners' Welfare centre, so I drove to Charnwood Forest, a "forest" with few trees, to see for myself the "prettiest part of Britain". It was not outstanding, simply a series of rocky outcrops giving a good view of the whole area. Rather than showing how farming and mining can co-exist, it showed just how incompatible the two are. In one direction farmland could be seen stretching eastwards into rural Leicestershire; in the other lay industrial haze and houses, while even part of the "forest" itself was being quarried. Worse still, the drone of the internal combustion engine was continuous and in places the grass had been worn bare by the feet of too many people. The area also seemed to be used as a dog latrine by housing estate dog owners living within driving distance. As I sat on a rock in the warm sun, several cars stopped to allow dogs and owners to tumble out, so that the dogs could run, sniff and squat. The family pets certainly viewed "the forest" as the "prettiest part of Britain"; with more trees it would have been paradise.

The Miners' Welfare in a big red-bricked building, was obviously making a large profit, presumably at the expense of "working people". There were rows of plain tables, with a bar to one side and a stage in the corner. Trade gradually built up and friends and families sat drinking and occasionally talking. It was not inspiring: "Beer's cloudy tonight, Joan." "Aye, I wonder why beer's cloudy tonight?" At the end of each pint, refills were fetched, but the conversation remained as empty as ever. Being a club children were allowed in, sucking at straws in bottles and eating crisps, so ensuring that beer and bingo would continue well into the future. If one of them had worn a helmet he could even have been a future mine manager.

I wanted to meet an official of the National Union of Mineworkers and he briefly appeared, wearing a smart suit and tie and smoking a cigar. Somebody who knew him explained his disappearance: "Oh he's got a Labour Party committee meeting now; they run this town." Eventually he returned and lit another cigar: "Oh yes," he said, "the union wants to mine the Vale of Belvoir to protect the jobs of my members." A few weeks before, a former area president of the N.U.M. had said: "Mining is a strength-sapping, unhealthy and hazardous job. Men start to age very rapidly. By the time they are sixty-five they're finished, washed up. He [the miner] is likely to be a physical wreck."

I asked the union man why he was so keen to send his members underground, when it was possible to mine coal with robots, or even wash it out, for now he had the opportunity of actually freeing his members from their hazardous job. I had wasted my breath, for his attitudes were firmly rooted in the Industrial Revolution, and the implications and possibili-

ties of technology had not apparently penetrated his conditioned mind: "My members want work; many of them are
earning £200 per week and we want to keep it like that."

But I was not simply listening to a latter-day Luddite, albeit
an affluent cigar-smoking one; it went further than that. When
the union movement first started it was deeply involved with
the actual welfare of working people; now, however, in many
instances, "the union" has simply become a base for political
power. Consequently, if "the union" worked in the best
interests of its members, it would be working to take the
miners out of the mines. But that would mean "the union",
through "the Party", ceasing to "run the town", and few men
in history have ever voluntarily relinquished political power,
even in the interests of their fellow workers.

The union man blew an impressive smoke ring from his
cigar: "We are going to have the Vale. The Duke of Rutland
has said that he will lie down in front of the first earth-mover.
If he does then I want to drive it."

It was the new aristocracy against the old; for the second
time I found myself agreeing with the mine manager's little
rhyme.★

★Inevitably the government has now given the go-ahead for two mines in
the Vale of Belvoir.

2

Cornfield Casualties

The fields around the Vale of Belvoir could face sudden disfigurement at any time, but over much of Britain change of a different kind has already taken place. Miles of hedgerows have been removed to increase the size of arable fields, so enabling larger machines to plough, sow and harvest. On most farms, harvest time remains a pleasant season, although its mood has changed since the days of horse-power, binders, and bands of gleaners collecting left-over corn for their back-yard hens. Now it is a period of intense activity, to combine the corn and to get it home dry. As soon as the grain ripens, and the sun shines, the work begins; it can be a time of anxiety, too, with concern over milling quality, machinery break-downs, and, most of all, moisture content, for if the corn is harvested damp, it can heat-up and be ruined.

To the casual observer, and even to some farmers and workers, the form of harvest has not changed since the progression from binders to combine harvesters; the machines have merely become larger, the pace more frenetic and nothing more. To those who pause to think and to remember, however, harvest has changed significantly; the change has been slow and subtle, but its effects have been just as harmful as those of coaltips and destruction, gradually spreading over the land with the increasing use of chemical sprays. The fields themselves have altered both in colour and in character, and what harvest has gained in yield per acre and efficiency, it has lost in beauty, feeling and simple harmony. Even in my own childhood, just after the Second World War, memory clearly retains sun, dusty driftways, ripening corn and harvest flow-ers, which grew in such profusion that they were picked in bunches and placed in large jam-jars for the wildflower competitions at the village flower show. Now many of the flowers have simply faded away, and, in some cases, to pick those remaining would be to break the law. The fields of wheat, barley and oats once contained a variety of flowering "weeds", which according to John Clare consisted of:

> Bright carlock blue cap and corn poppy red
> Which in such clouds of colours widely spread
> That at the sun rise might to fancy's eye
> Seem to reflect the many color'd sky.

Carlock still remains common, but "corn poppies" seldom splash the fields with scarlet, making only intermittent brief returns. Poppy seeds can remain dormant for many years, then when a cold spring leads to late germination, after the weedkillers have lost their potency, their re-appearance can give renewed colour to the harvest landscape, and the song of the lark seems to reflect more fully the warmth of summer.

Sadly, the cornflower and the corncockle are not so resilient and only knapweed and field scabious remind of summers now lost, giving colour to uncut verges, and to the sides of little-used farm tracks, well away from the poisoned drift of sprays. Occasionally the cornflower, with its ragged flowers of deep, bright blue, can be seen in country gardens. It is also known by several rural names, such as blue cap, bachelor's buttons, bluebottle, and, because of its hard, blunting stem, hurtsickle. Before exotic imports became available and fashionable, it was widely grown for its beauty, and for its medicinal properties, Nicolas Culpeper, the old herbalist, recommending it "against plagues and all infectious diseases and pestilential fevers".

The attractive corncockle is even rarer, and is now one of Britain's scarcest wildflowers. It can sometimes be seen in cornfields in my own county, by a road which winds from Cambridge into the flat Fenlands, towards the village of Burwell. These are not wild, but broadcast by hand in odd field corners by the farmer, who protects and cultivates his "wildflowers" with as much care as others devote to their crops. Each year the farmer carefully collects seed from his

Corncockle

corncockles, and now I, too, have a flowering patch in my summer garden. Orchids grow in nearby grassland and loosestrife, another flower loved by Clare, edges his ponds and ditches with purple:

> And oft long purples on the water's brink
> Have tempted me to wade inspite of fate
> To pluck the flowers.

The corncockle's decline has been remarkable; that fine little book, *The Observer's Book of Wildflowers*, first published in 1937, says of it: "Wandering through or round our cornfields any time during summer, one is almost sure to find this beautiful flower", but sadly, such an occurrence is now little more than a dream.

Not native to Britain, the flower was originally imported accidentally with seed corn from Southern Europe. It is a hairy plant, growing up to five feet tall, with a number of purple flowers, which are scentless, but rich in nectar; the nectar, however, can only be reached by butterflies and moths, with their long proboscises. The name corncockle is thought to come from "cockerel", as the petals are the colour of a cockerel's comb, and the flower looks over the corn like a "cock's head", one of its rustic names.

But the saddest casualty of the cornfields is not a flower, but a bird, again one familiar to John Clare: "Where is the school boy that has not heard that mysterious noise which comes with the spring in the grass and green corn I have followd it for hours and all to no purpose it seemd like a spirit that mockd my folly in running after it."

Most of the old country writers knew of the corncrake, or landrail, and from his Hampshire parish in the eighteenth century Gilbert White wrote: "After harvest some few land-rails are seen", while Richard Kearton, the early pioneer of bird photography, described its nest as being: "On the ground amongst mowing grass, clover, willow beds and standing corn, all over the United Kingdom – the bird sits close, and as a consequence individuals get their heads cut off by the mower's scythe or machine."

Its habits, however, remained a mystery to these writers; each summer the corncrake would appear and every winter it would vanish. They doubted whether it could migrate, for its flight is awkward, rather like that of a moorhen. Gilbert White expressed these doubts:

This is deemed a bird of passage by all writers; yet from its formation seems to be poorly qualified for migration; for its wings are short and placed so forward, and out of the centre of gravity, that it flies in a very heavy and embarrassed manner, with its legs hanging down, and can hardly be sprung a second time, as it runs very fast, and seems to depend more on the swiftness of its feet than on its flying.

In 1772 the Honourable Daines Barrington wrote "An Essay on the periodical Appearing and Disappearing of certain birds, at different times of the Year". He claimed:

> A landrail, when put up by the fhooter, never flies 100 yards; its motion is exceffively flow, whilft the legs hang down like thofe of the water fowls which have not web feet, and which are known never to take longer flights.
>
> Now thofe who contend that the landrail, becaufe it happens to difappear in winter, muft migrate acrofs oceans, are reduced to the following dilemma.
>
> They muft firft either fuppofe that it reaches Ireland periodically from America; which is impoffible, not only becaufe the paffage of the Atlantic includes fo many degrees of longitude, but becaufe there is no fuch bird in that part of the globe.
>
> If the landrail therefore migrates from the continent of Europe to Ireland, which it muft otherwife do, the neceffary confequence is, that many muft pafs over England in their way Weftward to Ireland; and why do not more of thefe birds continue with us?

The corncrake does in fact migrate, spending its winters in Southern Asia and Africa. A solitary bird whose voice resembles its Latin name, *crex crex*, it is remembered by some in my East Anglian village as a common sound of summer fifty years ago. In recent years its decline has become even more dramatic and now, in a normal summer, fewer than 1,000 birds come to England, Wales and Scotland, most of them making for the Western Isles of Scotland, where the growing season is late and old farming methods are still used. Flowers and birds in country areas need patches of marginal land and marsh, away from the sprays and machines of intensive agriculture, if they are to survive. Unfortunately on most farms they are given no chance, for even the odd corners are drained, or cut with flail mowers, to create the impression of efficiency.

Few people really want weed-filled fields or large areas of wasted land, but if room in a few wild places and hedgerows is denied to wild life such as cornflowers, corncockles and corncrakes, then modern harvests have lost far more than they have gained.

The plight of the corncrake and old countrymen's memories of it in our now-empty farm fields, led me to study a map of bird distribution and decide to visit the island of Arran, where I hoped to hear the *crex crex* for myself. During the long drive, I crossed a river bridge near Newark where parked cars showed the presence of many fishermen; the Trent is a depressing river, its smell suggesting that the careless angler could catch far more than fish. At Ferrybridge I passed cooling towers and slag heaps, signs warning of mining subsidence, and a pub called "The Fox". Since it was late July, holidaymakers' cars competed for motorway space with those of salesmen and heavy lorries. Further north hay was still being cut in the fields, and travelling at speed just gave a number of blurred images: the Pennines; sheep; the Lake District; lower; higher; greener; drier; then another pub, "The Highland Laddie", not only before the Scottish border, but also set in completely flat countryside.

The local roads of lowland Scotland remained in focus longer, with grass meadows, cattle and more hay. The season

Corncrake

seemed well behind that of East Anglia; clumps of ragged robin still flowered and knapweed was not yet out. But in some ways the season was also later, for touches of autumn were already visible, or at least of the time when seasons merge: a large flock of golden plovers flew over the road, several groups of lapwings flew lazily, and the colour of the leaves seemed to be fading.

The villages looked hard, cold and regular, built from local stone as if they had grown from the rock just beneath the surface. As evening drew on I arrived at the small port of Ardrossan, and there, across the Firth of Clyde, lay Arran, shrouded in cloud and surrounded by patches of silver sea. I found Ardrossan an unattractive town, again pervaded by a feeling of hardness, despite amusement arcades and putting greens to please weekend trippers from Glasgow. It seemed that Glasgow provided more than trade, for the people obviously transported their hatreds and habits with them. On a toilet door someone had written "Celtic", and above it another hand had scrawled "Fuck your"; the whole literary exercise had then been daubed with human excrement. On another wall, either as a threat or as a suppressed desire, yet another anonymous writer urged Anglo-Saxon sexual activities with the Pope and the I.R.A.; a peculiar way of expressing religious or political antagonisms.

Arran is thirteen miles from the Ayrshire coast and six miles from the Mull of Kintyre. Although associated with potatoes, its shape more closely resembles that of a bean; quite a large bean, being twenty-six miles long and twelve miles across at its widest point. For a corncrake, from Asia or Africa, with its ungainly flight, the journey represents an extraordinary achievement.

I boarded the car-ferry for Brodick under a grey dawn. The crossing gave an idea of what was to come, with views of ragged mountains, tumbling streams and small villages. Three gannets flew by, close and beautiful; they were so near that I could see virtually every feather on their long black-tipped wings, and even the light blue of their eyes clearly showed. Patches of bright green weed indicated the richness of the clear dark sea, as did large orange jelly-fish, trailing their tentacles behind them. Some of the other travellers were oblivious to their surroundings, for the ferry had its quota of caricature Scotsmen: peculiar people, wearing tartan caps, T-shirts and kilts, and already, in the early morning, drinking cans of beer. Without coats, their alcoholic inner-warmth made them glow pink in the cold.

The island had a calm, unhurried air, and the tartan brigade seemed simply to disappear. The roads were a pleasure after those on the mainland: narrow, winding, and virtually empty. I stayed in the north of the island at the village of Lochranza, where the small sea loch has provided a refuge for fishing boats over hundreds of years. Today most of the craft have sails or outboard motors, and are owned by holidaymakers from England. Once, Kilbrannon Sound was full of herring, and 400 men fished and processed the catch, but now tourism has taken over. The change in activities and people was typified at the village shop where over her ample chest the assistant had emblazoned: "I'm a virgin – this is a very old T-shirt". She spoke with a London accent and the age of her T-shirt was self-evident.

Outside a nearby cottage an old man leant on his stick and sucked at his pipe; his skin was dark and wrinkled, his beard grey and his eyes aware, yet distant. He wore a fisherman's jumper, and had been a fisherman all his working life: "There are only six old men and six old women left of the original village. All the young people have moved. The crofts have fallen into disuse and the houses have all been bought up by 'white settlers'; they want all the amenities of the town and don't understand the area. When I was young, herring was caught in the sound and the small boats sold them to market ships. Even salmon came upstream and we caught them with 'grapes' – gardening forks. We went long-lining too, with a mile of line and 800 hooks baited with shellfish. Now there are only a few fish for the tourists. The deer were controlled too in the old days."

I resisted the temptation to stay and talk, to find out just how much the village had changed in one man's lifetime, as I was anxious to hear a corncrake. In the north of the island the mountains rose to nearly 3,000 feet, with jagged ridges of bare rock, deer silhouetted against the skyline, and the ever-present smell of the sea. Towards the south the landscape became lower; yellow irises grew down to the shore, with foxgloves, yellow loosestrife, harebells and cotton grass inland. In the woods some gypsies lived in tents made from a framework of boughs lashed together with string and covered with canvas; inside, stoves burnt without chimneys and everywhere were dirty children, dogs, dampness and the smell of smoke.

At the little coastal village of Lamlash I met Howard Walker, a rugged-looking man with a Norse-like beard. For many years he worked as a gamekeeper on the island, but then he turned to conservation and now counts seals and watches birds. He heard corncrakes regularly until five years ago: "But they've gone. I heard them on Skye earlier this year, and the starlings imitating them. I wish I could still hear them on Arran, but the farming has changed and the birds no longer come." He has a pleasant life and looks after Holy Island, across the bay, with its wild goats and Sohay sheep. Highland cattle are also reared on the island and Howard tows over a wooden raft to fetch the calves. The distance is about a mile and wild mink have swum over, too. "They have killed most of the bantams, on which a study was being carried out, but they have also cleared the island of rats." He regards mink as a pest; it is said that they were brought to Arran for a mink farm, but when planning permission was refused, the owner simply released them. He also considers the gypsies to be a great pest: "They are Scottish tinkers; they receive social security and at the same time they get sixty to seventy pounds a week collecting whelks."

The gamekeeper who replaced him on the local estate had never heard of a corncrake on Arran; his main concern was the theft of his pheasants by mink. However, he thought that one local farmer would know if corncrakes were to be heard, and he directed me back towards Brodick. As I drove from the estate, I stopped by a small stone bridge over a rocky stream. There, thirty feet below was a heron, quite unaware of my presence, looking for a good place to fish. As it walked it slipped inelegantly on algae-covered stones, and for brief seconds it became a tangle of long legs and wings; it had never occurred to me before that herons, too, face simple difficulties as they go about their daily business.

Near Brodick a tall man in accentless English pointed to the farm: "It's the one that has a manure heap covered with a plastic sheet." Why would a farmer cover manure with a plastic sheet? It seemed a strange practice. The man must have been an English urban-dweller, for the "manure" was silage, made to feed the farmer's cattle through the winter. It had been several summers since the farmer had heard a corncrake, and he did not expect to hear one again. He ran a 150-acre dairy farm, but he made little hay; instead he cut his grass twice a year for silage, in late May or June, and again in August or September. Consequently no corncrake could successfully nest on his land.

Finally I called on Maggie Dunn, a teacher-cum-ornithologist, at her bungalow, at the end of a long country lane near Kingscross. She, too, reported the recent disappearance of the corncrake from Arran; what I had missed by a generation in my own parish, I had missed by a whisker on the island; but the result was the same – silence. She offered some hope, for a few days earlier she had been talking to an "old wifie" who claimed to have heard the call about a month earlier, near Blackwaterfoot. Maggie's husband, Alisdair, had once been a teacher too, but gave up his routine job to become a potter. He has made a success of this and feels he could never return to working for an employer from nine until four. Now during the summer he produces badgers, puffins, nightjars and pots, for the tourists, using a variety of clays and glazes. "But the island closes down at the end of September and I do my own work then." Like his wife he appreciates the wildlife of the island, including the birds, for there are eagles, peregrines, hen harriers, goshawks and many more: "But it was better for corncrakes on the island in the old days, when the farmers could live more easily on their subsidy, called locally 'subsidey'. They would plough a field, collect the subsidy, do no more work and the whole business would 'subside'. Now they are all cutting silage."

Towards Blackwaterfoot, the country was undulating, with more uncut grass, a promising habitat for the corncrake.

At a farm, with decaying stone outbuildings, the old farmer was shearing his sheep by hand; of retirement age, his lined, weathered face looked tired. Despite the hard, heavy work and the protests of the animals as he cut, he had no wish for change, or for electric cutters: he simply wanted different weather as he was being forced to make hay between the showers. Like everyone I had met, he had not heard a corncrake for many years.

At last I located the "old wifie", living in a small modern bungalow, another tribute to Scotland's awful architecture; oblong and ordinary, it seemed a concrete replica of the old crofts. She, however, was warm, pleasant and excited by my visit about the "wee bird", but she would not talk until she had produced tea and biscuits. She spoke with a broad accent, and told me she had heard the corncrake's familiar "crex crex" in the adjoining hay field from May until June 11th: "I first went oot in the gloamin, to hear the cuckoo. Instead I heard the corncrake in the brae. It crakes before it sits on its eggs; it was good of her to let us hear her call." Years ago she heard many more: "But I like the wee sandpiper as much as any. She sounds like the piper before he skirls his pipes." She was a pleasure to listen to, for she was also the sound of old Arran. Once her husband arrived, a retired farmworker with an even broader accent, I hardly understood a word.

Sheep and cattle occupied most of the farmland, although I had imagined the island to be full of fields growing potatoes – Arran Pilot and Chieftain – but Donald "Tattie" Mackelvie developed his breeds in small plots, and now they are virtually all grown on the mainland. Another surprise lay in wait for me along the road back to Lochranza, at King's Caves, for despite the Scots' legendry liking for money, access was free. The King's Caves are a series of caves in the cliffs by the seashore, where Robert the Bruce was encouraged by a spider, at a vital stage of his life; appropriately enough 101 types of spider are found on Arran, so his choice was wide. I passed bracken, foxgloves, ferns, liverworts and grassy banks where harebells grew; it was a peaceful, fragrant dusk, as the sun gilded the gently swelling sea with gold and silver as far as Kintyre.

For two or three days I wandered through the island; the

mountains offered spectacular views, with wide open valleys, great walled corries, slopes covered with scree, crystal-clear streams that flowed from dark, oozing bogs, the distant call of curlews and red deer, hinds with their calves, and groups of stags with their full-antlered heads, still in velvet. Alone in the hills I enjoyed a feeling of remoteness, where the complete cycle, harmony and rhythm of the natural order could still be felt.

My last evening on the island remains vivid. I walked from Lochranza harbour, in a wide circle to the sea and the Cock of Arran. The harbour was once of strategic importance, for a small castle stands close to where a stream flows into the sea; a pair of red-breasted mergansers slept on a half-submerged rock and it was quiet apart from several broods of eider ducks swimming idly by. Fences surrounded the nearby cottages, for deer wander at will around the village after dark, and gardens have to be protected. Wild honeysuckle was on flower, as were yellow irises which grew right down to the salty shingle.

Following the stream inland, I passed through water-meadows where sheep grazed and alders gave patches of darkness and light. Gradually the water narrowed, its stony bed adding music to the flow and, at a bend, a dipper was living up to its name and "dipping" on a stone. I was pleased to see it, for it is said that the bird has declined on the island since the arrival of mink. Running shallows were broken by deep pools with darting trout and as the bed became narrower still, the gradient steepened and the character changed. The leaves of the trees, hirsute hawthorns, covered with moss, and battered birches with twisted trunks, formed an archway of dappled light, giving a strange, surrealist beauty. On wet ground grew liverworts and lichens, close by pools, tumbling torrents and walls of sheer rock. In mud "slot marks" were visible, showing where deer had probably sheltered during the day.

Along a small tributary, climbing steadily, the terrain changed to open country, where a warm breeze blew. The bracken was still green, the gorse on flower, and then came coarse moorland grass, with harebells looking perfectly formed and delicate; it was easy to see why they are known as the "bluebells of Scotland". Tormentil was also common, a small buttercup-like plant with four-petalled flowers of bright yellow. It was once much valued in Highland areas as a medicinal aid, for the roots, boiled with milk, were said to cure both calves and children of stomach trouble. In addition, red dye was obtained from the roots, which could also be chewed to improve the gums.

It was pleasant seeing sheep grazing down in the valley, with their distant bleats coming in on the wind, and in one field they had been joined by deer. Higher up on the moorland a kestrel flew; I always have difficulty in identifying Highland kestrels, for they seem to fly lower and glide more than those I normally see hovering over our lowland fields. Higher still the ground turned to bog, with heather and attractive patches of white-tufted cotton grass. The summit itself gave a sudden sweeping view of the sea, islands and far-off farm fields caught in the bright shafts of the setting sun.

I descended steeply down towards the sea, waist deep in bracken. Two hinds with their calves were grazing quietly,

Red deer hind and calf

their summer coats shining with health. Ahead, by a deserted, tumble-down cottage, another hind and her calf were lying down. The wind was blowing in the wrong direction for me, but I crawled beyond the bracken and then pulled myself slowly over short grass towards a small jutting rock overlooking the pair. It was a slow, tense journey, but successfully stalking a wild animal always produces a peculiarly satisfying sensation. I lay just thirty yards away; the mother was chewing the cud, and the calf, with its "bambi" spots, was doing nothing in particular. Then the wind suddenly and briefly swirled, the hind turned her head and looked directly at me. She barked, a low gruff bark, and mother and baby ran to longer grass from where the hind studied me with interest. Other deer were watching from the slope behind me and they barked too; it seemed that I had given them some form of entertainment.

Close to the sea grew a clump of birches, their gnarled trunks covered with layers of granite-like lichen; two kestrels flew from them, calling as they went. The coast was rocky, strewn with boulders and tidal pools and with the gentle swell of the sea. Three grey seals were basking on a submerged rock, giving them the appearance of floating without effort. On seeing me two dived, to watch inquisitively from deeper water. As the light faded a curlew called as it flew towards a far-off peninsula of land. Two bobbing sandpipers still fed among rocks, and oystercatchers flew and cried out in alarm. By the time I had walked past the fishermen's crofts, darkness had fallen and the scent of honeysuckle was sweet and rich. From the village the sound of Scottish dancing floated over the harbour, while nearer at hand it sounded as though drunks were trying to break into a garden. They were quite sober, however, for I had startled a group of four or five stags, with full antlers, wanting to include roses in their diet.

I had not found corncrakes, but I had found an island of great charm and beauty. Unfortunately, others, too, have found Arran; they want to use it as a dumping ground for nuclear waste.

3

Plagues, Puddings and Peaks

Flowers, both in the garden and in the hedgerow, give enormous pleasure. The wild rose is a flower of love whose flowering signals the approach of harvest; its petals can be made into scented water, and its seed-heads can be used in country medicines and wines. Most flowers have similar associations and uses, and as each month passes, so different plants bloom, forming a year-long procession from the hazel catkins of January to the Christmas roses of December.

When wild flowers were more plentiful they featured in many country celebrations: St. Valentine's Day, May Day, and Midsummer Day, as well as at flower shows and harvest festivals. In the Peak District, in Derbyshire, they are still used to decorate wells as part of an ancient thanksgiving for water. One of the most popular well dressings takes place each year at Eyam, a small village made famous by "the plague", in the seventeenth century. The Eyam well-dressing is on the Saturday before Plague Sunday (the nearest Sunday to September 1st), and the following Saturday the celebrations and commemorations are completed with a carnival.

The Peak District itself forms a rolling and at times rugged upland area of about 540 square miles, hemmed in between the great industrial conurbations of Sheffield and Greater Manchester. It lies well north of the Vale of Belvoir, from which it is separated by mining villages, motorways and spasmodic development.

It can be a most appealing place, and although Defoe described it as a "howling wilderness", he liked its wildness and its people. The area is made up of valleys with small farms and stone-walled grass meadows, sheep and cattle, villages, woodlands, fast-flowing streams, reservoirs, moorland, crags and high peat bogs. In weekdays during the winter or even in early summer it can be almost empty apart from local people going about their business – farming, quarrying and mining – but in high summer or at weekends it fills with visitors, walkers and "earnest anoraks", looking for picnic sites, "scenic routes", and the Pennine Way.

I drove into the Peak District to see Eyam's flower-covered wells and its carnival. From Sheffield, in early morning, the high hills were bathed in mist under a weak sun and on the roadside verges some wildflowers gave natural decoration with clumps of rosebay willow herb and ragwort; in general, ragwort is a much-despised plant, for it is mildly poisonous and its leaves have an unpleasant smell when crushed. Consequently it has a number of uncomplimentary names including stinking nanny, dog stalk, and mare fart. On closer examination, however, it contains much beauty, and John Clare wrote of it:

Ragwort thou humble flower with tattered leaves
I love to see thee come and litter gold.

Before making for Eyam I drove to Hope and then along a narrow winding road to Edale, a small village I had visited several years before. It had changed: double yellow lines attempted to keep parked vehicles off the village streets and a large, ordered car park had been created. A local woman did not like it: "It's mad here, every weekend it's worse than a football match. We get thousands – that's right, thousands – drinking, shouting and clogging up the roads. And then there are those 'earnest anoraks' with their new boots, socks and bright coloured coats. Even if they're only going to walk a hundred yards they'll bring an expensive rucksack to carry with them."

She did not exaggerate, for I remembered a day during the hot summer of 1976, "the great drought", when I drove through the National Park, people and cars were everywhere: picknickers with collapsible chairs, sunbathers on airbeds, and the repetitive refrain of "Wonderful Radio One". In a stream, unorthodox fishermen caught crayfish with plastic badminton

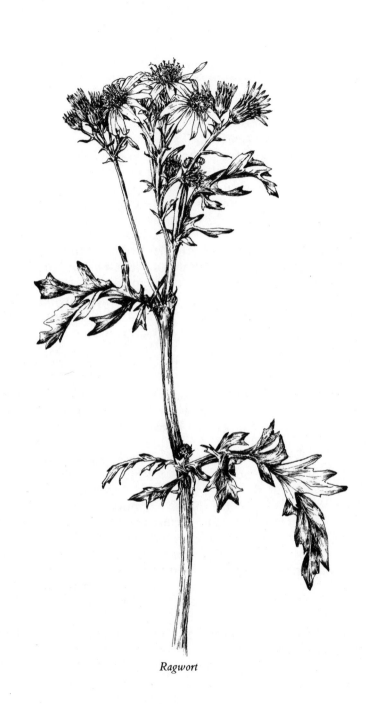

Ragwort

rackets, and from the hills, once-a-year-climbers shouted to their friends and relations below. It could have been a holiday camp at Skegness, not a place of "outstanding natural beauty", and the ice-cream vans added to the illusion.

Early in the morning, however, Edale was almost empty, and with time to spare, and despite the mist, I walked by a stream at the beginning of the Pennine Way. The smell is part of the appeal of high places, an aromatic mixture of pines, sheep, water, moorland and, by a farm, silage also added to the blend. The air felt cool and damp, and as I climbed upwards, so the stream flowed down, tumbling and falling along its rock-strewn bed. In places, too, where the passing of many walkers had worn the vegetation from the soil and rock, water had tried to convert the path into a tributary, until the flow of feet and rain had made the ground slip away.

A wheatear flitted to a rock, its white rump showing clearly, and a large lamb ran bleating to its mother. The car parks and picnic sites were worlds away as the mist closed in; it seemed that even in an area with millions of visitors each year, it was still possible to get away from the crowds. Gradually the mist appeared to glow, a deep marine blue. Rocks and moorland slowly emerged, washed in watery blue sunlight; I had the impression of being underwater. Then suddenly the haze rolled away, leaving the land below white and hidden, but above me was clarity, sheep, grassland and rocky crags. There, too, on an outcrop of high rock, stood about thirty hikers, who had shouted as the visibility cleared; they wore brightly-coloured anoraks, blue, red and yellow; I had not been alone after all. One threw an empty can down towards the stream and they began to study maps; it became strangely quiet, with no birds singing in the valley, and then the whole process went into reverse. The mist swirled back, engulfing everything; I was not sorry, and again I seemed alone.

By the time I had returned to Edale along the worn and eroded path, the sun was stronger, the mist had cleared and the drive to Eyam was brief but pleasant. It is an attractive village, with cottages and terraces and country gardens; although the houses are built of stone, they lack the hardness to be seen in Scotland, and strings of bunting gave them a festive air. The three wells were decorated with rowan berries, leaves and flower petals, most of the flowers having been picked from gardens, not the open fields. They were stuck on to large squares of clay to make pictures and each year the designs are changed to depict a new biblical or contemporary scene. This custom was revived in 1951, Festival of Britain year, as part of the celebrations to commemorate the plague, for Eyam is a "plague village", devastated by bubonic plague from September 1665 until the autumn of 1666. The disease began with the village tailor, who had received a parcel of cloth or clothes from London, where the plague was rampant. The tailor soon died, and misery and suffering swept through the small community. The parish rector, William Mompesson, worked bravely and selflessly among the people, as did his predecessor Thomas Stanley, who had become a Dissenter, and so had been ejected from his living. Nobody was supposed to leave the parish and food was left well away from the houses; payment was made by placing money in running water to cleanse it. All contact with the outside world was avoided to prevent infecting other communities, and out of a population of about 350, only eighty-three survived. Among the victims was Mompesson's wife, and by the end of the year every family understood the meaning of fear and grief.

Some of the present-day villagers can trace their roots back to the time of the plague in Eyam, among them Clarence Daniel who had three relatives die during plague year. On account of the links he feels with the past he has turned his house into a private museum with many old documents and reminders of the period. Several anti-plague recipes in old English hang from his walls, including:

If there do a botch appear; take a Pigeon and pluke the feathers of her tail, very bare and set her tail to the sore, and she will draw out the venome till she die; then take another set too likewise, continuing so till all the venoms be drawne out which you shall see by the Pigeons, for they will die with the venome as long as there is any in: also a chicken or hen is very good . . . All should studiously avoid dancing, running, leaping about, lechery and bathing.

An old apothecary claimed to have treated a female patient in another way: "I laid a great Mastiff Puppy Dog upon her breasts two or three hours together, and made her drink Dill, Pennyroyal, Fennel and Anniseed Water, for she was a fat woman and could bear it."

Another interesting document from the past is a certificate from the Eyam Penny and Halfpenny Burial Society, of which Clarence Daniel's father was president for forty-eight years until 1969. Oddly, despite the Welfare State, the club still flourishes with a membership of 600, although it is now simply known as the Penny Club.

Before his retirement Clarence worked in the local fluorspar mine, where they both mine and quarry. Thousands of tons are crushed for the chemical and steel industries, and some variations of it are also used as semi-precious stones. The museum has on display many geological specimens and relics from the early days of mining; even in those days pilfering occurred, for which the punishment was:

> For stealing ore twice from the minery
> The thief that's taken, fined twice shall be.
> But the third time that he commits such theft
> Shall have a knife struck through his hand to the 'heft
> Into the stone, and there till death shall stand,
> Or loose himself by cutting loose his hand.

The church is at the centre of the village and a Methodist chapel still represents the old Dissenters. Even now, the strength of the two is evident, for, according to a notice, the village playing field is closed on Sundays. In the churchyard stands a magnificent eighth-century Celtic cross, carved in stone, together with the famous headstone for Harry Bag-shaw, who died in 1927 after playing cricket for Derbyshire and the M.C.C. from 1888 to 1924. When I asked the old churchyard sweeper where I could find the cricketer's grave among the many stones, he replied: "Why does everybody want to see that? Geoff Boycott has done far more, but I'm sure people won't want to see his grave when he's dead."

On Harry Bagshaw's gravestone, his stumps are

Eyam Celtic cross

spreadeagled by the ball and a finger above points heaven-
wards. Then comes a slight misquotation of the famous lines:

> Well played
> For when the one great scorer comes
> To write against your name
> He writes – Not that you won or lost
> But how you played the game.

The carnival began as soon as the pubs opened; some of the
local beer was good, but I could not agree with Defoe, who

wrote: "Not forgetting the ale, which everywhere exceeded, if possible, what was passed, as if the farther north the better the liquor, and that the nearer we approached to Yorkshire, as the place for the best, so the ale advanced nearer to perfection."

By mid-afternoon the village seemed to be full, with people milling around, waiting for the procession. The bunting flapped in the breeze and there was a genuine feeling of warmth, happiness and anticipation. Eventually the procession appeared, with bands, money collectors rattling boxes, and many floats, bearing men and women in fancy dress. On one, men were dressed as washerwomen, with the inscription: "Big Bertha – she washes all day and all of the night, but still her clothes are never white." Another concerned foreign aid to Arabs and camels: "We neuter our camels with two bricks", and behind it trundled an "Irish Camel" – a small donkey on wheels with its front and back feet pointing in different directions. More topically, a group wearing white coats, stained with blood, proclaimed: "Super Organ Transplants – only two sizes – Big and Whoppers." Then came a criminal vicar advertising his work: "Rentokil Episcopal Division – Shotgun Weddings a Speciality." Also in the procession were a fire-engine bike, gorillas, rabbits, enormous babies in prams, and carnival queens from neighbouring villages – serious and superficial – and outshone by far prettier girls in the crowd. On a small patch of grass a large queue had formed in front of the lamb roast, for slices of mutton, bread rolls and mint sauce. One of the carvers appeared to have already consumed much liquid refreshment, his work punctuated by cries of: "Come on, Harry, more ale."

At the Bull's Head people were still staggering out with pints of beer. Ironically, opposite the pub, pinned to the church door was a notice which read: "Thirst Aid – Jesus said – whoever drinks the water that I give will never suffer thirst any more." It seemed, however, that the locals still had real thirst.

In addition, another irony became obvious, for during the plague people kept well clear of Eyam; now, each year, despite the piece of modern graffiti which says "Avoid Eyam like the Plague", thousands of people pour into the village, and into

the whole of the Peak District. The day of the carnival, the
roads were lined with parked cars, the "botches" of the new
plague. On nearby trees other modern day marks were visible
for many of their green leaves were covered with a fine coating
of white dust from a nearby quarry. There, limestone was
being blasted out of a hill, shattered by dynamite charges and
then carried away in huge trucks to be processed elsewhere in
the quarry. It was crushed amidst conveyor belts, rollers and
flying dust, for use in building, industry and cement-making.
On the site, too, some of the smaller stones were covered with
tar for use in road construction. The quarry walls were high
and sheer, where rock had been cut and carted away; it was like
a huge amphitheatre for men and their giant rock gouging
machines. Trees and grassy banks screened the hole from the
road, and the quarrying company had undertaken some land-
scaping, yet its presence seemed remarkable; the Peak District
is a National Park, an area of great beauty, but it is gradually
being allowed to succumb to the competition and demands of
people and industry.

Bakewell lies close to Eyam, and on a windy, cloudy day I
parked in the centre of that small market town, for I had heard
of more competition, this time between wallabies, sheep and
people. Surprisingly, it was not simply imagination, as
there have been wild wallabies in the Peak District for many
years.
Bakewell itself is built on the River Wye, where an ancient
stone bridge with five pointed arches takes the road over the
water. It is a leisurely place, with old shops, streets and inns,
which combines a feeling of antiquity with that of a genuine
community. It also contains controversy, for it is the home of
"Bakewell Puddings", for which two local bakers both claim
to have the original recipe. However, although running rival
firms, they agree that the correct title is "Pudding" (although
in a momentary lapse, Mr. Bloomer did refer to tarts) and that
anything described as "Bakewell Tart" should be avoided at
all costs. A true Bakewell Pudding is said to be made of puff
pastry, with jam plus a secret ingredient with sugar, eggs and
almonds.

Probably the most original of the two "original" puddings can be tasted at Bloomer's bakery, where a sign informs: "Bakewell's Famous Puddings Made Daily in our model Bakery From Original Recipe Over 100 Years Old." According to Mr. Eric Bloomer, son of the founder, the pudding was first made in 1860, when the cook at the White Horse Inn, now the Rutland Arms, was asked by the mistress, Mrs. Greaves, to make a new pudding with jam at the top. The cook put the jam in first by mistake, but the result tasted so delicious that thereafter she continued to make it in the same way. When the cook made her will, she paid for the service by giving her lawyer the recipe, who in turn passed on the secret to Mr. George Bloomer. Another story, based on gossip, suggests that the recipe was obtained in quite a different fashion, and that the cook and the founder of the bakery shared a common interest far divorced from cooking.

Although well into his seventies Mr. Eric Bloomer still worked in his old bakehouse, which he showed me round with pride. He also showed me the tattered piece of paper on which the recipe's ingredients were written, but he would not let me read it. The precious mixture, stored in a plastic bucket, looked very yellow, rather like a liquid egg custard. All the puddings are made by hand; 200 small and 200 large are made each day by the seven or eight local employees. Traditional pork pies were also made on the premises, from traditionally-reared pork, for two pigsties at the back housed several pigs, fed on the bakery's waste. The bread tasted excellent too, and the smells and warmth from the ovens produced an appetising atmosphere. Mr. Bloomer was proud of his family firm: "We never make for the public what we wouldn't eat ourselves", nor was he worried by the local opposition, for he was sure that he possessed the original recipe. However, he did complain about his own name: "Things were all right until some lady invented those things for women to wear when riding bicycles."

The "Old Original Bakewell Pudding Shop", built in the seventeenth century, is quite close to Bloomer's. The owners claim that their recipe is the original from the Rutland Arms; the same cook passed the recipe to the wife of a tallow chandler who lived where the shop stands today, and she liked the pudding so much that she set up a business of her own to make them. Since then the recipe has always been sold with the business. The manager was proud of his product and claimed to have had a large helping of Bakewell Pudding for lunch that very day; indeed from the size of his expanding waistline he was probably right. Both puddings were tasty, but obviously made from different recipes, with the Bloomer pudding containing the most almonds.

All the secrecy is to no avail, however, for other local people also claim to have the recipe, said to be based on puff pastry, raspberry jam, 4 eggs, 4 ozs of sugar, 4 ozs of butter and 2 ozs of ground almonds. The jam should be spread on the pastry and then the filling prepared. The eggs and sugar should be mixed, the melted butter added and then beaten. Finally the almonds are added before the mixture is spread on to the jam. The pudding should be cooked until it has set.

Just past the pudding shop, I was surprised to see a much younger establishment, "John Brocklehurst, The Countryman's Outfitter". John Brocklehurst is an interesting man, for at a time when the trend is for larger shops and stores selling mass-produced clothing as cheaply as possible, he gives personal service, selling well-made clothes. His story is unusual; he left school at fourteen, as he did not like it, and his masters had written him off as a failure. The countryside around Bakewell interested him far more; ferreting, tickling trout, and rough-riding a neighbour's pony. He obtained a job with a local butcher, but did not like that either: "All I saw of the customers was when they were striding over me as I scrubbed the floor." He then worked for an outfitters, where he established a country round: "But I couldn't get my boss to buy the right things. He would concentrate on fashion, but country people weren't interested in fashion, they wanted practical things. Moleskin trousers – made from soft cotton, that farmers like; Derby tweed, made in Yorkshire, and corduroy." So he set up on his own. "I had a wife and baby and I spent all my money on a van, a tank full of petrol and a week's rent. The only person who would give me credit was a Jew who had a warehouse. I said to him: 'Being of the origin you are, why have you given a Gentile credit?' He replied: 'I like your face, my boy, you will pay me', and I did.''

He has been so successful that he now owns two shops, as well as a £24,000 articulated lorry, in which he visits country shows during the summer, while during the winter he takes time off to hunt three days a week. "I have the lord of the manor and the poacher coming in here, for we have all the stuff for grubbing about in hedge-bottoms and smart suits as well.'' With his countrywide reputation he is proof that hard work and originality can succeed; that the "little man" can still compete with the giant, and with imagination and initiative he can win.

Although John Brocklehurst was experiencing good times, the wallabies were finding things hard. I was told about them at the Nature Conservancy Council's office at the headquarters of the Peak Park Joint Planning Board. In many government departments plush office suites help to give the impression that money is no object, but although politicians talk about the merits of conservation, their interest seldom extends beyond the spoken word. Consequently the Nature Conservancy Council is kept short of money, and their representative in Bakewell had a small, spartan office; he had to borrow a typewriter, and his petrol allowance did not allow him to cover the area as he would have liked. He told me that the wallabies inhabited a wild place of rocks and heather called the Roaches, and had been in the area for about forty years, after being released from Swythamley Park, the estate of Sir Philip Brocklehurst (no relation to John Brocklehurst). The year before the colony had numbered about forty, but a cold winter had cut the population by half. Competition from grazing by sheep was now the greatest threat, as the owners of the land were increasing the size of their flock.

The journey to the Roaches went north-westwards through the Park, and as Buxton approached the road wound through a small gorge where masses of broad-leaved butterburr grew by a stream. Then came more quarries with dust, dirt, heavy lorries, the large leaves covered with thick dust. Beyond Buxton the road ran higher, where the hills and valleys had been cut and smoothed by glacial ice, and more quarries gave harsher, angular intrusions. By a large outcrop of rock, a country road lined with heather and sheep led to Roaches End. The road ceased, but the rocky outcrops continued as a long heather-fringed ridge, and with the wind blowing coldly, it seemed a hostile place for animals to live, especially those more suited to the hot sun. As I walked over the ridge, knee-deep in old heather, three grouse flew, but they did not call. The heather was on flower, but in poor condition through a mixture of neglect and over-grazing. Then came birch scrub, with peeling bark and lichens; it was sheltered and quiet, apart from the hum of flies. Pines grew higher up and with the taller trees the silence became deeper and stronger. A narrow gorge, where Luddites had once hidden, was damp and cold, mosses and grasses growing from its walls. As I passed through more heather and birch, a hare ran off, pausing briefly to sit up, with its ears aloft; but I saw no signs of wallabies. The remains of a dead sheep lay decomposed by a brackish pool, and paths worn by sheep cut through the heather. On top of the ridge it was colder still. Wallabies could have hidden in many places but all I saw was yet more sheep.

In straightforward terms the wallabies in Derbyshire are irrelevant. They are not natural to Britain and their status in other places is assured. However, if they are to be starved out of their isolated, infertile outpost, for no real reason other than the false economies of intensive moorland grazing, it is again a

Grouse flying

sad reflection on modern-day values. Perhaps, as flowers are used at Eyam to celebrate, some could be left on the rocks of the Roaches as a memorial wreath.★

★After the hard winter of 1981–82 only a handful of wallabies were left. Visitors to the Peak District are therefore requested not to add to their difficulties by searching for them. They should be left undisturbed in the hope that their numbers will recover.

4

Butterflies and Bustards

Butterflies are attractive ephemeral creatures, whose evanescent beauty evokes memories of summer – small meadows, flower-filled gardens, hedges, heat and floating iridescent wings.

Each year as the cold of winter dies, so the first butterflies appear, sometimes as early as March, the sulphur-coloured brimstones flitting over fields and gardens. Soon afterwards the warmth awakens others, small tortoiseshells and peacocks that have over-wintered. Then, as spring turns to summer, the holly blues and orange-tips can be seen, and so as the year moves on the colours change with each brief life. Indeed John Clare's words on life, could equally well apply to butterflies:

> And what is Life? An hour-glass on the run
> A mist retreating from the morning sun
> A busy bustling still repeated dream
> Its length? A moment's pause, a moment's thought
> And happiness? A bubble on the stream
> That in the act of seizing shrinks to nought.

Yet their fleeting lives of sunlight, nectar, and gentle breezes have become more vulnerable. Although butterfly numbers appear to be high, particularly during a hot summer, memory seems to fill the days of childhood with far more colour and variety. Such a view is not based entirely on nostalgia, for at about the same time, John Moore wrote *The Brensham Trilogy*, a fine evocation of country life, in which Mr. Chorlton, a local schoolmaster, collected a plentiful variety of butterflies and moths. Now, however, in many parts of England collecting would be futile, for memory is not wrong, and although a few butterflies remain common, others have declined, and some, like a bubble on a stream, have disappeared. Again the destruction of our wayside flowers ("weeds") is the most likely cause, through modern agriculture and even garden sprays, leaving few plants on which the butterflies can feed or lay their eggs. In the 1950s the large blue could be counted in thousands, but in 1979, it was thought by some to have become extinct in Britain.

The "skippers" are another family that have declined rapidly. Just twenty-five years ago the chequered skipper was to be found in reasonable numbers in and around the woods of Northamptonshire, Bedfordshire and Buckinghamshire; now, the only chequered skipper in England is to be found on a pub sign hanging from the Chequered Skipper Inn, at Ashton, near Oundle, the home of Miriam Rothschild. I heard of the pub in conversation and knew nothing of its history; consequently I wanted to visit it, to discover the reason for its name and swinging sign.

Late May is usually one of the most pleasant times of the year, and in the soft sunlight the small villages looked picturesque, with the "may" out, cow parsley on flower and the churches and houses half-hidden by foliage. I drove through Little Gidding, the hamlet where Nicholas Ferrar lived in the seventeenth century. Elected a Member of Parliament in 1624, he gave up his career almost immediately to spend the rest of his life in prayer and the service of God: "Counting the lowest place in His house better and more honourable than the greatest crown in the world".

Today values have changed, for in most of the nearby political constituencies, the majority safe Conservative seats, ex-public school stereotypes, with tenuous local links, have moved in to take the assumed glory of representing the people. Many of them appear to have chosen politics as a career in much the same way as others choose accountancy, carpentry, or scrap-metal dealing; philosophy and conviction rarely seem to be the main driving forces, and politics has been turned into a circus by the search for a safe seat.

When Nicholas Ferrar abandoned ambition and personal

power, he founded the Little Gidding Community, which, with a small church, a few houses and six acres of land still exists. The members of the Community, married and single people, eat, work and pray together, living as an extended Christian family. As I wandered around the churchyard a male chaffinch sang from the top of a hawthorn tree and a tethered Jersey cow – being used as a lawnmower – quietly chewed the cud.

Of the roadways around Little Gidding, T. S. Eliot wrote:

> If you came this way,
> Taking the route you would be likely to take
> From the place you would be likely to come from,
> If you came this way in may time, you would find the hedges
> White again, in May, with voluptuary sweetness.

Alas, between the villages little "may" can now be seen, for most of the hedges have disappeared, ripped out, and replaced by cultivation and spraying right up to the roadside verges. Between 1946 and 1970 the area lost ninety per cent – 5,000 miles – of its hedgerows. Richard Jefferies made this plea for hedges in the late nineteenth century:

> Let not the modern Goths destroy our hedges, so typical of an English landscape, so full of all that can delight the eye and please the mind. Spare them, if only for the sake of the 'days we went gypsying – a long time ago'; spare them for the children to gather the flowers of May and the black-berries of September.

A few hedges have been spared from total destruction, but as I drew nearer to Ashton I saw a large stretch of hedge which had been slashed, battered and reduced in size. It had been flail-mowed; the flowering may had disappeared, as had most of the foliage, and the "hedge" had been left with tattered bark, torn limbs and stumps of fresh white wood that looked like many fractured bones. It did not "delight the eye", or "please the mind", and the action had served no useful purpose. A well-developed hedge is a living thing and during the month of May it will contain and conceal many nests with eggs and feeding young. When children steal eggs or smash the nests they are punished for breaking the law and referred to as hooligans, yet farmers who hack away their hedges at nesting time are congratulated on their efficiency and tidiness. Their action has no agricultural merit and the reason for it is simple: towards the end of May there is often a slight lull in the landwork and so the men are sent to cut the hedges "to give them something to do". It reflects both ignorance on the part of the farmer, and the absurdity of the tax system, for after a good year some farmers buy pieces of equipment, such as flail mowers, that they do not really want or need, simply to reduce the size of their tax demands.

The immediate approaches to Ashton, grass meadows and well-grown hedges, made a complete contrast to the previous acres of feelingless farming. Ashton itself had thatched cottages, a village green, and mature horsechestnut trees reflecting the season in their candelabra flowers. The Chequered Skipper, its butterfly sign made from the painted heads of hundreds of nails, also had a thatched roof. The fame of the pub exceeds the limits of its name, for it was once the centre for

The Chequered Skipper

the World Flea Congress, and on the second Saturday of October it is also the venue for the annual National Conker Championships.

The pub and the whole village have been in the Rothschild family for many years, and they are now managed by Miriam (properly called the Honourable Mrs. Lane). Both she and her house were easy to find from a villager's description: "Oh, the Honourable Miriam Rothschild; she may be an Honourable but she looks more like a gypsy peg-seller. She lives down the road; as it's the only house along there the road becomes their private drive. There is a set of large iron gates, but don't go through them – they lead to another set of iron gates on the other side of the estate – her father erected the gates first and then decided on a different site for the house."

Her father was Nathaniel Charles Rothschild, founder of the Society for the Promotion of Nature Reserves and a leading authority on fleas; he possessed the largest collection of fleas in the world, and discovered which type of flea carried the plague. His daughter has retained his interest, being herself an expert on fleas; her particular speciality is the rabbit flea and its sex-life, but her interest in natural history extends much further, to butterflies on which she is an authority.

Her large, stone-built house, covered with roses and climbing plants, is set among trees and overgrown lawns. I was ushered in by a man wearing wellington boots and taken along a corridor, one wall of which was lined with bookcases containing leather-bound volumes. He showed me into the library, where there were more handsome old books and birds cast in bronze; the room had a lived-in look, however, as a collection of attractive daughters and grandaughters engaged in their Sunday afternoon leisure. Some were sitting on the floor, talking and laughing in front of a large open fireplace where elm logs burned, while one played classical music at the piano; it was a scene of dishevelled refinement – an updated glimpse of Victorian England, complete with buttered toast, thinly cut sandwiches, chocolate éclairs and tea.

Miriam herself was instantly recognisable, reclining on an old sofa and wearing a head scarf, smock and yellow galoshes, but without the basket of pegs. Immediately she began to talk about butterflies, showing evident enthusiasm; indeed in 1967 her butterfly passion led her to change the name of the local pub from the "Three Horseshoes" to the "Chequered Skipper". Once the chequered skipper thrived in the 500 acres adjoining the house, for it liked the mature woodland with its long grass and flowering bugle, where it could feed and breed. Gradually, however, it disappeared, possibly because the meadowland around the wood was converted to arable use, and drifting or seeping sprays spread poison, indiscernible to human senses, but sufficient to kill butterflies.

Surprisingly, in 1974 a swallowtail butterfly was seen drifting through Ashton on a light June breeze, but it did not indicate a change in butterfly fortunes – for during the winter a local cottage had been thatched with Norfolk reeds from Hickling Broad, and a chrysalis arrived with the reeds. One day Miriam Rothschild hopes to reintroduce butterflies by more orthodox scientific methods, breeding them in captivity for release when the habitat has been restored: butterflies such as the wood white, white admiral, and silver washed fritillary. She admitted the problems involved: "Many people consider butterflies to be unimportant, but they can be of great benefit to man. Their numbers reflect the good health of an area and they are good monitors of climate and long-term climatic trends. They are also important, for it is vital to keep a genetic pool; recently a scientist discovered twenty-one new antibiotics from the stomachs of butterflies which could be important to us." Her main motive for wanting to restore butterfly numbers was much more straightforward however; she simply wanted them for the aesthetic pleasure they give.

Part of this pleasure is created by the flowers required by butterflies, and she ushered me through the french windows to show me her lawn, long and uncut, with flowering plantain, daisies, clover and buttercups among the grasses. It was a genuine "wild garden", kept to encourage birds, bees, plants and butterflies. Nearby was a small grass meadow, again full of flowers: cowslips, fritillaries and orchids. But she had still more to show me and led me into the large walled garden; there a notice on the door asked visitors to keep it closed to prevent a vixen and her cubs from wandering out. Breeding owls stared as we passed some greenhouses and then we came upon rows of cultivated cowslips, poppies, cornflowers, cuckoo flowers, violets, harebells and many more: "I am collecting all this seed so that people can grow their own wildflowers and I am going to mix some with grass seed and call it 'farmer's nightmare'." By so doing she hopes to reverse current trends, for in her opinion roadside verges should be planted with wildflowers as they are in some American states, and farmers should be given encouragement, through compensation, to retain their hedges. The verges and hedges would then act as they did in former years, as corridors linking woods, marshes and special reserves, so that wildlife would not be restricted to isolated areas surrounded by hostile arable land. She would then be able to release her butterflies with confidence in their survival.

Despite being in her seventies, she bubbled with enthusiasm as she spoke about her flowers, the chequered skipper, an old water mill that she was converting into a fishing museum, and the future. Strange then, that in view of her serious work and hopes, many people still see only the scarf and the galoshes, nothing more than an eccentric old lady obsessed with butterflies. The need for her obsession showed clearly as I left, driving slowly through her private wood, its floor carpeted with the creeping stems of bugle, blue with flowers, but there were no signs of the butterflies that should have been feeding on the nectar.

In today's political climate some would no doubt argue that Miriam Rothschild's enthusiasm developed from her privileged background, with money buying time in which to indulge in an interest irrelevant to the twentieth century. But in Hertfordshire lives an artist who is just as deeply concerned by the destruction of the countryside, and butterflies in particular, who came from a working-class home, left school at fifteen, and developed his knowledge, concern and skill while working with his hands.

Gordon Beningfield lives at Water End, near Hemel Hempstead, a depressing journey from Ashton, passing through Northamptonshire, Bedfordshire and eastern Buckinghamshire. Bedfordshire must be almost the dullest county in the country; much of the land is of heavy clay and its coldness seems to draw itself into the landscape. The villages, of red-bricked cottages and tiled roofs, lack the character of beams and thatch found elsewhere, and the roads are overburdened with heavy lorries. Just over the border into Buckinghamshire is one of the ugliest places ever conceived; my first view of Milton Keynes was of a wide area of rooftops in low undulating land. There was no apparent reason for its situation; no church tower, no castle, no cathedral and no bridge, around which settlements usually develop. But Milton Keynes had no natural birth, for it was simply spawned by planners, politicians and developers who decided to build a "new town" in rural Buckinghamshire. The "new town" was evidently still growing, and appeared to be divided into areas to suit several degrees of bad taste and income levels, from box-like flats for workers, to better-class mock-Georgian homes for executives, complete with panelled doors and two garages. In Milton Keynes plastic garden gnomes seem quite in order; its marriage breakdown rate is one of the highest in the country; it has an abundance of smartly-dressed men wearing dark glasses and driving Ford Granadas, with coat hangers swinging in the rear, and it even has a group of concrete cows; needless to say it has won numerous architectural awards for concept and design. Everywhere is claustrophobic landscaped sterility but, surprisingly, people live and work there. Yet it seems so regimented and artificial that ant-hill society looks liberal and individualistic by comparison.

After the new and antiseptic, I arrived at Bletchley, a drab blot on the landscape – a mixture of old industrial housing and semi-detached suburbia. As I reached the outskirts I passed a young goldfinch lying dazed against the kerb; I wanted to stop but the road was narrow and an articulated lorry pounded impatiently along behind me. The annual carnage of wildlife as well as of people on the roads is enormous. Close by was a signpost pointing to Leighton Buzzard; in the wild, buzzards would efficiently scavenge the injured, but they were driven from this part of England many years ago.

Once away from these two man-made scars, the countryside became more rural, with the Chiltern hills rising steeply on my left, the green fields and hedges broken by a large white lion carved into the hillside, showing the position of Whipsnade Zoo. Off the main road were narrow lanes, farms, woods and quiet villages with names such as Little Gadesden, Nettleden, Ashridge and Cheverell's Green. The River Gade wound through a wide fertile valley, flowing over a number of small sluices, passing houses with beams and old gardens, redolent of the age of genuine horse-power and the country squire.

At an arched bridge a small cottage nestled away from the road, an old farm cart parked by the door; it was Water End. It seemed an ideal place for a country artist to live, and Gordon Beningfield's paintings reflect his closeness to the countryside and his love for it. He paints landscapes as well as butterflies, and all branches of natural history, the canvasses possessing a feeling for the subject that few other artists can match: with a bumble bee on a bramble flower, the sights and sounds of the hedgerow again become a reality, and with deer at dawn, it is almost possible to hear the breaking of twigs as hooves move on and feel the shock as a cold dew-soaked leaf brushes the cheek.

Although his paintings are outstanding, his background is most unusual; no fine education, finishing at a top art school in London or Paris, nor the leisured experimentation and observation of a middle-class Edwardian lady. He literally learnt his art in the fields and developed it while undertaking a full-time job. He failed the eleven-plus, attended an ordinary secondary modern school, and even escaped National Service: "They thought I was mentally deficient and would make no contribution to army life." In fact Gordon Beningfield is to modern-day art what John Clare was to nineteenth-century English literature. His paintings are simple and expressive, and all convey the message of what the countryside could be, if only people and politicians cared.

He was born in London, where his father worked as a tugboat-man on the Thames, but the whole family moved out to Hertfordshire when Gordon was three because of the war. He grew up in London Colney, near St. Albans, then still a village, in a small terraced house overlooking farmland: "It was one of the best times in rural England, they were still using binders, and I remember the marvellous time stooking up the corn, chasing the rabbits and butterflies and picking wild-flowers; we took all these things for granted."

On leaving school he wanted to become an artist, but his parents could not afford to send him to an art school, and the most likely alternatives seemed to be farmworker or gamekeeper. Fortunately, at that time an opportunity arose at Faithcraft, a studio in St. Albans, which created ecclesiastical art and furnishings: "It was perfect. I worked with extremely good craftsmen and learnt to handle a great variety of ma-terials. I got to know how to cut wood, mix paint, apply gold leaf, work at heraldry, mural painting, lettering, layout and the preparation of faces on candlesticks." In addition he went to St. Albans Art School for two days a week, and during lunch hours, evenings and weekends, he would work on his private painting and drawing: "I would draw landscapes; the country churches where we were working; natural history, and I was always harking back to my schooldays, with farms, animals and country scenes."

By 1968 he had enough private commissions to last six months. Consequently he took the gamble and gave up his job; his first London painting exhibition followed soon after-wards and was a success. He has been painting ever since and as we spoke he confessed to a backlog of work that would take at least three years to clear.

Altogether he has held numerous London exhibitions, com-pleted memorial windows in stained glass for the Household Cavalry, the Coldstream Guards and the Parachute Regiment; he has had two books published and has taken part in numer-ous television programmes. Just before my visit he had been commissioned by the G.P.O. to design four butterfly stamps, for butterflies have almost become his trademark: "Initially I became interested in butterflies by accident. Being very fond of the traditional countryside, particularly old meadowland, large hedges and mixed woodland, it was very hard for me not to notice butterflies. I began to look at them closely and discovered a wonderful small world, with beautiful shapes and forms. I saw butterflies in their environment, and thought they would make a fascinating subject. I didn't want to paint them as book illustrations, I wanted to paint pictures of them – eavesdrop on a butterfly world."

Eavesdropping on butterflies is made easier by his over-grown garden, which he showed me with great pleasure. There was cow parsley, "Queen Anne's lace", on flower, and stinging nettles in abundance. "I have roses, but I also have all sorts of wildflowers to attract wildlife. I have stinging nettles for tortoiseshell and peacock butterflies, ivy for brimstones and holly blues, and jack-by-the-hedge and cuckoo flower for orange-tips. I also have a jungle to give them plenty of cover, and I might even have dormice."

He has been both saddened and angered by the fall in butterfly numbers: "A few years ago the chalkhill blue was common on the Chilterns, but now you have to look hard for it. The trouble is hedges have been ripped out and farmers are spraying without thinking of the consequence. Do you know, if an ordinary person goes into a field and digs up a flower, he can be prosecuted. If a farmer sprays a whole field of rare wildflowers, it is quite legal. It's not the farmers' fault, it's all to do with economic pressure, cheap-food policies and over-population. It causes me total depression that can last for days or even weeks. But farming, leisure and life in general can co-exist with nature, if only people will make the attempt. I have made it work in my garden."

Gordon is a keen fisherman, and a member of the syndicate that stocks the streams flowing past his front door with trout. In marshy ground along one bank lady's smock was on flower, and he bent down to show me the small orange eggs of the orange-tip butterfly, that had been laid on its "food plant". As he did so he noticed something else – a youth on the bridge surreptitiously trying to poach trout with a hand-line: "Oi!" he shouted. "What do you think you are doing?" and as the youth fled he set off in pursuit.

Soon he returned, unsuccessful and panting, and we went into his small studio, built in the garden, to sit down to home-made cakes and tea. Among drawings and paintings were signs of his other interests; old sheep-bells, docking irons and shepherds' crooks, and, surprisingly for somebody considered to be "thick" by the army, shelves of books including many by Thomas Hardy. "I have been fascinated by Thomas Hardy for several years, and if you are interested in the English countryside you cannot avoid him. *Far from the Madding Crowd* is probably my favourite novel, as it introduced me to Gabriel Oak, the shepherd, and it was probably Thomas Hardy who got me interested in shepherding of the past. I have also been to look for the countryside of Thomas Hardy, and because of it I have discovered Dorset. It is a wonderful county. You still find old meadowland, hedgerows, wildflowers, small farms and absolute silence. It is the world I dream of, and I find it there. If I go to a location that Hardy wrote about, and still find it as I hoped it would be, it is a great joy. I went to the Frome valley recently; it was lush water meadows, with cattle standing in the river, reeds, and old willow trees. It was late afternoon, with lemon light and mist; it was superb and very emotional."

As I left I looked at the solitary picture on Gordon's drawing board; there, in precise detail was a magnificent large blue. It is extremely sad that in Britain such a butterfly can now only be seen as a painting or as a postage stamp.

The large blue, apart from being strikingly beautiful, is a most unusual butterfly, with a remarkable life cycle. It lays its eggs on wild thyme, the leaves of which are eaten by the young caterpillars. After a few weeks the growing grubs secrete a substance found attractive by certain red ants, myrmica, who carry them into their nests. In return the thankful caterpillars eat the ant larvae, until they pupate in the spring; in midsummer they emerge as fully developed butterflies. The disappearance of the large blue has been caused both by the intensification and modification of agriculture, and by myxomatosis. In the past, rabbits kept much grassland closely grazed, which provided an ideal environment for the red ant. Now, large tracts of grassland have fallen to the plough, while most of the rest is too long for the ants, and so one of the vital links in the metamorphosis from caterpillar to butterfly has been severed.

Butterflies should be on the wing between June and August,

so I delayed the final part of my butterfly journey until mid-July. Then I travelled to Compton House, near Sherborne, just inside the Dorset border, to meet Robert Goodden, the founder of Worldwide Butterflies where he breeds both indigenous and exotic species. He became interested in butterflies at the age of four, and since then his enthusiasm has developed into a dedicated effort to preserve them.

A mild man, bald, bespectacled, and concerned, but with a ready smile, he founded Worldwide Butterflies in 1962 after a trip to the Far East to study butterflies; previously he had subsidised his interest by selling saucepans at Harrods. The venture was so successful that in 1978, Robert, his family, and his butterflies, moved to the old family home of Compton House. It was an ironic twist, for Robert Goodden was not the eldest son but, due to the crippling expenses of maintaining a country house, the family seat was due to be auctioned. But then Robert, who had been building up his collection of butterflies, took the risk of buying the property in order to display his collection to the public in more suitable surroundings, and butterflies proved to be the catalyst that saved the Goodden link with Compton House.

The manor house at Compton, dating back to the sixteenth century, is set back from the main Sherborne to Yeovil road, in mature rolling parkland. Inside it has been turned into a butterfly centre, with specimen butterflies, butterfly models, butterfly pictures, and "the jungle" and "the palm house" – two heated rooms with luxuriant vegetation where tropical butterflies live. Silk worms also thrive, and are fed on locally-grown mulberry leaves. In the grounds food plants, where swallowtails, orange-tips, peacocks and tortoiseshells breed, are protected by butterfly cages.

Away from the house Robert took me to one of his most important ventures, where he was experimenting with the large blue, for he believes that a serious attempt to reintroduce the continental strain of the butterfly might have to be made if no British butterflies reappear. His reasons for wanting to preserve the large blue are simple: "Someone has to take care of the countryside for others to enjoy. People just couldn't manage without the countryside and beautiful creatures." He is wrong of course, for many people are oblivious to their surroundings, or the wildlife struggling for survival, but at least his motives are admirable.

In nearby meadows, among grazing sheep, he showed me colonies of the required red ant, into which he had introduced a number of large blue caterpillars. If these survived, they might emerge at any time, so he had covered the ants' nests with pyramids of muslin to ensure that the large blues were not lost. We looked at all the nests; the ants were busily going about their business, in Milton Keynes fashion, but there were no signs of butterflies:*

Robert Goodden is trying to offer protection and ensure continuity both to butterflies and to his family home. It would be a pleasant thing if, in years to come, Gooddens and butterflies still lived at Compton House.

Two hundred and fifty years ago Wiltshire was one of the last strongholds of the great bustard, a bird whose name, according to Sir Winston Churchill, should be "enunciated with relish but discretion". Gilbert White often saw the bird in Sussex, it was also to be found in Yorkshire, East Anglia and Dorset and it gave its name to the Bustard Inn on Salisbury Plain. But, like the large blue, the bustard could not cope adequately with change, particularly the switch to mechanical methods of agriculture, and the change from rye to wheat, and so numbers dwindled until it finally disappeared during the middle of the last century. Its demise was hastened by its reputation for making an excellent meal, and it was considered to be an ideal quarry for coursing dogs. Unfortunately as the bird does not have a preen gland, after heavy dew, rain, or frost, it cannot get airborn and so provides good sport for greyhounds and lurchers.

In 1900 an unsuccessful attempt was made to re-introduce the bustard to the Breckland of Suffolk, and so for many years the only bustards to be seen were on the coats of arms for Wiltshire, Cambridgeshire and South Cambridgeshire District Council. Then in 1970 the Hon. Aylmer Tryon, who established an art gallery in London, decided to make an

* No large blue butterflies emerged.

Arthur, the great bustard

attempt to re-introduce a breeding herd to Porton Down in Wiltshire. After meeting with no success in my quest for the large blue butterfly, I made the short journey to Wiltshire, to his home in the village of Great Durnford, hoping to hear better news of the bustards. Aylmer lives in the old eighteenth-century mill, which he has renovated and converted into a house. He can just remember it being used to grind corn in his early childhood, but then, like most of the water mills, it was replaced by electricity and allowed to fall into disrepair. Situated on the river Avon, he has called it Kingfisher Mill, and has constructed a mud bank by the mill stream in the hope that kingfishers will nest in front of his living-room window. An idyllic home, the mill is permeated with the sound of running water and the scent of summer roses. In nearly all the rooms hang paintings of wildlife and landscapes, and by the stairs is a special area of plain wallpaper where each visiting artist adds an item to a country scene. He shares his house with a young spaniel named Drake, and each day a friendly lady from the village helps in the home.

Aylmer Tryon is a mildly eccentric man, who once went searching for truffles around his home with a trained truffle pig; alas the venture was unsuccessful. It was entirely in character, therefore, that in 1970 he decided to form the Great Bustard Trust as his contribution to European Conservation Year, to re-introduce bustards, for their numbers are declining throughout Europe. The Trust leased a ten-acre area of downland from the Ministry of Defence at Porton Down, and acquired a number of cock and hen bustards from Portugal, as well as one hen bird found exhausted on Fair Isle in January 1970. The birds were then released into their enclosure during the spring – but nothing happened. If male and female coots, cats, or even human beings are put together, they will breed; bustards are more discerning, however, and will not. Unbeknown to the members of the Great Bustard Trust, they had chosen one of the most difficult birds to breed in captivity.

The great bustard itself is extremely handsome; a large, very shy bird, rather resembling an elegant rufous-coloured turkey. The cock has Gladstonian side-whiskers and can reach a weight of forty pounds, which makes it the heaviest flying land bird in the world, with the possible exception of the mute swan and the African kori bustard.

By 1975, with an air of indifference and abstinence continuing to hang over the enclosure, Dr. Nigel Collar of Oxford University was appointed as research officer. It was an unusual choice, for he obtained his doctorate not in science, but in English, writing a thesis on the Literary Climate of the 1930s. His interest in bustards developed when he was teaching in Spain, where he often drove through the heart of bustard country. Some years ago his father, also a doctor, had produced a learnéd paper in conjunction with a Dr. Tie; in addition to his interest in bustards, therefore, Nigel's other ambition is to outdo his father by producing a document written by Drs. Shirt, Collar and Tie.

He studied wild bustards for the Trust in Portugal, and discovered that cock birds do not reach maturity until they are about nine years old, and that the birds divide into single-sex flocks during the winter. Consequently in the winter of 1978–79 the sexes at Porton were separated; the birds were considered old enough to breed, but to ensure success Arthur, the one tame cock, was given a hormone injection of testosterone. In the spring a full display followed and fertile eggs were laid. Unfortunately marauding rooks smashed the nests; one egg was rescued and placed in an incubator, but the chick died two days after hatching.

The courtship display is vital for successful breeding, as the male fluffs out his feathers and inflates his chest like a balloon, in order to impress the female. The inflatable area is known as the gular sac and is blown up by forcing air through a hole beneath the tongue. In the nineteenth century Thomas Bewick misunderstood its purpose, for he wrote:

This singular reservoir was first discovered by Dr. Douglas, who supposes that the bird fills it with water as a supply in the midst of those dreary plains where it is accustomed to wander; it likewise makes a further use of it in defending itself against the attacks of birds of prey; on such occasions it throws out the water with such violence as to baffle the pursuit of its enemy.

79

In fact, in the spring of 1980 I had already travelled to Porton in the hope of seeing Arthur's display. By coincidence Eric Hosking and his son David had arrived the same day and were already installed in two photographic hides inside the enclosure. The sun was shining but a bitterly cold wind blew even in the shelter of the permanent wooden hide. Paul, a biologist who looked after the birds during the summer, assured me that Arthur would begin his display at about five thirty p.m., as he had on recent days. At five thirty one of the younger cocks walked directly in front of a hide and sat down. Later a stoat, dragging a rabbit behind it, hurried by, but there was no sign of Arthur. Paul then decided that because of the open skies the display would probably begin at about six thirty. At seven a strange white patch showed through a bush, giving it the appearance of blackthorn on flower; it moved – it was Arthur.

Slowly Arthur moved from behind the bush; he was an incredible sight, like a large unstable meringue with legs and feathers. It was almost as if he were trying to turn himself inside out, with his erectile whiskers vertical, his sac inflated, and both his head and tail bent up over his back. A hen approached, but showed no signs of interest, despite Arthur rocking backwards and forwards seductively. Finally he tired, his feathers returned to normal and he began to feed. It is thought that the cock bird mates just once with each hen, and that they have some form of sperm storage which allows all the eggs to be fertilised.

Because bustards are so shy, Paul had to walk to each hide, to frighten the birds away, for the sudden appearance of a figure from inside would have caused great alarm. Eric Hosking, an agreeable dumpy little man, emerged from the hide beaming with pleasure. Even after a long career of photographing exotic birds all over the world he said: "It's been a wonderful day," and he meant it.

In July I drove from Kingfisher Mill to meet Paul again at the Pheasant Inn, and he accompanied me to the Chemical Defence Establishment at Porton Down. A notice at the check barrier informed "Germ Warfare Division", but the paddocks of sheep and cattle scarcely looked sinister. Away from the buildings, fields gave way to undulating grassland with a few pine trees, gorse bushes and hawthorns. The ground was carpeted with small yellow flowers, skylarks sang, and only the tank tracks were out of place. Beyond the bustards' pen the rolling downland descended to large flat fields, like an ocean of arable surrounding an island haven. Inside the pen an area of barley and tares had been covered with netting to keep off rooks, and as we walked through the seeding grasses towards it, clouds of butterflies, common blues and marbled whites, flew on flimsy wings. Porton is one of the old relic downlands, with a wealth of plant and insect life; it is strange that such a rare and rich place should be given over to the army to develop ways of inflicting death and to play war games.

The bustards remained well away from us and Paul showed me where one hen had laid in the barley. This time the eggs had been taken and placed in an incubator, but the temperature had been slightly wrong, and again the chicks had died shortly after hatching. We then waded waist deep through the barley to where another hen had been incubating, but she had apparently lost interest; Paul had seen no signs of eggs. The

Marbled white

nest site had been in a small depression, and there, to one side of it, hidden by grass, we found a large mottled egg. It was cold, rotten and infertile.

So it had been another unsuccessful year, and next summer, to avoid rooks and incubators, any eggs will be placed under bantams, who usually make excellent foster mothers for chicks and even ducklings.★ As far as the bustard is concerned, however, there is another ray of hope. Just as agricultural change helped to reduce its numbers, so a more recent change could actually help. In the last ten years rape has been grown in increasing quantities, particularly in East Anglia; it is planted in the autumn and could provide ideal food in the winter and cover during the summer. If the sea of green surrounding Porton gains patches of flowering yellow during May, then, with help, the great bustard has a chance of returning as a breeding bird to Britain.

★ In 1981 two chicks hatched, but again they died soon afterwards.

5

Otters and Immigrants

The journey to Dorset and Wiltshire was not simply to see butterflies, Arthur the great bustard, or the lost world of Thomas Hardy, so dear to Gordon Beningfield. I had also hoped to see a wild otter, an unfulfilled ambition for many years. Like so many other creatures the otter was plentiful throughout Britain until a rapid decline began in the 1950s and accelerated in the '60s as dieldrin and various other toxic chemicals were used with insufficient knowledge or concern. The disturbance caused by four million anglers has not helped the otter, nor has the attitude of many water authorities whose quest for efficiency and tidiness has turned many once-healthy rivers, streams and quiet country brooks into featureless drainage channels, almost devoid of life, by the removal of all plants and bankside trees. Otters need clean, healthy rivers, where disturbance and interference are at a minimum; these they can seldom find in over-crowded England, where sewage effluent and excess fertilisers are flushed into our water systems, and where millions of people seek their recreation on boats and river banks.

Otters are now entirely absent from Central England, and nor is one to be found in the area covered by the Thames Water Authority. They are only present in the north, south and south-west, the coastal parts of East Anglia, and the Welsh border, although they remain comparatively plentiful in Scotland. As Dorset still supports a few otters I wanted to visit an "otter haven" on a quiet, clear-flowing country river, in the hope of seeing, at last, a wild otter.

The drive to Dorset had flow of a different kind, and it seems that "havens" for people are already required near several of our major roads. Watford is the real beginning of commuter land, where each day streams of cars head for London – "the great wen" that Cobbett regarded as a blight on the countryside, sucking both people and money to its fashionable, unwholesome centre. The houses of suburbia are so numerous that I find it difficult to imagine real people living in them, or real occupations to keep them employed. Gradually turbans and saris became more numerous as I approached an area where immigrants have settled in quite large numbers, bringing their traditions with them. By the time signposts appeared for Heathrow Airport the roads were almost solid with vehicles of all shapes and sizes; one car bore the slogan: "It's quicker by Air" – very true. The visitor who flies in to Britain could be excused for thinking that the whole country is covered with motorways, ring roads and housing estates.

At Windsor, with its castle and river, the visual quality of suburbia improved, and then I drove through Windsor Great Park, with fences, parked cars, people and their dogs. Again it seemed to have taken on the role of dog latrine. What unfortunate lives urban and suburban dogs are forced to lead; some even undergo operations to prevent them from barking. The residents of neighbouring Ascot do not like the term "commuter", for theirs is stockbroker country, complete with a racecourse and golf clubs, whose car parks were full on that Tuesday afternoon.

Motorway driving followed, until I came to the A30, a straight, undulating road cutting through the heart of downland. In the days of the large blue and the bustard it must have made a memorable summer journey, and today it is still pleasant, but now much of the land has been converted to arable farming, as wheat brings in a greater return than sheep. Even the remaining grassland has lost its character, for new strains of faster growing grass, encouraged by fertilisers and sprays, have pushed the old grasslands out.

The destruction of the downland has been steady, stretching back over many years;* even Cobbett saw it and was disheartened: "We came by some hundreds of acres of ground, that was formerly most beautiful down, which was broken up in

* A quarter of Dorset's chalk downland was ploughed up between 1967–72.

84

dear-corn times, and which is now a district of thistles and other weeds. If I had such land as thus I would soon make it down again."

Most people travelling along the A30 continue on to Devon and Cornwall, but I turned south, to travel for the first time into the depths of Dorset. The county was an immediate revelation, for despite changes it is still a place of hedges and meadows, old wooden field gates, clear streams, small villages and wooded hillsides. It has both the look and the feel of the traditional English countryside, which in so many places has been destroyed, and the names conjure up its country character: Fiddleford, Smugglers Lane, Gallows Corner and Fox Warren.

I intended to spend the night at Blandford Forum, conveniently situated in the centre of the county, but in the meantime I meandered along the roads and lanes visiting three quiet villages; Child Okeford, Shilling Okeford (now called Shillington), and Okeford Fitzpain (which is still known locally as Okeford Fippany – 5d). The names date back many generations to when an orphan child was looked after in Child Okeford, and the other villages paid a shilling and fivepence for its upkeep.★

At Child Okeford I stopped by a newly-built stone farmhouse; it looked extremely prosperous, but there were no farm fields leading from the yard, not even a proper farmyard, just a number of long low sheds; it was a mink farm with 10,000 mink. Although well into the evening the farmer was still working, injecting the animals to protect them from botulism. Each time he picked up an animal it squealed vigorously and bit into his strong leather glove. John Harbour had been farming mink "man and boy for twenty-eight years" on the farm started by his father. He considered it hard work: "I have to work seven days a week, but it's a good thing, for it means that I never get that Monday morning feeling." The mink themselves were attractive creatures; healthy and alert with soft black coats. A few were brown in colour, while the most striking were a smooth steel grey. As we stood by one cage a

★ In the days when 12d made one shilling.

mother with three "kits" scolded us in agitation: "They are brave little things – fierce too. The males fight, and superficially it seems that no damage is done. Then one of them might die two days later; if you examine the corpse you will find teeth pricks in its neck or balls. They usually go for the balls. Not very friendly of them, is it?"

Every male has four females, and each female usually gives birth to three or four "kits". These are kept in small cages and fed daily on chopped-up chicken-heads, day-old cockerel chicks, and entrails. The surplus, plus the bodies of any skinned mink, is sent away to be made into soap and cosmetics. When the mink are wanted for their skins, they are injected with barbiturates to kill them; a good skin is worth about fifteen pounds and an average of forty skins are needed to make a coat. After "pelting", the number of animals on the farm falls to about 2,000, and the only other quiet time of the year is just before "kitting".

Mink have been living free in England since the late 1940s, and they can now be found in most parts of the British Isles. An American member of the weasel family, there is no doubt that the original wild mink escaped from fur farms. Some naturalists and countrymen want all wild mink exterminated,

Mink

arguing that it is a destructive, alien creature that kills birds, animals and fish in large numbers, and has no place in the British countryside. They also claim that the presence of mink, competing for food, has contributed to the decline of the otter in England. Others take a totally different view, believing that Britain has a shortage of predators, and that the wild mink will settle into our wildlife and become accepted, in exactly the same way as the rabbit, little owl and the fallow deer.

Although John Harbour kills mink for his livelihood, he actually likes them and does not believe that they are as destructive as some suggest: "They are not as savage as they are painted and there is a place for them in the wild. They are very territorial and once they reach a natural balance their numbers will not increase." He was quick to point out that none of his animals had escaped into the Dorset countryside. Some get out of their cages, but boundary fences prevent them going further, and they are all re-captured on the premises. It seems a harsh way to make a living, killing animals to produce the furs of high fashion; yet he was a pleasant, amusing man, and at least fur farming is more defensible than taking skins from the wild. When he heard I was travelling on to Blandford Forum he commented: "Oh, what a place; if local people decide to have an evening out in Blandford, they go somewhere else."

Behind the farm Hambledon Hill stood green and misty, and at the next village, despite heavy drizzle, white-clad figures were playing cricket. I felt it really was the world of Thomas Hardy, with country people, rural accents, woods, fields and a feeling of calm.

The tranquillity was not evident in Blandford Forum, a peculiar town, with narrow streets and a steady flow of heavy lorries. Built on the River Stour, its name originated from the word "Blagna", the Old English word for gudgeon. Visitors crossing the fine arched bridge should beware, for an iron plaque in the centre still proclaims: "Any person on wilfully injuring any part of this COUNTY BRIDGE will be guilty of FELONY and upon conviction liable to be TRANSPORTED FOR LIFE." The bridge is also said to have its own ghost in the form of a dog, and a headless sheep apparently lurks around the old market.

Despite being so close to water, almost the entire town was burnt down in 1731, after a fire started, appropriately enough, in a candle factory. Fortunately, the inhabitants included members of the unfortunately named Bastard family, who were builders and architects. After a special act of Parliament, they rebuilt the town in the classical style, and buildings, such as the Town Hall, bear the inscription "Bastard Architect". They also built the parish church, a particular favourite of Sir John Betjeman, and close by, they erected the Town Pump to prevent another fire; that, too, has an inscription.

In Remembrance of God's dreadful Vifitation by Fire which broke out on 4th June 1731, and in few Hours reduced, not only the church, and almoft this whole Town to Afhes, wherein 14 Inhabitants perifhed, but also two adjacent Villages. And in Grateful Acknowledgement of the Divine Mercy that has fince raifed this Town like the Phoenix from its Afhes, to its prefent beautiful and florifhing State, And to prevent by a timely Supply of Water (with God's Blefsing) the Confequences of Fire hereafter.

This Monument of that dire Difafter and Provifion againft the like, is humbly erected, by John Bastard, a confiderable Sharer, in the general Calamity. 1760.

The town could desperately do with another fire, for the combination of narrow streets and heavy lorries has completely destroyed its character. I stayed one night at the King's Arms Hotel, which despite its grandiose name, is a rather ordinary pub, standing on the site of the "tallow chandler's", where the great fire started, and which I found most uncomfortable, since every time a lorry passed by, it seemed as if it must come through the bedroom wall.

A better night was spent at a small terraced cottage in Alfred Street, the home of Angela King, an attractive smiling girl, with short, fair hair, and kind, light blue eyes. She had an interest in water, too, since for several years she had worked to create the first "otter havens" – stretches of undisturbed river, and banks, suitable for otters – one of the earliest being in Dorset, on the River Piddle. Otters like clean water, plenty of cover from overhanging trees, and root-made caverns in the banks in which they can rest, breed and rear their young. The spreading roots of oak, ash and sycamore are found to be particularly good for otter holts.

Angela's cottage, full of pictures of whales, otters and butterflies, all "endangered", and books on a wide variety of birds and animals, showed where her interests lay. In her back garden books and pictures gave way to real creatures; small frogs that one day she hopes will breed. Her concern for life was also to be seen in her vegan diet, for she will not eat animal products. She gave up eating meat at the age of eleven: "I could not disassociate the meat on my plate from the animal in the field."

On leaving school she had no idea of what she wanted to do. As a consequence she drifted from one job to another: interior designing, selling crackers at Harrods, a disc jockey at a night club, and she even held a disastrous one-man art exhibition in South Kensington. Finally she became interested in designing clothes for pop stars, when her clients included such "golden oldies" as Long John Baldry and Elkie Brooks.

The turning point in her life came when work took her to America in the late 1960s: "The whole ecology movement was growing and was rather trendy and when they had a series of 'Earth Days', I became interested and joined." On returning to London she became a member of Friends of the Earth and helped to start their wildlife campaigns: "We wanted to stop people wearing the products of endangered species, and we began campaigning to save the whales and we also started off the demonstrations against Schweppes non-returnable bottles. The Establishment thought we were a load of cranks, who would go away if they ignored us long enough. But after a while they learnt that we wouldn't, we became more professional and so people came to respect us." She then met the Honourable Vincent Weir, a quiet middle-aged bachelor, who founded the Otter Haven Project as part of the Vincent Wildlife Trust, and at his suggestion she joined with another Angela, Angela Potter, to begin her work with otters. They became known as the two Angelas, and bore the brunt of much unwarranted criticism, as many people took them to be simply "anti-hunting", when in fact they were anti everything harmful to otters, including fishing competitions, boating and wildfowling. They travelled all over the country, walking along river banks and through salt marshes, searching for signs of otters; then they would contact landowners and water authorities in an effort to create "havens".

The work continues, but both Angelas have moved on; Angela King is back with Friends of the Earth, researching wider threats to the countryside, and Angela Potter is with the Devon Naturalists' Trust. Living at Blandford, however, Angela King is still very much interested in otters and the River Piddle haven. On a warm day she took me to see it, on the way driving through the heart of Dorset, with rolling woodland, forest and far-off heath. Near Wareham we turned on to a track between tall pines and then walked through grass meadows to the river; the water was clear with wandering arms of flowering water crowfoot trailing in its flow. Sand martins and house martins flew low, occasionally dipping beaks to drink, and damsel flies were drying and stretching their fragile, delicate wings as part of their new incarnation. As we waded deep through pollen-spreading grasses, some of the damsel flies lifted off into easy flight and meadow brown butterflies joined them, almost flopping through the thick humid air.

Two artificial holts in which otters can take refuge had been built into the banks; both were concealed by reeds, so it was impossible to see if an otter was in residence. Small trees had been planted, cattle grazed in the neighbouring fields, few people were around, and the water of the Piddle was so clean that a salmon fisherman was casting with confidence. At one point the local water authority had even left a fallen tree to form a bridge over the water; ideal for birds as well as otters – unfortunately few authorities are so enlightened. In such a river there is still hope for the otter and although, walking along the bank to the sound of water and willow warblers calling, I did not catch sight of one, it really did seem to be an ideal "haven".

Damsel flies

During our walk, Angela waded into the water, and by a
small sand bank found an old otter dropping – a spraint –
confirming the presence of otters. She picked it up and smelt
it for confirmation, for apparently they smell sweeter than the
droppings of mink. Such a method can have its dangers; once
in North Norfolk when Vincent Weir was collecting otter
spraints to discover the diet of the local otters, he was watched
carefully by an old lady as he collected and sniffed. Eventually
she approached him and simply said: "You disgusting man."

Undeterred, his "disgusting" research continued and yielded much useful information.

Research into otters has also taken place in the West Country, at Exeter University. Exeter is an agreeable, clean city, with an outstanding cathedral, and the journey there from the River Piddle is a pleasant one through undulating country with trees, pastureland and fertile fields. It is a gentle landscape, easy on the eye and relaxing to the mind.

Ian Linn is a lecturer in biology at Exeter who fits perfectly into his surroundings; he looks like a gentlemanly African explorer, with a beard, a smile and a slight Scottish accent. On his door a note contained ideal advice for explorers, whether in Africa or Britain:

> If in Danger
> Or in Doubt
> Run in Circles
> Scream and Shout.

Despite his affability, the claustrophobic atmosphere so typical of universities seemed to filter through from the adjoining buildings. Indeed, the unaware academic or student is open to many dangers, for it is a small, restricted and specialised world they inhabit – rather like that of the otter.

Ian Linn was pessimistic about the otter, attributing its decline to human disturbance, pollution and habitat destruction by water authorities. He had little time for water authorities: "They have a large under-employed workforce who turn pretty streams into ditches when they have nothing better to do. Rather like the farmers of Exmoor who are now killing their beech hedges with flail mowers."

Ian Linn does not agree with the view that incoming mink have driven out otters: "The mink is very resilient, the otter is not, that is the difference. They do not compete; at Slapton, in Devon, they live side by side. In any case the otter is larger than the mink, and in Russia two cases have been reported of otters eating mink." Unlike many people he has a soft spot for mink, and although he does not like the idea of introducing alien species into Britain, he considers that in a country with

Standing otter

few predators, there is a place they can fit into without causing too much damage. "In England and Wales the mink has established a niche for itself which is not fully exploited by any indigenous carnivore, including the otter. In the early days, twenty years ago, if forty or fifty thousand pounds had been spent, the mink could have been eradicated, but nobody was prepared to spend the money. Now it would cost many millions of pounds. The occasional mink acquires a taste for chicken, but in general they do not do a lot of damage. Their diet is one-third mammals and one-third birds and 5.8 per cent is rats. They can hammer ornamental duckponds, but fishing is not affected. If they do cause problems they can be trapped easily but they should be prevented from getting on to some of our off-shore islands, for they could create havoc among sea bird colonies."

He thinks that part of the countryman's dislike for mink is based on the fact that people need something to hate, and the mink conveniently fits the bill: "People have to have a hate object; if they don't have something to hate they get repressed; in the country it's animals – in the towns it's people."

Just to the south-east of Exeter lies the village of Otterton, where the River Otter flows towards its estuary at Budleigh Salterton. The otter, after which the river and the village are both named, was once commonly found along the valley. Although the river is not a "haven", I walked from its arched bridge to the coast, in one final effort to actually see the animal that for me had remained elusive for so long.

The Otter is typical of many West Country rivers, winding through luxuriant water meadows down to the sea. There were deep, clear pools, divided by shallow races where the water murmured over the smooth, rounded pebbles, and in places the pebbles formed long spits and islands, thrown together by the power of the river when in full spate. An old gamekeeper told me that at one bend the local water authority, in its wisdom, had moved the bank of pebbles to the other side, but after the first heavy rain they were all washed back again. Along the bank, alders and willows gave occasional pools of shade and dark water, and on a dead branch a kingfisher perched, before flying off in sun-scattering flight. Nearer, a grey wagtail flitted delicately, almost dancing from stone to stone, in pursuit of insects. Grey wagtails are agile, graceful little birds which I only see occasionally in Cambridgeshire, as they pass through in the spring. With their bright yellow breasts they deserve a far more descriptive name than grey, and in the West Country, because of their association with fast-flowing streams, they are called "dishwashers".

The cliffs of sandstone on the far bank held the nesting holes of sand martins, which joined house martins and swallows flying low over the water. Several pines clung precariously, with exposed roots nearby, and where the slope of rock was less severe, oak, sycamore and beech provided a canopy of fresh green, from which came the melodic calls of warblers and the double-noted song of the chiff-chaff. The laughing cry of a green woodpecker filled the warm air, and then tribulation erupted as blackbirds scolded a tawny owl that changed its perch.

Wild flowers of many sorts grew down to the water's edge, including yellow irises, comfrey (the famous healing herb), yellow rocket, speedwell and red campion. Himalayan balsam was also plentiful, yet not on flower; an interesting plant, it was originally brought to Britain from India. Due to the shape of its flowers it is commonly called policeman's helmet, and when the seed-pods ripen, they explode, scattering seeds over a wide area, giving rise to yet another country name of jumping jack. As a result, its spread has been rapid and it has colonised the banks of many rivers and streams in the south-west. In the meadows themselves ragged robin, a distinctive plant with a reddish stem and pink, ragged and dishevelled flowers, grew profusely in the marshy ground. Because of their attractive but scruffy appearance the flowers are also known as bachelor's buttons, drunkards, shaggy jacks and wild williams.

From an old iron bridge down to the sea public fishing is permitted, but by mid-morning a group of four fishermen had already given up. The oldest was about nine and they had been fishing for trout. The only catch was held by the youngest in a large jam-jar; an elver that had been caught in a net. A more orthodox fisherman had problems close by, for he had succeeded only in catching the far bank, and was tugging in vain. However it can be a good river for fish, with trout, mullet, sea-trout, and the occasional salmon to be caught. Eels are very plentiful, and the locals still go "clatting", as they have done for generations, best done after a thunder storm, when the water is cloudy. Mustard is put around large worm holes, to make the occupants surface, and they are then threaded through with wool, before being folded over into a bunch, a "clat". The "clat" is fixed to a pole, "about as thick as yer arm", and dangled into the water: the eels get the wool caught up in their teeth as they eat the worms and can be hauled out. With plenty of eels, otters' favourite food, and covered and ex-posed tree roots touching the water, the river should be ideal for otters.

Heron feeding

By a group of twisted willows with moss-covered bark, I watched another fisherman at work, as a heron stalked slowly through the water. Then, on a fallen branch almost opposite, I caught sight of a different movement and I instantly thought "otter". I was wrong, for it was a mink, small, black and alert, against a backcloth of flowering irises. Despite its reputation it was attractive, and soon it was joined by its mate; they worked their way busily along the far bank, before taking to the water, swimming, and diving from view. I found it an unexpected pleasure, and although it is classified as vermin, my first mink has remained clear in my mind, like my first views of foxes, badgers and deer.

Few moorhens were to be seen along the river, and the locals attribute their disappearance to the arrival of mink, although two mallard ducks, one with nine half-grown young, and the other with six, appeared to be doing well. They managed the fast current easily, and seemed almost a different breed to the mallards that inhabit parks and village ponds. Among more comfrey, bees worked the bell-shaped flowers and on the stems of grasses I found countless turquoise damsel flies in metamorphosis; they almost glowed, and it seemed as if they too were drying their new, lace-like wings before discovering flight.

The soothing sound of the wind in the trees mingled with that of surf on the seashore and at the confluence of tide and fresh water the smells of salt, marsh and sea, mixed with those of grass and grazing cattle. The river banks gave way to salt marsh, pans of mud and pools of brackish water; a buzzard circled effortlessly overhead. Across open water a group of Canada geese waded in to swim and a few shelduck dabbled in the slime.

The river wound by a high shingle ridge and into the sea. A sudden shower of rain swept in from banks of heavy cloud, yet it was not unpleasant, as I stood at the meeting place of river and sea. That small stretch of river had given me much enjoyment, but it was clear that in the River Otter, otter had been replaced by mink.

On returning to Otterton that view was confirmed by an old man, with an ancient bike, who was leaning on the bridge watching the water flow by. He had a rich, warm Devonshire accent, punctuated with laughter: "Have you seen any of them mink down there?" he asked. During his working life Charlie Hawke had been a gamekeeper, but in retirement he had become a part-time water bailiff, and as a result he hated mink. "They should not be tolerated. I don't know about exterminating them, but I don't like them. They don't serve any useful purpose. They kill hens, as many as they can, as well as ducks and moorhens. They hide up all over the place too; someone cut a tree down recently and one ran out of the top. A neighbour had one in his garden and it climbed right up the wall of his bungalow. They are easy to catch, especially in March when they are mating and have no sense at all. Mink came here just over ten years ago, when I caught one, but there was no quantity until about 1975. In 1976 I caught twelve. I haven't seen an otter around here for years."

I walked with him along the village street where a small stream flowed by the footpath beside attractive whitewashed cottages. A thatcher was working on one of the roofs, repairing it with reeds, not from Norfolk or Suffolk, but from Austria, as he considered them to be stronger than English reeds. They cost £3.50 for a metre bundle, whereas local wheat straw cost £250 a ton. It is strange to go to an old Devon village to find alien mink in the river, measurement in metres, and even foreign thatch on some of the roofs.

At Charlie's small house he produced a sack with a dead mink inside; he had trapped it earlier in the day. Its coat was dark and far coarser than those kept in captivity. During the winter he can get £3 for a good skin or £1.50 for a "second". He was a good-natured man who likes living in Devon and wants it to stay as it is, with its villages, its people and its countryside, minus the mink. He is proud, too, of his accent, but he thinks that, like everything else, its days are numbered: "They have outside teachers in the schools now and they make the children talk posh." Nevertheless his wife writes poems in dialect for the local Womens' Institute.

Charlie Hawke is part of old Devon but, as elsewhere, things are changing and village cottages are being bought as holiday homes, or by professional people who commute to work. Consequently even in places such as Otterton local people are being replaced by newcomers of a very different type.

Back at the bridge another carload of tourists arrived at the watermill, recently restored and again grinding wheat into flour. It was once an important part of the village scene, and to see the wheel turning and to hear the wood creaking is to feel the living links with a past that goes deep into history.

The otter is also part of that past, but it cannot simply be restored by the signing of a cheque, or even the creation of a "haven". Unfortunately in many parts of England, due to the intrusions of man, otters have probably gone for ever.

6

Beer and Badgers

One of the pleasant surprises for those who travel through Britain is the regional food and drink that can still be tasted and enjoyed. To be avoided are places along motorways and holiday routes where the usual fare is chips and peas with processed pies, and bread that resembles plastic, all washed down with weak tea or coffee in cardboard cups, or cans of gassy beer; yet away from the service stations and assorted roadside "Chefs", it is possible to find traditional food and drink of high quality. By the time my journeys took me to Dorset I had already enjoyed Stilton cheese, Scottish shortcake, Bakewell pudding and a fine meal in the Vale of Belvoir; while travelling in Dorset and Devon the unexpected gastronomic pleasures continued.

Cobbett, who greatly enjoyed good food, wrote: "The people of England have been famed, in all ages, for their good living; for the abundance of their food and goodness of their attire. The old sayings about English roast beef and plum pudding, and about English hospitality had not their foundation in nothing." English beer also has a well-established reputation and Cobbett became very concerned when he saw it being replaced by tea, a much inferior beverage:

The drink, which has come to supply the place of beer has, in general, been tea. It is notorious, that tea has no useful strength in it; that it contains nothing nutritious; that it, besides being good for nothing, has badness in, because it is well known to produce want of sleep in many cases, and in all cases, to shake and weaken the nerves.

In Blandford Forum, William Cobbett need not have worried, for the brewers, Hall and Woodhouse, have been making beer there for over 200 years. They now make Badger Beer, not from the waters of the River Piddle, but from the River Stour. The brewery was built close to the river in 1900 for £28,000, a huge sum of money in those days, and today it produces 70,000 barrels a year, as people still seem keen to part with their money so that water, hops and barley can be blended into alcoholic unity.

The assistant brewer showed me around his brewery, starting at the guests' bar to sample some of the produce; wearing a white coat he looked more like a doctor than a beer expert, and was proud of his trade: "The brewery has been in the town for a long time; people complain about the weather, the government and the local brewery, but they don't really mean it." Apart from one highly-polished old steam engine, now driven by electricity, the whole brewing process seemed to be extremely technical and complicated, and far divorced from the locally brewed ale of years gone by. The terminology, however, remains the same as it has been for many years with "mashing", "sparging" and "straining", all involving a variety of complex pipes and containers. The amount of barley used in the malting process came as a shock; in reality it means that acres of downland have been ploughed up to produce barley, simply to enable the area's beer-drinkers to add to the water levels of the Stour and Piddle. It does seem to be a misuse of land and a waste of good crops.

Nevertheless the beer did have a distinctive taste, which we enjoyed again at the end of our circuit. The strength of the beer was also confirmed by my host, for as we spoke he revealed that he was very interested in natural history and Dorset's rich flora and fauna. After another bottle of barley wine he became almost lyrical about orchids – bee, butterfly, and green winged, which could all be seen close to Blandford: "You can see much more," he continued, "partridges, possibly otters, and bustards". Bustards in Dorset? While observing the effect of the beer the creature that came most readily to mind was the newt.★

★ The coarse association between newts and drunkenness probably comes from hibernating newts in winter. If disturbed they stagger and totter as if drunk.

Badger beer can be sampled in pubs throughout Dorset, among them one at the side of a long, wooded road, called the Silent Woman. It is the Quiet Woman of Hardy's *Return of the Native*:

> The inn known in the neighbourhood as the Quiet Woman, the sign of which represented the figure of a matron, carrying her head under her arm, beneath which gruesome design was written the couplet so well known to frequenters of the inn:

> > Since the Woman's quiet
> > Let no man breed a riot.

Badger beers can also be purchased in Wiltshire and the West Country, which is most appropriate, for it is there that real badgers have been most numerous for many years. With grass meadows, dry banks, hedges and spinneys, it forms ideal badger country, and they have therefore become well entrenched, not only in the countryside itself, but also in folklore. The badger is a charming animal, with a black and white striped head, a large snuffling nose and a slightly rolling gait that helps to give an overall bumbling appearance. In some parts of the country it was once believed that badgers had longer legs on one side than the other, to enable them to run faster along hillsides and furrows. They eat anything that becomes available, including worms, beetles, rabbits, eggs, and occasionally farmyard hens. They are even used as evidence by country weather forecasters when they become fat, for it is said: "When birds and badgers are fat in October, expect a cold winter."

Unfortunately for the badger it can be eaten too, and at one time badger hams and pies were popular. They were also dug out of their setts for sport, badger baiting once being a common country pastime. Now the badger has other problems for it has been suggested in some areas, and in the West Country in particular, that it spreads bovine tuberculosis among cattle, and so thousands of badgers, innocent and affected, have been slaughtered. Some remain, however, and

Badger cubs playing

after visiting the brewery I set off to see real badgers away from the illustrations on the side of beer bottles. The setts were outside Blandford, by the River Stour, where it meanders in a great U to skirt a wooded hill. The hillside was a perfect place, of oak trees and undergrowth, and there among the shadows I saw several well-used holes. The day died almost silently as darkness came and a light breeze wafted warm air gently and erratically through the leaves; sufficient to warn the badgers of a human presence and no animals emerged.

As well as beer, Dorset also boasts good food including Hubble Bubble, Hopel-Popel, and Rumble Thumps, and a collection of these, and similar delights has been produced by a few of the locals of Piddletrenthide, under the name of *The Piddle Valley Cook Book*. Like so much of Dorset the Piddle Valley still has the feel of genuine rural England, with spinneys, meadows, quiet lanes and country cottages. In earlier times, to save Queen Victoria from embarrassment, some of the names were changed to "puddle", so creating Turner's Puddle, Affpuddle, Tolpuddle, and Puddletown, although further along the valley the old names remain, such as Piddlehinton and Piddletrenthide.

The name of Tolpuddle has become deeply rooted into the traditions of the Labour movement, as it was there that George

Loveless formed a union which adopted initiation ceremonies and oaths for its members. In 1834 they were prosecuted and deported for their trouble, and so became elevated to the status of political martyrs. As in so many country places, the people of that time were an independent breed, similar to those whose activities were described by Richard Jefferies: "Betting, card-playing, ferret-breeding and dog-fancying, poaching and politics, are the occupations of the populace. A little illicit badger-baiting is varied by a little vicar-baiting; the mass of the inhabitants are the reddest of the Reds." Times have changed, however, for Tolpuddle hardly gives the impression of being a focus of social discontent, and Conservative coffee mornings would seem to be more in keeping than intrigue and union cards. The Piddle flows peacefully through the village, there are small cottages such as "Little Noddings" and "Sweet William", and on a July day a feeling of summer somnolence pervaded the warm air.

Vicar-baiting too would bring little reward or satisfaction these days, for already the vicar of Piddletrenthide is a most unusual man. From the outside the vicarage appears to be an ordinary Victorian house with a large garden, including a lawn where wild badgers are sometimes seen, but inside it is the centre from which the *Piddle Valley Cook Book* emerged, in addition to various other unusual publications.

The vicar's wife, Heather Parry, invited me in and plied me with coffee and delicious Dorset apple cake. In the comfortable living room I noticed a booklet of poems on the coffee table – *Poems from the Piddle Valley Parsonage* – already reprinted six times. They were the work of Mrs. Parry, and I picked it up, expecting to read verses like those from a sugary Patience Strong; I was wrong:

> I live in Piddletrenthide
> And the mighty Piddle flows
> Through the bottom of our garden,
> Round a little isle it goes.
>
> In the winter it's like crystal,
> So it does no problem pose,

But in summer it gets murky
As the vegetation grows.

I'll be wading in the river,
Digging up each weed that shows,
Hoping one day I will clear it –
Will I ever? Goodness knows.

If I do somehow achieve this,
And it unimpeded flows,
Come and paddle in the Piddle –
It does wonders for the toes.

No doubt her predecessors at the vicarage would not have taken kindly to such poetry, but then money for the church was more readily available in earlier days. Another amusing lady, Muriel Pike, also visited the vicarage that day and she too was busy editing a book,* the proceeds from which would again help to maintain the ancient churches of the Piddle Valley.

The vicar arrived while the coffee was still warm; he was in a very good mood and had just returned from conducting a funeral. At least he had arrived on time, unlike one Rogation Sunday's "beating the bounds" when a car managed to park on the hem of his cassock; as the people moved off towards the parish boundary to sing hymns and to pray, the vicar found himself firmly rooted to the ground. He is a popular man, and his popularity is helped by the fact that he does not agree with long sermons. His philosophy is simple: "Preaching is like North Sea exploration; if you haven't struck oil in ten minutes, stop boring."

Boredom is not a condition known to many of the vicarage visitors, for apart from the food, the vicar and his wife, it contains a war museum. There, in a place associated with prayers, Bibles and words of peace, one of the vicar's sons has amassed over 600 items linked with war and violence – gas masks, uniforms, knives, medals, posters, and "Government loo paper, not used 1939–45".

On leaving the vicarage and heading away from the Piddle Valley another surprise is in store, the Cerne Giant, cut into

* *The Piddle Valley Book of Country Life*, Hutchinson.

the hillside near Cerne Abbas. He is a naked, immodest, 180-foot chalk giant, his white figure standing out clearly against the grass. One day, across the valley, he could be given a mate, for a local farmer has threatened to excavate the figure of Marilyn Monroe lifting up her skirts. His planning application for a house had been refused, and so he promised a modern fertility symbol in retaliation. An old shepherd liked the idea, but did not think the farmer would succeed: "'Eem only havin' a bit of fun really."

On into Devon, food and drink continue to be an enjoyable feature, with Devonshire cider and cream teas, which, with the West Countryman's flair for business, can be purchased all day long. The cream is "clotted", made by simmering naturally cooled milk; when eaten with strawberry jam on newly-made scones it tastes delicious. At Otterton Mill there is the perfect gastronomic irony; cream teas and health-food flour side by side. Cream teas are also served at the tea rooms in nearby Newton Poppleford where, as you eat, chaffinches wait impatiently for crumbs.

It was while eating a cream tea at midday that I was told: "The best food anywhere in the world is obtainable at the King's Arms in Winkleigh". Winkleigh is a picturesque village on a hillside twenty miles north-west of Exeter on a road leading to nowhere in particular. On the outskirts of the village, past the winding high-banked lanes, and old thatched cottages, Inch's cider factory produces real Devonshire cider. In a large shed the cider can be bought from a youth wearing one ear-ring: "What do you want? You can taste it first you know." Various bottles were produced, ranging in flavour from sweet to dry, together with a large flagon of "scrumpy", whose taste approached that of vinegar with an equally distinctive kick. Liberal helpings of several varieties of cider were served to the handful of customers, but it was not wasted, for most made substantial purchases, and unusually, smiled as they parted with their money. According to John Evelyn, the seventeenth-century diarist, cider gives far more than a feeling of happiness: "Cider excites and cleanses the stomach, strengthens digestion and infallibly frees the Kidnes and Bladder breeding the Gravel and Stone."

I wanted to look over the factory to see how the cider was made, but the youth could not help: "You'll have to see the boss for that."

The "boss" was an elderly man, with a mischievous sparkle in his eyes, a trilby on his head, and a fine accent: "What do you want to write about us for? We don't want to give all our secrets away. Anyway, you can't look round without an appointment, and we've got no time for books and papers here."

"How do I get an appointment?"

"You have to write me a letter."

"Then you will tell me when I can come?"

"Oh no, 'cause I probably won't read it."

He too gave a broad smile, with no alcoholic assistance, and left. Most people fall over backwards to help writers and people involved with the media; what a refreshing change to find that the "boss" still had things in perspective.

The King's Arms, white walled and thatched, was in the centre of the village, but on this particular evening its approach was dangerous; suddenly, cheering started, hooves clattered and local youths began shouting: "Go on, Walter!" "Get up!" The noises were not the effect of cider in my head, for an old man came into view driving a pony and trap like a charioteer. As he passed, he too shouted and flicked his whip; he had a ruddy, cider-apple complexion, his cap perched precariously on the back of his head and his eyes shone with well-intentioned wickedness. The sound of hooves on the metalled road was a pleasant addition to the village scene, but the cart was completely silent, with pneumatic tyres.

Sonja, the waitress at the King's Arms, knew the driver well: "Oh he's Walter; he's a pleasant old eccentric who talks and laughs for hours, but he drives his pony and trap like a maniac." Inside were old beams and soft lights. At one time the bar and restaurant had been a cottage and stables, and the elevated wine cellar, containing the best of wines, had been the hay loft. When Dennis Hawkes first moved into the village, with his partner, he had not wanted to run a "launderette or a shoe shop": "I wanted to do something different that would be acceptable to the local people, and so I chose a restaurant. I wanted people to enjoy a high standard of food and service and to give them a memorable evening without chips or peas. We serve dinner at 8.15 and anybody who is late is not allowed in. When people first arrive they are disappointed, as they think it is an ordinary pub, but then they go into the dining room where everything is laid out properly and the food is excellent." The dining room itself is small with polished tables and pictures on the walls, but although its reputation has grown and people travel regularly from Tavistock, Ilfracombe and Exeter just to eat there, Dennis Hawkes is not entirely happy: "We also do excellent bar snacks, yet with all this good food and good value we get tourists come in, take one look at the menu and say, 'Ploughman's lunch please'."

The chef is a local boy, whose grandfather had run his own baker's shop where he baked hand-made bread. Melvin started in the bakery, and then, with no additional training, moved to the King's Arms. His speciality is leg of lamb cooked in hay, and he travels regularly to the Lake District for new ideas, as he considers it to be the best area in Britain for food. Being too late for the restaurant, I was nonetheless served with asparagus, spiced chicken and Sharrow Sticky Toffee Pudding, all accompanied with wine; the perfect way to round off a long day.

The Sharrow Sticky Toffee Pudding was an unusual but delicious sweet and, unlike many chefs, Melvin Popham actually passes on some of his recipes to his customers. The pudding is easy to make:

Sharrow Sticky Toffee Pudding

2 oz butter, softened
6 oz granulated sugar
½ lb flour
1 tsp baking powder
1 egg, whisked
6 oz dates, stoned
½ pint boiling water
1 tsp bicarbonate of soda
1 tsp vanilla essence

For the toffee coating
2½ oz brown sugar
1½ oz butter
2 tbsp double cream

Cream the butter and sugar together. Sift the flour and baking
powder. Beat the whisked egg into the creamed mixture with
some of the flour. Continue beating for a minute or so before
mixing in the rest of the flour. Flour the dates lightly and chop
them finely. Pour the boiling water over them. Mix in the
bicarbonate of soda and vanilla essence. Add this mixture to
the batter and blend well. Turn it into a buttered cake tin (11 by
7 inches). Bake for about forty minutes in a moderate oven,
Gas Mark 5, 375° F.

For the toffee coating, heat the brown sugar, butter and
cream and simmer for three minutes. Pour over the hot
pudding and place under a hot grill until it bubbles.

N.B. The coating burns easily.

It would have taken a major renovation to transform Walter's
farm buildings into a restaurant. The farmhouse had walls of
crumbling clay and a thatched roof, half covered with luxuriant moss. The sheds and stables were similar, helping to
create the illusion of the 1920s, complete with horses at the
gate, hens and bantams scrapping for grain, and the sound and
smell of pigs. In the entrance hall were bridles and whips.
Walter sat in the kitchen, his cap still in place, next to an unlit
stove over-flowing with ash. The table was clothless, littered
with empty milk bottles and a cold cup of tea: "So you want to
know about horses, do you?" he said eagerly. "Well, that
piebald you saw yesterday had only been between the shafts
three times, believe it or not, but it was completely under my
control. I've a way with horses, I was born with reins in my
brain."

Before taking up farming, he had driven a horse-drawn
bread van for many years, taking in the villages around
Otterton and Newton Poppleford: "I like working with animals forty times better than people, as they are honest. When
you deal with people it's always different; they'm trying to

have you, and I'm always trying to have them." To show off his driving prowess he was keen that I should ride in the trap with him: "Some people get frightened driving with me, but everything's all right. Sonja at the King's Arms won't come with me anymore. I think she damped herself last time, she was so frightened. But there's no danger, my horses are so well trained that they automatically stop at white lines on the road. I've had a happy life. If I go out, I hope I go smiling."

Still smiling, he picked up a whip and we went to a stable to let one of his horses into a field; on opening the door a family of bantams led the way out: "Before going to the fields we must get a bowl of nuts, for the young piebald's jumped into the field with the mares as one of them's in season. He's being hopeful; he was gelded three weeks ago but it seems he still think he's got his stones. He'll soon come for food."

It was a large field, sloping down to marshy ground, with oaks standing in a fine hedge. At a fenced-off gap, bullocks watched as if anticipating entertainment. Under a hot, bright sun, and a fresh breeze, the pasture was lush, with buttercups and fading ragged robins, and larks sang. Walter called the horses; they were not interested in him or the nuts. "We'll corner them, that's what we'll do." We cornered them, close to the bullocks, but they cantered between us easily. Then we chased them, with Walter shouting and cursing, but they galloped excitedly into the wind, their manes and tails flowing. The louder he shouted, the less they appeared to listen: "I'll get my dog to chase them, that'll tire them," but the border collie tired first. After an hour, his smile gone, Walter gave up: "I want a rest and a cup of tea. That pony's not going to let me catch it now, the beggar." He may have been born with reins in the brain; he really wanted them in his hands.

In the nearby village of Chulmleigh I visited an even more surprising farm, surrounded by an unusually high perimeter fence in a small valley. Dating back to the twelfth century it was then used by a professor of Toulouse University as his summer home. Now it is owned by Dr. John Henshaw who has converted it into a Wildlife Research Centre. His main interest is deer, and from the front of his house the view took in almost all his seventeen acres of grassland and his herd of fifty red deer. He believes that it is possible to farm deer in exactly the same way as sheep or cattle, and that deer should not simply be regarded as highland animals. In the wild they thrive best in lowland woods and he is therefore convinced that red deer on lowland grass are an economic proposition. He gives them extra rations, and, unlike Walter's horses, as soon as nuts were spread on the ground, stags with fine antlers, still in velvet, and several hinds with young calves trotted over. They were surprisingly tame and his main problem is not his own deer trying to break out, but wild stags trying to break in, during the rut. His grass field is dissected by a stream and a pond, and there he tries a more traditional type of husbandry by keeping geese and ducks. Cattle and deer are susceptible to liver fluke, passed on by a certain type of snail; geese and ducks eat snails, and so his deer have been completely free from the parasite. John Henshaw is as unusual as his deer farm. He left school at sixteen to become a merchant seaman and reached the rank of third mate before going to Gambia and Zaire where he became a crocodile hunter. This aroused a great interest in wildlife management, in which he obtained a doctorate in Hungary. He then spent fifteen years in Alaska studying moose, before finally settling in rural Devon. If deer farming succeeds, then it may be possible one day to sample venison rather than lamb cooked in hay at the King's Arms.

Another local farmer hopes that more traditional forms of farming will prevail. Indeed he became so worried by changes in livestock and farming fashions that he decided to collect all the old types of British sheep. Now, on his farm along the Chulmleigh road, outside Winkleigh, he has all forty-eight breeds, from those of Devon, such as the Devon Longwool and the Exmoor Horn, to the more exotic sheep of St. Kilda and the Badger Face. He shows his mixed flock to visitors by whistling Bob, the border collie from the farm next door who enthusiastically drives them through a small field. When his work is finished Bob is told to "Go home"; he reluctantly obeys, with several pauses, hoping for a change of mind.

In addition to sheep Roy Blackford has founded the Ashley Countryside Collection, a wide range of old farm tools and machinery that he displays in his barns. There are ploughs, carts, thistle cutters, a cider funnel, butter churns, and a whole range of relics from an age that died just a generation ago. In one shed he also has a reminder of badgers; a spring trap that gamekeepers and farmers would once conceal at sett entrances.

Like Dorset, Devon has a long tradition of digging and baiting badgers. Although such activities are now considered to be cruel, it is easy to understand their popularity in the past; then, instant entertainment was not available at the turn of a television switch and the old fighting sports often brightened up otherwise dull days. Even Thomas Bewick, a very sensitive man, could see nothing wrong in them; commenting on the baiting of "Foumarts [polecats], Otters and Badgers", he wrote: "In the fierce conflicts between them and the Dogs, there was something like an exchange of retaliation and not unfrequently the aggressors were beaten – and I have with pleasure seen that wonderfully courageous Animal the Badger (with fair play) beat all the Dogs of a whole Neighbourhood (one after another) completely off."

Now Devon is the centre of badger gassing, and sadly, in its wake has come a resurgence of digging and baiting, and badger hams, sandwiches and pies can again be purchased surreptitiously in a few country pubs. On talking to a farmer in what appeared to be good badger country, I was told: "If you want to find out about the badgers round here you should go and see the badger lady on Dartmoor."

On the road from Winkleigh to Dartmoor is a sudden, unexpected view, for there, on a hilltop, is a granite castle, Castle Drogo. It is not an ancient castle, but a folly designed by Sir Edwin Lutyens and built between 1910 and 1930 for Julius Drewe. A wealthy man, he started his first shop in 1878 and in 1883 he moved to London, where his trading was so successful as The Home and Colonial Stores, that he was able to retire from active involvement after six years, at the age of thirty-three. When he discovered that he was related to a Norman nobleman called Drogo, or Dru, who had given his name to the parish of Drewsteignton during the reign of Henry II, he decided to build a castle in his ancestor's parish, overlooking

The Drewe Arms

the gorge of the River Teign; Castle Drogo is the splendid result. The Drewe Arms in Drewsteignton itself is not so grand, but just as unusual; whereas Castle Drogo was consciously built to resemble an earlier age, the Drewe Arms has simply survived as an old-time pub. It has a thatched roof, wooden benches and a dark corridor leading to many rooms. The landlady, aged over eighty, shakily filled pint mugs, with the dog's bowl beneath the barrels to collect the spillage. Some customers walked behind the bar for service, and an even older man sat drinking, claiming to be responsible for "tidying-up". The barmaid, only just into her sixties, was considered to be the "youngster", but she was allowed to take over as the landlady shuffled off to cook lunch. The pub is now owned by a large brewery; if they ever turn it into a place of bright lights, gassy beer, one-armed bandits and plastic fittings, then Drewsteignton will have gained another "folly" within its parish boundaries.

After undulating farmland, Dartmoor itself looked formidable in wild weather, its boulders and tors showing through mist, shafts of sunlight and slanting showers of rain. Yet it had softness too, with the duns, browns, and pale greens of early summer uniting to make a strangely contrasting landscape. A backward whitethorn, still flowering in a hollow exposed to the wind, showed how the season lingered. The small road to the "badger lady" threaded its way through a group of bedraggled Dartmoor ponies, standing with their tails towards the rain, and over a narrow arched bridge above a rocky stream. Through silent pine forest a gate opened out to small, wet meadows filled with buttercups and daisies, and then came a farmyard, with a stone bungalow overlooking forest, field and stream. Laughter Hole Farm nestled beneath Laughter Tor, and below it lay a steep combe with a real echo; for "laughter" probably comes from "lafter", the Celtic word meaning echo.

I was greeted at the door by Mrs. Murray and invited in. Almost immediately I realised that the bungalow was bursting with badgers, for cubs were kept in the kitchen, the study and even the bathroom. Ruth Murray became interested in badgers when she was very young, and clearly remembers travelling from her home in North London to an uncle's farm in Devon, where she saw badger skins on a sofa. She was fascinated by them and kept asking why they had been killed. The answer seemed most unsatisfactory: "They do bad things to pheasants." Even at that age she was puzzled: "I could not accept the logic. If people shot pheasants, why kill animals that eat pheasants that are to be killed anyway? At least that is the question that posed itself in my mind." She saw live badgers for the first time at the age of five or six, when she was taken to London Zoo: "I thought they were such wonderful animals that they couldn't get me any further to see the lions and tigers."

At school she was very keen on natural history and sciences and decided to become a vet, as few jobs in conservation or with wild animals existed at that time. Unfortunately the war interrupted her plans and while waiting to go to college she started to work as a milk recorder for the Milk Marketing Board. One of the farms she visited was run by David Murray, and there among the milking machines, Red Polls and dairy nuts, she fell in love, and in 1948 she married. Her husband ran a mixed farm of 200 acres with thirty cows, and in nearby Hatfield Park she could watch wild badgers.

David lost much of his land when De Havilland's aircraft-factory expanded and so in 1955 they moved to a sixty-acre dairy farm near Okehampton in Devon. It was a move to a more attractive area, made better by the fact that badgers actually lived on the farm. The milk recorder who visited the farm was a badger digger and, without warning, in 1956, he gave Ruth her first badger cub. "Ticky" was a delight and stayed as a family pet until she died at the age of nineteen, the oldest badger ever recorded. Because of her interest in badgers Ruth was invited to see a badger dig and was appalled by what she witnessed: "The scene was horrific; it was just as Henry Williamson described in his *Tales of a Devon Village*. I was sickened by it and decided to fight to get the badger protected."

After that she watched a badger sett on the farm every night for eight years, simply to learn more about their behaviour. This enabled her to give much help to Lord Arran in preparing the 1973 Badger Act: "At last we thought we had won; badger digging was banned under the Act and illegal digging quickly fell away." Her hopes for the measures were short-lived, however, for in 1971 the body of a T.B. infected badger was found in Gloucestershire, and tests carried out by the Ministry of Agriculture led them to believe that twenty per cent of some badger colonies in the South West were infected with T.B. Consequently, although the badger was protected, almost immediately after the passing of the Act, the Ministry's gassing policy was implemented in areas where T.B. was found. Since then it has been estimated that about 10,000 badgers have been killed officially, out of a total population of approximately 50,000. The policy is surprising as no other European country slaughters badgers because of a supposed link with T.B. in cattle. In Britain the incidence of T.B. in our national herd was reduced from fifty per cent in the 1930s to 0.03 per cent in 1970 without killing a single badger. In addition bovine T.B. is only responsible for 0.3 per cent of tuberculosis in humans and the medical profession does not regard it as a problem or a threat.

Ruth Murray was disgusted by the gassing: "It was terrible; the Ministry's policy seemed to imply that all badgers were a threat. Illegal badger digging escalated, and when caught, the culprits would simply say, 'We thought we could kill badgers as they spread T.B.', and local magistrates let them off. Now the Ministry is even employing former badger diggers in their gassing teams and so they know of all the setts. Badger hams are being eaten again; when I hear of it I ask them, 'Would you really eat badger hams if you thought the animals had T.B.?' In all my years I have not been given one badger with T.B. alive or dead and I have had post-mortems carried out by properly qualified people." She also regards the use of gas as cruel: "Although experts, including the R.S.P.C.A., are in favour of gassing, I have grave doubts about it and consider it to be most inhumane. I have found setts opened from the inside after gassing in Devon and Gloucestershire and I have found half-gassed badgers that have staggered out, still alive, to die later." Advocates of gassing animals on humanitarian grounds claim that it takes effect instantaneously and without suffering. Yet even a Ministry report contains a suggestion that gassing does not cause an immediate end: "Death from the inhalation or ingestion of lethal doses of cyanide is the result of histotoxic anoxia and usually occurs within a few minutes of the cyanide entering the animal."★

Despite advances in medical and veterinary science the Ministry also claims that tests for T.B. in badgers are inadequate except in post-mortem examinations and stipulates that all badgers caught or injured cannot be released; they either have to be kept in captivity or put down. As a result, Laughter Hole Farm has become a home for badger waifs and strays.

In a room containing a collection of gruesome badger snares, as well as a pair of badger tongs, Ruth opened a large box and took out the inmates, Sam and Tom, two fine, half-grown boar badgers, lively, inquisitive and playful. Sam was rescued from an illegal badger dig, and Tom was taken during a legal dig. His sett was on a river bank where water authority men were working and he was named after one of the Water Babies.

Trundling down the corridor to the kitchen their excite-

★ *Bovine Tuberculosis in Badgers*, Second Report by the Ministry of Agriculture, Fisheries and Food, December 1977.

ment increased, for inside, three Basset hounds were trying to sleep in their baskets. Their rest was rudely disturbed, but one old sad-eyed bitch, Emma, tolerated their romping with almost motherly patience. Four more were released, Bella, Beau, Timothy and Tess. They had been in a sett on land to be developed by a housing association; various conservation bodies, the Ministry of Agriculture and the R.S.P.C.A. were all uninterested and so Ruth Murray had to intervene. In another room, in yet another box, were Bonnie and Clyde; they were larger cubs, as they had been found very early, before Christmas, by a man walking his dog. They had been by their dead mother at the sett entrance, slowly starving to death. The sow had died of enteritis, probably through eating grain treated with insecticide.

Order returned to the kitchen when only Sam and Tom were allowed to stay for feeding. Biscuits in a large jar on the table almost went crashing down as Sam tried to steal a custard cream, and Tom greedily sucked at a baby's feeding bottle held by David Murray. In his eagerness he stood on his hind legs, clasping at the bottle with his front paws; and milk streamed from his lips as he sucked. Sam then gave a similar demonstration of gluttony and had to be dried with a towel afterwards. All the cubs are fed on Lactol, a milk powder, and they thrive on it. Tea was finished with biscuits, causing the two playmates to compete in a greedy scramble, squealing in warning and annoyance as they did so.

Outside in the garden, pens contained adult badgers; some collected as orphans and others as casualties. Butch and Sundance were just over a year old, beautiful, full-grown animals in fine condition. They too had been found as cubs, starving by the body of their dead mother who had been caught in a cruel self-lock snare. How many badgers were held at Laughter Hole Farm, the Murrays refused to say for fear of the Ministry of Agriculture's attitude, but they have been taking them in since 1975. At the time of my visit they had received nine badger cubs during the course of the summer, and simple arithmetic suggests that they must have well over fifty. It is an absurd situation, for the animals came from setts with no record of T.B. yet on "principle" the Ministry of Agriculture is opposed to release. Ruth Murray is dedicated to her badgers, but is both angered and saddened by the situation in which she finds herself: "It is tragic; when I first saw badgers in London Zoo I remember thinking how wrong it was to keep such beautiful animals shut up in cages. Now I am forced to do exactly the same thing with my animals."

Of course one way to protect cattle from T.B. is to vaccinate them, but such a solution seems to be much too easy. As I left, the rain fell again as dusk approached. In the woods and fields around Laughter Hole Farm the badgers should have been waking for another night of foraging and freedom. Instead they were being fed, settled, and the bolts of their cages were being slid firmly into place.

7

Carvings and Kites

Although over-intensive agriculture and too many people have, through the years, changed the face and feeling of Britain, in a few remote regions there remain sights that are among the most moving and spectacular in the world. They are to be found on the coast, away from the crowded summer beaches and candyfloss stalls, where the sea surges against ancient rocks and each year thousands of sea birds – guille-mots, razor bills, shearwaters and puffins – return to nest and rear their young.

My favourite island for birds is Skomer, at the southern end of St. Bride's Bay in Pembrokeshire. It is not the country's most outstanding haven in bird numbers, but it exerts a great emotional pull on me. I "discovered" it by accident one summer, after arriving at a small bay, where a fishing boat was offering to take a few holidaymakers over to the island for the day. There I saw for the first time rows of ledge nesting birds amid high cliffs, pounding seas and a hot sun. I felt I was looking into the past, at the earth when it was young, before the land and the creatures that thrived on it had been changed by the activities of man. It was an unexpected experience that did not confine itself to the senses, but went much deeper, stirring the inner rhythms of the spirit.

For much of the year the birds live on the open sea, leaving the cliffs deserted, but for centuries they have returned each spring. They can be seen most easily between April and mid-July, and whenever possible, I visit the island during that time.

My return to Skomer began in the early part of June, but I intended to see more than birds and cliffs, as I knew that my journey would take me through South Wales, close to "kite country", where for a hundred years the kite has been on the verge of extinction. Unlike the birds of the open seas, many birds of prey have been severely affected by the restless advancement of man; the landscape they favoured has been changed, and because they kill game, they have been shot and their nests destroyed. Over the years the red kite, to me Britain's most majestic bird of prey, has been particularly hard hit.

The story of the red kite is a remarkable one. In medieval times it was common in both town and country, and in 1544 an early writer recorded that the kite was "abundant and remarkably rapacious. This kind is wont to snatch food out of children's hands in our cities and towns."

It was a scavenger, hence one of its country names was "carrion kite". During the nesting season it also became a thief, even stealing rags and clothing for its nest, and Autolycus in a *Winter's Tale* warned: "When the kite builds, look to lesser linen." As late as 1777 nests could still be found in and around London, but subsequently, numbers rapidly fell away; kites had always been killed for stealing straying chickens – a habit confirmed by Bewick: "It is particularly fond of young chickens, but the fury of their mother is generally sufficient to drive away the robber."★ Yet improved shotguns and gamekeeping turned control into persecution. Game shooting became extremely popular during the nineteenth century, when all birds with hooked bills and talons were considered to be vermin.

By 1900 only about four pairs and twelve individuals remained in Central Wales where game shooting was neither popular nor possible, in a region of small valleys, sheepwalks, marshes, oakwoods and few people, which is where they remain today.

I took the motorway to Wales, with the Severn Bridge giving easy access. The Severn estuary is not attractive; a

---

★ Bones from archaeological sites and the writings of early naturalists have confirmed that the British bird has always been the red kite and not the black kite, which is also a scavenger. The black kite can still be seen stealing chickens in many Indian and African villages.

mixture of murky water, mud flats and low areas of drab land that some people call islands – a poor end to a fine river. Lowland Wales, by contrast, was fresh and green, its livestock in grass meadows enclosed by hedges, one of which had been recently "laid", by expert hands, showing that this dying craft is not yet completely dead. At one time Wales was known for its craftsmen, but now, like the kite, they are an endangered species. At Cardiff I turned away from the main road to find St. Fagans castle, the home of the Welsh Folk Museum, where efforts are made to keep alive the ancient traditions and skills of Wales. The sprawling building, extensively restored, dates back to Norman times. In the outbuildings and stables the old crafts such as spinning, weaving and tanning are practised.

In one room a wood carver was working, making a simple spoon from a block of sycamore, using only an axe, a knife and a spoke-shave. Around him were examples of his work; walking sticks, a collection of household gadgets including needle-holders, shaped like miniature rolling pins, bobbins and silk holders. He had made many love-spoons, but only one bowl containing fruit, carved out of their own wood – cherry, plum, pear and apple. The similarity was remarkable, and even the Victoria plum had a pink tinge, exactly like the real fruit.

Gwyndaf Breese was born at Aberangell, in the Dovey valley in Mid-Wales, and the lilt of his accent matched the hills and vales of his home: "We had a sprinkling of craftsmen in the family – rural craftsmen and farmers, so I have a mixture of slate dust and earth in my blood. My father was a quarryman and my grandfather a country carpenter. I often used to go into his shed to look at his tools. In the village there was a cobbler and a wheelwright and the idea of working with wood took a grip very early." He decided to become a carpenter and started his apprenticeship, but then grew less keen, as to put it to use would have meant following his friends into factory work in England.

Fortunately he instead obtained a job at the museum where he has been for over twenty years, spending his time developing and researching the traditional wood carving and turning of Wales. He makes walking sticks, using coppiced hazel, and

Love spoon

love-spoons, with balls inside the stem and links of chain, all carved from a single piece of wood: "I can spend up to twenty-five to thirty hours making a love spoon, but I only charge about a pound an hour. To be commercial you would have to work fifty to sixty hours a week and still live a very spartan existence. There are only a few genuine wood carvers left in the villages and you would have to look hard to find one. There are plenty who turn out things commercially, but they are not the same. They put daffodils and leeks on love-spoons, but they were never on the traditional ones, nor were horseshoes, which developed with Valentine cards. Some love-spoons are even made of metal now – soon they will be appearing with 'made in Hong Kong' on the back." As he spoke, he continued to work, creating shape out of shapelessness: "I love working with wood, especially sycamore, and I make bowls, spoons and butter-prints from it, because it is tasteless, colourless and stainless. Fruit wood is a lovely wood because of its grain pattern, its colour and its texture, and the working quality is excellent. One of my favourites is laburnum. It is a traditional Welsh tree and the hedgerows of Cardigan are beautiful when it is on flower, like rows of gold chains."

The simple spoon was nearly finished and he scanned it with an expert eye: "I enjoy my work but I am always trying to

improve; my best piece of work is always the next. I think
wood carving will become more popular with people again, as
they want to create; it is an instinct." It seemed a great pity that
he should have to practise his skill in Cardiff, away from the
hills, the country roads, and the "rows of gold chains".

Travelling on to Port Talbot and Swansea, the world of
craftsmen and cottage industries seemed far away, amid more
motorway, heavy lorries and a long strip of development. It
offered ranks of "works" and council housing, a British Steel
foundry giving out a drifting haze quite unrelated to summer
heat, and only the Aberdare rugby club and the names of
Jones, Evans and Davies above many of the shops showed the
difference between ugly English and Welsh urban sprawl. It is
little wonder that cottages in Mid-Wales lie empty, bought
by Englishmen as holiday homes, for it seems that the average
Welshman prefers the illusion of wealth away from the hills,
complete with supermarkets and fish and chip shops.

Along the valleys tip heaps merged with valley sides, and
rows of Coal Board houses formed tight communities. Somehow the Welsh cottages seemed brighter, warmer and cleaner
than those of Scotland. The town of Ammanford marked the
end of the industrial zone and the countryside opened up into
rolling farm land with grass, stone walls and hedgerows,
where the elder tree and guelder rose added large inflor-
escences of white. Red campion and ox-eye daisies stretched
above the vergeland grasses, and once more there was the
chilled yet fragrant smell of meadow, sheep and cattle.

The farms were small, hemmed in by hedges and divided by
streams and marshy land. They formed a living landscape,
where the creative hand of man still worked and animals had
their place. Good farmers are also craftsmen who care for and
shape their land with love and physical labour.

A back road wound from the village of Bethlehem between
farm buildings, through an open stream, and came to an end at
a farmyard, where terriers barked and the farmer hobbled with
an arthritic limp. The house, painted bright orange, and set in
a garden full of flowers and vegetables, lay above the farm.
Peter, a former computer salesman, slowly walked over to
greet me, his accent betraying his army and suburban back-

ground. At an age when most people would be thinking of retirement, he had opted for a small farm, believing in the philosophy of Virginia Woolf: "The peasants are the great sanctuary of sanity, the country the last stronghold of happiness. If they disappear, there is no hope for the race."

"You must stay and see the farm," he said warmly, and after an afternoon tea, of tea, bread and strawberry jam, we strolled around his land at a leisurely pace. Of his fifty-five acres only thirty-five to forty were productive, his grass meadows full of clover, sorrels, yellow rattle, buttercups, orchids and natural grasses. The rest were oak woods, marsh and stream, but this did not worry him and he had no plans for drainage or tree felling: "Today, high-input farming is decimating the countryside. It is being despoiled with land being used just as an outdoor factory, with a pig unit going up here and a cow unit fifty yards from the church. Farming is a more gentle and creative occupation than that. High-input farming is bad for the land and bad for the people; the countryside should be a populated place. The ideal situation is an educated peasantry enjoying a little of everything – manual work and some high life as well."

Ironically, because of his arthritis and the scarcity of labour, his dream life had faltered and he had recently let his land and sold his eighteen Jersey cows to two young men of hippy appearance. Brian had earned his money on an oil rig, and opted out, while the other still worked on the North Sea but journeyed to Wales at every opportunity. How "high life" was possible with just eighteen cows, being milked two at a time, soon became apparent, for Peter had developed a market locally for cream and yoghurt, thereby doubling the income from each cow. The method of making yoghurt seemed fast, simple and unhygienic. The milk was skimmed and as it flowed into a bucket a farm cat drank from it while another repeatedly dipped in a paw and licked it clean. The bucket was then placed in a boiler for the start of the yoghurt process.

An early "sundowner" on the terrace followed; Peter with pastis, a cigar and *The Times*, whisky for his wife, and I had a glass of wine. The life of an "educated peasant" had much to commend it. After supper, breast of lamb cooked in herbs, with whole cabbage leaves, served from an earthenware pot, Peter sat in a deep armchair in his study and talked. A log fire burned brightly and the walls were lined with books on the countryside, farming and travel, from Henry Williamson and Hugh Massingham to Laurens van der Post: "Since leaving suburbia we have chosen to live in voluntary simplicity, with limited material resources and a minimum of capital expenditure. We try to produce little waste or pollution, we live without unnecessary hardship, in reasonable comfort, without excessive outside stimulants. We have shown anyone who wants to see, or know, that it is quite possible to sell your suburban house – the only asset we had – in latish middle age, and live a quite healthy, rewarding life, on a poor soil farm in a sixty-inch rainfall area. All this without recourse to social security and avoiding the irresponsible opting-out sloppiness and squalor of the hippies.

"Small farms could provide many solutions to problems at this time. Ten farmers on 1,000 acres are much better than one farmer working 1,000 acres. A garden is more productive than agricultural land and small farms under a hundred acres are twice as productive as big ones.

"The rural communities should be living instead of dying, with local people doing the engineering and contracting for jobs like baling. With all the unemployment there is about, farming should be labour intensive – big landowners should be taxed to make more land available to those wanting to come into farming. The National Farmers Union is not interested in small farms and the Ministry of Agriculture encourages farms to get bigger all the time. France is strong because they have small farms." He was content, for he had proved to his own satisfaction that a life-long dream could become a reality. We talked of farming, country life and Africa until the fire died to glowing embers. The night was still, deep and silent, the silence only broken a few hours later by the dawn chorus and Brian calling his cows for their early morning milking.

The next night was far different, following a day of driving through wide valleys and wild open country where I saw a kestrel hovering and several wheatears, but no signs of kites. In a valley of woods and fields I stopped at another small farm which offered a caravan "To Let" in the yard, at £2.50 a night, including breakfast in the farmhouse. The night was rough with teeming rain and howling winds, but the caravan was comfortable and dry. Breakfast was a Scottish and English mixture – porridge, followed by egg and bacon. Thomas, the farmer, claimed to have Spanish ancestry, yet his clear blue eyes and broad Welsh accent seemed as Spanish as leek soup. By a field gate he showed me his sheep dogs. He sells his puppies: "I only send them to places in Wales though, because they only understand Welsh swear words. We like the English; those people who burn down their cottages are cranky, and those who daub signposts with Welsh should have their faces daubed." He, too, had laid a fine thorn hedge, complete with wands of willow plaited at the top. He viewed it with pride and said unexpectedly: "If you want to meet a real craftsman go and see Dan, up the valley. He's one of the best wood carvers in Wales and he even made a shepherd's crook for the Queen Mother."

The gate to Dan's farm, held together with baler twine, opened on to a winding track that passed between stone walls and hazel hedges. At a bend, an ancient plum tree was propped up by a post to prevent it from splitting in two, and some of the outbuildings were in disrepair, their brick work broken and slates falling from the roofs. By a well-rotted heap of manure a do-it-yourself "muck cart" rested, made from a sheet of corrugated iron, a rickety wheel, and two wooden handles. Two redstarts flew from a bush by the back door and nearby stood several hand-reared lambs, one with a broken leg held by baler twine and plaster. The flower garden was overgrown, with garden flowers showing through a complete wilderness, but beyond them vegetables thrived in weedless soil – beetroot, potatoes, peas and beans.

Two border collies raced up the track through the drizzle, followed by Dan, walking wearily yet steadily with the help of his crook. His face was gentle, weathered and deeply lined, for the life of a hill shepherd is hard, and Dan manages the sheep on his seventy-five acres with only the help of his five dogs. He was the last of a line who for many generations had worked on the family farm.

Above the farm, jackdaws, crows, ravens and buzzards lived in the woods, and spring water from a field flowed down to a tap at the back door. The door opened with difficulty into the small, dark, flagstoned kitchen, where boots and groceries lay in disarray. The front room was darker still, a single bulb casting a meagre light. A kitchen range stove was out, but full of winter's ash; the wallpaper was faded and discoloured and in places hidden by Victorian pictures depicting Biblical scenes. Old papers and copies of *The Field* and *Country Life* littered the table, and two large sideboards displayed numerous cups and trophies won for carving, quoits, growing vegetables and sheep-dog trials.

He began to speak of his boyhood, remembering his father in the same house, weaving baskets. Dan taught himself to carve, and uses only a pocket knife, a sharpened screwdriver and a file. No signs of his carving were visible and it seemed almost impossible that he could work in surroundings so bare and dark. He spoke of the local wood, sycamore, blackthorn and hazel, that he cut from his hedges, and how he spends winter evenings carving, sitting by his stove. Gradually reserve left, and every so often he opened a sideboard drawer to reveal the contents; first, walking sticks with carved handles, then thumb sticks, ornate shepherd's crooks and love-spoons. His work was beautiful, of the highest quality, and each new drawer yielded more treasures: stools, axe handles, bowls, spoons, forks and salad-servers. Finally he went into another room to fetch besom brooms and hay rakes made from ash. He handled his creations with loving care and it was touching to see such workmanship produced with simplicity and humility. The mood was caught by a poem, framed and hanging on a wall, written by a Welsh girl who had moved away to live in an English town:

White is the heart of the sycamore tree,
Warm is the heart that carved for me
My heart's desire from the heart of the sycamore tree.

Green are the flowering banks of Carmarthenshire,
Sweet are the Twyin waters, slipping between.

High over the water, the house on a bank of green
Where skilled hands carved the white wood to my heart's
  desire.

Grey is the heart of my city; I long to go
Where the hedges are splashed with the milk of the thorn in
  flower,
Where the river is bright and the bright fish dart below,
Where the young lambs gambol and skip in the playtime
  hour.

Grey is the heart of the town; but I take in my hand
The heart of the sycamore, carved to my heart's desire,
And my mind's eye sees the green of the lovely land
I am home in the valleys and hills of Carmarthenshire.

These are my thanks, to him who carved for me
The white wedding spoon from the heart of the sycamore
  tree.

I found it sad; cups with nobody to admire them; skills with no one to learn them, and long winter evenings alone. Yet he seemed happy and content.

As I left, Dan took me to the tractor shed next to the house: "Look, four nests, a pied flycatcher, a swallow, a wren and a thrush. When the flycatcher had young I watched the thrush trying to feed them with a small worm. She put it in the mouth of each one, and they all rejected it. Once the female flycatcher even climbed over the thrush's back to get to her young. The thrush finally gave up and dropped the worm outside. You see, in life everything has got its place – the thrush for getting worms and the flycatcher for insects." Men with gentleness, understanding and skill, like Dan, should also have their place, but in an increasingly harsh, materialistic world they are a rapidly disappearing breed.

The valley of the River Teifi took me further into kite country, and to the small market town of Tregaron, a settlement that grew out of cattle and sheep droving. In this remnant backwater of old Wales, I stumbled upon two craftsmen of a newer generation. One was a middle-aged clogmaker, whose front room had been turned into a workshop, with a bench and "clogging-knives". He makes the clogs from sycamore and alder, but survival is difficult and he relies on mail order for most of his business: "I think I'm the only one left making clogs in Wales. There is another in England and two more in Yorkshire." So, although times were hard, for him anyway, Yorkshire had gained its independence.

The other was a young man, Arthur Lewis, who makes copies of medieval stringed instruments. In his workshop lutes, a long-necked lute and an English cittern, made in six weeks from cherry wood hung from the walls. He left school at fifteen where he was hopeless at woodwork, but has since developed his skill and a sympathy for both his work and his surroundings. How his education managed to stifle such sensitivity and ability is a wonder in itself.

He lives in an old vicarage and stables which he is converting into a home, and in addition to his musical instruments he helps out on local farms for extra money. His wife works as a nurse and without her additional income he would not be able to continue. Tregaron is the ideal area for his work: "It is wonderful here and often we can see kites from the window." He produced a pair of woodcock wings, shot by a friend; they were like autumn leaves, dark and fallen: "Some of the farmers kill far too much; last year I found dead crows and buzzards around the body of a sheep that had been baited. If anything happens they always blame animals. When a local farmer saw a cow with a badly-torn teat he blamed it on a dregnog,★ claiming that it had tried to get the milk. In an area as beautiful as this I just don't understand it."

He told me of other valleys where kites could be seen and so I journeyed on. I stopped in a small village consisting of a church, two chapels, two pubs and grey, stone cottages with slate roofs, where I found accommodation. Once more the owners were respectable English drop-outs who, tired of the rat race, had opted for a different life style in late middle age, offering bed and breakfast and selling home-baked cakes and jewelry made from hand-painted stones. The couple were

★Welsh for hedgehog.

content, not wishing for anything more, and brightened up a damp, dull evening with tea and Welsh cakes (*cage bach*). Despite being English she sells large quantities of Welsh cakes to the local people; a novel variation of coals to Newcastle. The reason for the demand was obvious, since the cakes were tasty. Here is her simple recipe:

Welsh Cakes

1 lb plain flour
1 tsp baking powder
pinch of salt
10 oz margarine
6 oz sugar
½ tsp mixed spice
3 oz currants
3 oz sultanas
1 egg, beaten

Sieve together the flour, baking powder and salt. Rub the margarine into the flour, and add the sugar, spice and the fruit. Mix to a firm dough with the beaten egg. Roll out the pastry to ¾ inch thick and cut into rounds with a pastry cutter. Cook in a lightly-greased pan over a medium heat, making sure that they cook right through. Serve warm with butter.

As it was Saturday night they recommended that I should visit the Black Cow, rather than the Red Cow: "You will see some strange things there, including a dog that eats money." The pub was dimly lit, but warm, with beams, benches and chairs. Most of the assorted occupants were speaking Welsh. An old man in a long dark coat, with a cap and thick-lensed glasses, sat drinking beer, looking bored and mildly inebriated; his terrier sat next to him, wearing a similar expression. A local shopkeeper and an old farmer were engaged in banter, until they turned to me and spoke in English about the valley. At the mention of foxes the old man suddenly stirred, and even the terrier looked interested: "Foxes – we've a lot of foxes here. They get in the woods. If a fox kills a lamb, as it's worth only

£5 and the fox fur is worth £25, they let the fox go until October, to make more money. If it does more damage they will get the hunt in. When the hounds meet, up to fifty people turn up with guns and surround the woods. If the foxes run out they open fire." The shopkeeper then flicked a 2p coin on to the floor and the terrier pounced. It spent the rest of the evening alternately chewing the money, and digging for it in the seat: "One night he had 15p in his mouth all in ones. He gives it to me when we get back home."

The conversation turned to kites and the old man and his dog slipped back into boredom. The shopkeeper saw them often: "You see kites up the valley road and even from this pub. The pub should be called 'purcid'.★ The best place to see them is from the bar window with a pint in your hand." He also claimed to be a deacon of one of the local chapels: "Why didn't you become a deacon, Dai?" he asked the farmer.

"Because I like drink and it's not right to drink and be a deacon."

The deacon was drinking a succession of pints of beer and whiskies, justifying his excess by saying: "There's nothing wrong with drink, because it only hurts you, it doesn't hurt others. The things you should worry about are those that hurt others such as love of money and greed."

There had been a wedding at the chapel that afternoon and the "disco-reception" was being held in a room at the back of the pub. At eleven p.m. the bride and groom walked into the bar; he with tattooed arms, black tie and waistcoat, and a cockney accent; she with an off-white wedding dress and looking at least five months pregnant. The groom ordered a round of drinks and spoke to his wife: "Shall I get half a bottle of whisky to take home?"

"Where's home?" Dai asked.

"Where we were before."

Dai was not impressed.

A group of small boys arrived and the groom gave an eleven-year-old a glass of whisky. To show off to his friends he gulped it down in one; he swallowed hard, struggled for

★Welsh for kite.

breath, and tried to conceal his discomfort with a grim smile. Joining in the sport the deacon – "alcohol only hurts you" – gave him another whisky. Again the boy swilled it down. For the next twenty minutes drinks flowed to all but the boy; he stood motionless with a fixed grin, leaning against a table with an acute list. Relations then came looking for the happy couple, wanting them to cut the cake before they left: "It's traditional for the bride and groom to leave first."

"Oh, go and cut the cake yourselves. Cheers!"

Sunday morning was quiet. Would the deacon be at chapel with a sore head and a guilty conscience? "You can go if you like, but the service will be in Welsh. They might sing one hymn in English specially for you."

I walked away from the village along a road bounded by stone walls and clumps of ash, sycamore and hazel which followed a long, winding valley of grass meadows, sheep and murmuring water. On higher ground oak woods had leaves the colour of autumn; they did not reflect the true season, but had been eaten by thousands of caterpillars, many of which hung on long silken threads. Within the woods were also beech, birch and hazel, with trunks made wrinkled and ancient by mosses and lichens, and some even had ferns growing from wet hollows and bowls. The road turned to track, where the prints of horses' hooves showed the farmer's method of transportation. A male chaffinch sang his restful, repetitive song from the top of a silver birch, and higher still buzzards and crows circled. Then, suddenly, there was a kite, soaring on open wings and showing the clear silhouette of its deeply-forked tail. It was one of those moments when the present becomes transfixed into memory; the bird seemed to hold the wind with its wings and flex its tail around the hidden currents of air. Another wheeled higher, before drifting away; the sun burst into a wild sky making the kite glow a brilliant rufous red.

I crossed the valley floor where cuckoo flowers (lady's smocks) still bloomed and orchids and forget-me-nots thrived in the dampness, untouched by harmful sprays. Through the oak woods more caterpillars hung in countless legions and a pair of flycatchers were feeding their young, safe in a hole in a rotting branch. Food was plentiful and their trips to the nest were frequent; flitting after flies, the black and white male looked dapper and distinctive. There were redstarts too, active birds with rich red-brown tails that fanned and quivered, proving the suitability of many of their country names such as fanny redtail and fire tail.

Higher, above the tree line, I sat in the grass, where tormentil grew and a solitary bumble bee flew by, seemingly oblivious to altitude. Around me were the blue, single flowers of butterwort, looking like small highland violets, and wild yellow pansies, the perfectly formed hearts'ease. The flowers and the sight and sound of distant waterfalls softened the wildness; the whole valley uplifted the spirit and offered values long rejected by the twentieth century.

Two more kites flew across the valley, to perch in an oak tree below me, and a solitary magpie tried lethargically to mob a buzzard, wisely staying above its talons. As rain came I walked over the crest of the valley side into another darker world. At first there was grassland with pansies, but then came a solid block of planted pines; dense and black and devoid of life. The wealth of one valley and the sterility of the next came as a jolt. Although it is assumed that the planting of pines is a modern phenomenon, even Cobbett encountered it: "The oak is the thing to plant here; and, therefore, this whole country contains not one single plantation of oaks! That is to say, as far as I observed. Plenty of fir-trees and other rubbish have been recently planted; but no oaks."

Even pines can be planted in harmony with the land, creating glades, belts of birch and oak, and open spaces where buzzards and kites could search for food, but these plantations were as programmed and featureless as the minds that planned them.

At last, I came to a road and another valley as drizzle gave way to sunlight. More water meadows with marsh marigolds, foxgloves and small farms. At one, the farmer appeared in his wellington boots, old jacket and cap. He had kites on his land and offered to show me their nest, a dishevelled heap of sticks in the oak woods close to his farmhouse. As we approached a large tree the adults glided just above the dappled light and the

Kite

canopy of leaves. They accept him and his sheep dog without fear, as they see them every day. Each year he has to eject trespassing visitors who try to approach the nest when the eggs are being incubated and the birds are at their shyest. Recently one of his kites died on a neighbouring farm, after eating poison: "Fortunately the remaining bird soon got another mate. But there is no need for them to use all this poison." It had been a successful year and the partially feathered youngster could be seen in the nest: "Tomorrow they are going to ring it, then we will be able to see how it gets on." He was proud of his kites, and from observing their behaviour and diet he did not consider them to be a threat to his sheep.

"They", turned out to be Peter Davies, of the Nature Conservancy, who lives close to the Tregaron Bog, a great "raised mire". He has studied the kites of the area for several years and was reasonably optimistic about the birds' future:

"But it will be a long uphill struggle. We have had our best summer this year*; twenty-one pairs reared twenty-seven young, and the population is about 125, a fifty per cent increase since 1972. Kites do not compete with farmers; they live on much carrion – dead sheep and lambs, and also magpies, blackbirds, woodpigeons, jackdaws, rabbits, field voles, moles and even worms and beetles. In winter they eat offal from slaughterhouses." It is strange that kites should include moles in their diet, for how they catch them remains a mystery; it is poison bought for moles but illegally put into carcasses to kill foxes and crows that kills so many birds of prey. There is little doubt that some of the birds are poisoned quite deliberately.

Peter Davies does not consider Wales to be ideal kite country: "East Anglia and Sussex are much better, but gamekeepers are still the big problem and the main reason for the decline in the first place." In the past three years poisoned kites have been found not only in Wales but also in Kent, Somerset and Sussex. The area around Herefordshire, Worcestershire and Somerset is ideal for colonisation by the expanding Welsh kite population, but until poisoning ceases expansion will be prevented. Yet there are simpler and safer ways of controlling foxes, crows, and moles, and with modern methods of rearing young gamebirds, pheasants and birds of prey can co-exist quite easily.

I found it immensely rewarding to see kites, and at Carmarthen, on the River Twyi, I came upon more Welsh rarities; men fishing for salmon in coracles. They fished in pairs on the wide placid river, a net slung between them as they drifted on the current. Four pairs were working on a long bend, but they were all out of luck: "It's been a bad year; there's hardly any salmon and it's made worse by the seals. They come right up the river here and can rip up the nets and have us in the water." They use coracles not for effect but because they consider them to be the most suitable boats on the river and handle them with great skill. One made an unusual comment however: "I don't like fishing, but it's a tradition in the family, so I've got to keep

*1980.

doing it." Yet some traditions had died, for the boats were made of fibreglass instead of skins and cost about £40 each: "Like everything else, it's expensive to fish. Nets are around £30 each and the licence is another £36. They only grant twelve each year now."

At a hotel just outside the town a board advertised "Coracle Racing". Again the coracles were of fibreglass, but the participants were local businessmen rather than fishermen. They nearly all seemed to be upper-middle class, or "made-good", from English backgrounds, trying hard to impress each other. Their clothes, including cravats and silver bracelets, appeared to have come from the same mail-order brochure, and their braying laughter seemed to get higher with every drink. I was once again reminded of Cobbett:

> If I had been brought up a milksop, with a nursery-maid everlastingly at my heels, I should have been at this day as great a fool, as inefficient a mortal, as any of those frivolous idiots that are turned out from Winchester and Westminster School, or from any of those dens of dunces called Colleges and Universities.

An old lady and her sheep dog briefly watched from the opposite bank, with obvious distaste, and a dipper flew to more peaceful waters. After the quiet meadows, Dan's skill and the soaring kites the scene seemed cheap, superficial and nasty.

Coracles

8

Harbours and Havens

Pembrokeshire, now inappropriately part of the conglomerate called Dyfed, is a warm, rich county of undulating greens – arable fields, meadows, hedgerows and trees. Although it forms the most western part of Wales, somehow it does not seem to be Welsh, but a pleasant English appendage. Away from the main roads it is quiet and soft, like Devon and Somerset, with the vast expanse of the Atlantic Ocean washing its shores and islands. On his journey through Wales, Defoe also found the area attractive:

> The next county west is Pembrokeshire, which is the most extreme part of Wales on this side, in a rich, fertile, and plentiful country, lying on the sea coast, where it has the benefit of Milford Haven, one of the greatest and best inlets of water in Britain. Mr. Cambden says it contains 16 creeks, 5 great bays, and 13 good roads for shipping, all distinguished as such by their names; and some say a thousand sail of ships may ride in it, and not the topmast of one be seen from another; but this last, I think, merits confirmation.

The state of Milford Haven today is simple to confirm. Its large, natural, deep-water harbour is ideal for oil tankers, and super-tankers of up to 275,000 tons discharge their cargoes there, while on the surrounding land oil refineries convert crude oil into the various fuels and chemicals on which the developed West depends. Each year about 4,000 ships enter the Haven, of which over 3,300 are tankers, carrying twenty-six million tons of oil.

After the farmland, villages and rural calm, the oil installations came as a sudden, metallic intrusion. Beyond Pembroke, the vast Texaco complex appeared as a technological forest of tanks, towers, pipelines and torches of burning flame, amid green fields and part of a National Park. It dwarfed the nearby parish church of Pwllcrochan, deserted and incongruous. Once Roundheads and Cavaliers fought in its churchyard, but its new neighbour confirms more recent battles, modern gods and changed values. Within the nine-mile perimeter fence construction work was in frenzied progress to increase the capacity for North Sea oil. The scale and the technical expertise were astonishing, and driving through the site I viewed the activities and the structures with awed incomprehension. The manager was proud of the work, and there is no doubt that man's journey into the technological age has been rapid and spectacular. The activity was constant; men in helmets driving Land Rovers, working cranes and welding. Some went at a more leisurely pace, simply watching the others work; these were local pensioners employed as fire watchers: "We could have taken on more locals too, for there was quite a lot of unemployment when we came here. Do you know, it's stayed the same; they didn't want to work and we had to get labour from outside."

The names of the processes which transform crude oil into petroleum fuels, such as "catalytic cracking", "isobutane decarbonising", and "furfural refining", adequately convey their complexity. By comparison the jetties where the tankers were unloaded seemed simple and the structures almost fragile. A patch of hardened oil on rocks by the shore gave ample indication of the risks. The cost of using petrol in manpower, equipment and technology is enormous, and although it is easy to decry our dependence on oil, I, too, was using it to get to Skomer.

Narrow undulating roads led away from the Haven and even in the early morning the saffron splashes of flowering gorse and broom were vivid against the backcloth of mist that obscured the broad sweep of St. Bride's Bay. In the High Street of Marloes a small cluster of village women stood waiting for transport to take them to casual work in the fields, and beyond the village loomed grass-topped promontories, islands, and the sea.

The road, by now a mere track, petered out at Martin's Haven, where a path led down to an inlet of rocks, pebbles and water, bathed by a warm sun that quickly lost its strength over the sea in the lingering blanket of fog. A group of people, with coats, anoraks and picnic baskets were waiting. Then a fishing boat chugged in to the bay; an inflatable dingy sped to the shore for its customers and the short final journey to Skomer began. The sea was calm as we passed rocky headlands, except where white water betrayed the presence of reefs and the treachery of the currents. Soon Skomer appeared, shrouded in mist with a horizontal plateau of white cloud above; puffins flew by, fast and direct, and floating guillemots washed, causing bright clouds of irridescent spray. The cliffs seemed to have escaped the influence of man; the world of wage claims, political divisions and the wonders of economic growth seemed irrelevant.

Skomer

Fully loaded with sleeping bag and food for several days, it was a hard scramble up the path to the clifftops. Puffins appeared from holes among foxgloves and sea pinks, and gulls called. The warden, a large bearded man, met us at the top to direct the day visitors to the path that would allow them to circumnavigate the island; I made my way to the old farm buildings in the centre, where basic shelter and communal cooking facilities were provided. Settlement on the island's seven hundred acres dates back to Iron Age times, but the harshness of Skomer's winters, with their Atlantic gales, has won in the end. The last farmer-fisherman left in 1950 and the old farm buildings show the ravages of wind and rain in their crumbling walls and battered roofs. A rusting Fordson tractor reminded of earlier days, as did the warden's hens. Livestock of a different kind was evident in the clear water of the spring, and when washing, drinking or cooking, it was important to avoid the newts and their tadpoles.

As the sun climbed, so its strength gained; the warmth sweetened the air with the scent of bluebells that formed pools of blue among the bracken and belts of red campion. I set out to complete a circuit of the island; a rabbit darted across the path, to disappear in one of the numerous holes, a lizard scuttled in the undergrowth, and a pipit perched on the top of a frond of bracken. At South Haven the mist was melting and floating away seawards in great rafts of towering white, like giant icebergs. A raven stood on a rocky outcrop, looking large and sleek, its low throaty call distinguishing it from its black relatives. Lighter glowing wings of copper dropped on to sea pinks, as a fritillary, a large, fast flying butterfly, apparently unaffected by the buffetings of sea breezes, found nectar. Below, flotillas of puffins rested on the sea, made calm by the Haven's protective horseshoe of sheer cliffs. Away to the south in open sea the neighbouring island of Skokholm remained half-hidden in mist, as close by, a large oil-tanker moved steadily towards Milford Haven.

The path descended into a small valley where water seeped through peat, and brambles and clumps of tall flowering water-dropwort grew in surprising profusion. Somewhere, concealed by leaves, a wren sang clearly and continuously, making an unusual contrast to the surge of the sea and the calls of the seabirds. On a ridge, holes, and short grazed turf again showed the presence of rabbits, while sudden cries of alarm and warning signified something more. Curved wings cut through the air to fall below the level of the cliffs and out of view. As the peregrine falcon sped over I had stopped involuntarily, at the sight of its majestic, savage and primitive form in an ideal island haunt. By contrast a swift flying by, low and alone, seemed quite out of place.

At High Cliff a strong wind met a warm thermal rising against the rock face. Gangs of jackdaws were hurling themselves downwards into the turbulence, with wings held back, as if enjoying the sheer pleasure of tumbling through troubled air.

A small, steep path dropped down to the sea, giving close views of a great granite wall where fissures and ledges harboured rows of nesting guillemots and razorbills, their low barking cries mingling with those of kittiwakes as they called "kittiwake, kittiwake". The sound of island life is part of its appeal. Halfway down, a group of fulmars were resting on a grassy bank, just six yards from me. Another wheeled by, before allowing itself to stall and drift backwards, with wings held into the wind, to land near its companions. Fulmars are such graceful, quiet birds that by comparison the noise and clamour of breeding auks★ are most undignified. On the water groups of puffins, guillemots and razorbills floated peacefully, while others washed and preened; it was a perfect place to be.

As the sun began its downward journey its strength was hidden by the fresh sea breeze, bracing as I walked over the short grazed turf; in places the grass was littered with the remains of Manx shearwaters, their bones picked clean by gulls. Each new cove, bay and headland held fresh beauty, until over a rise came a sight so far unequalled; a carpet of soft, white sea campion, puffins standing outside their burrows, and then the land dropped vertically to a long wedge of water, far below, to form the Wick. On one side sheer basalt cliffs fell more than two hundred feet to the sea and housed hundreds of birds. In that vast natural chamber of rock, the tones of their calls gained in clarity as they mixed with the sound of the ocean to give a wild, haunting symphony. I walked opposite the tumult, where great slabs of smooth rock went more

---

'★The auk family includes the guillemot, the black guillemot (not on Skomer), Brunnick's guillemot (rarely seen in Britain), razorbills and puffins.

gently down to the sea, and there the wind ended its Atlantic journey by lifting the surging surf into sheets of glittering spray.

Puffins emerged from their burrows, very close, as I sat among the flowers; they seemed quizzical but unafraid. With their orange beaks and feet their alternative name of "sea parrot" seemed very well suited. The wind was so strong that some of the birds were repeatedly blown fractionally off balance, so that they appeared to be tapping their feet.

Rabbits ran, herring gulls called to their chicks among boulders, a pair of wheatears bobbed on a lichen-covered rock and the sun continued to shine from a now cloudless sky. The sea was a mixture of pools and patterns of metallic blue and turquoise, with "white horses" on the wave tops showing the strength of the wind. Six miles out to sea the small outcrop of Grassholm could be seen clearly through the light haze that had replaced the thick mist. In spite of its name it was not green, for every summer thousands of nesting gannets turn it white. There were no gannets close to the Skomer shore, but through binoculars large white birds could be seen milling around Grassholm: the island looked distant and mysterious and I decided I would like to visit it.

High above the Garland Stone, I sat again; the sun was turning the sea to rippling gold and silver, and below, grey seals were basking on their backs in lethargic bliss. Bees worked among the sea pinks, the piercing cries of oystercatchers showed their displeasure at an unseen threat, and a seal scratched its stomach with a flipper. Large wings flapped briefly from a crag below me as a buzzard found a thermal and was hoisted high over the island. I could think of nothing I would rather be doing and thought it strange that despite technology, computers and silicon chips, the human hand was still considered necessary to file bank statements, screw nuts on to bolts, and dig for coal. For the first time in human history, people could be freed from work; they too could share the pleasure of time and space on a long summer day. Yet the traditional social and political attitudes in favour of full employment and the need for routine at least ensured that I found comparative solitude on Skomer. A marvellous experience, for in summer, Britain's remote islands offer some of the most unique and spectacular wildlife to be found anywhere in the world.

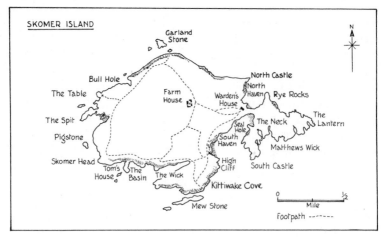

By the time I moved, an empty oil-tanker had anchored in St. Bride's Bay, riding high on the water. I turned inland over marshier ground. Curlews bubbled, and from the top of a large clump of heather an adult bird called "curlew". Over an area of dense bracken, other silent wings appeared with a fluttering, light and buoyant flight. Occasionally as the short-eared owl quartered the ground it angled its wings upwards to hang motionless in the air. One of the most beautiful and skilful of all hunting birds, it too breeds on the island, and from deep among the bracken came the wheezing calls of its young. Almost back at the farmhouse a pair of pheasants ran for cover; in the company of owls, gulls, buzzards and peregrines their presence seemed remarkable and any chicks must have lived a precarious existence.

With evening the light became more gentle; the day-trippers had left, and the deputy warden, his nose red and peeling, suggested a communal evening meal, cooked over an open fire in the old farmhouse. There were few people staying; Richard Anderson, of Scandinavian name and appearance, who worked as a conservation officer for a naturalists' trust, a

Swedish hiker, a schoolmaster from Winchester, and a domineering woman with military manners and bearing. Potatoes and sausages were produced and smoke joined the twilight through the roofless building.

Richard was visiting the island to see storm petrels but added: "The birds you must see are Manx shearwaters. There's no moon tonight, so they'll be coming in as there is less chance of the black-backed gulls getting them on a dark night. They were massing out to sea this afternoon." Manx shearwaters are mysterious birds; there are thought to be over 100,000 pairs on Skomer, nesting in rabbit burrows, and while one bird incubates, its mate flies off to feed on sardines in the Bay of Biscay. Some experts say that the birds are away for three days, and others suggest six, then, under cover of darkness they fly in to exchange roles. As they approach they call, and are answered by their waiting mates underground.

The barbecued food was reasonable, and the schoolmaster produced a bottle of whisky: "Here, this will keep the moths out until the birds take off." Richard obviously enjoyed Skomer: "There is one word that everybody learns who visits this island – onomatopoeic; it means that the call of the bird is the same as its name. Curlew is onomatopoeic because the bird calls 'curlew'. The kittiwake calls 'kittiwake' and the chiffchaff calls 'chiffchaff'. Then of course there is the Manx shearwater, which is not onomatopoeic. Can you imagine a bird flying through the air crying 'Manx shearweater, Manx shearwater'? In fact its call is more absurd because it calls 'cup o' cocoa, cup o' cocoa', so it should have been called a cup of cocoa bird." Others who had heard the call of the shearwater confirmed its strange, plaintive cry. Richard now had another word to explain: "If you really want to impress others, then you should use the word 'chlorotic'. It sounds disgusting; it means green, but sounds so much better. I heard a serious botanist use it once; I use it all the time now."

Shortly after midnight the first faint cry came in. It really did sound like "cup o' cocoa, cup o' cocoa", similar to a pheasant with breathing difficulties. Soon the cries were all around us; outside, wingbeats would suddenly pass close to our heads. Everywhere ghostly calls sounded, some coming from beneath the ground among the bracken. Torchlight revealed birds scrambling with difficulty on the ground for, like many birds of the open seas, shearwaters find moving on the land extremely difficult. They were attractive, sooty birds with dark eyes and hooked beaks; once grounded they looked lost and helpless. My face stung as a bird flew into me but it continued on its way unhurt. It was astonishing to see hundreds of birds, apparently lost and clumsy in torchlight, yet each one homing in to its own burrow among many thousands of holes.

The few days on the island passed quickly and I envied the warden his summers, living in a bungalow overlooking North and South Havens. Each evening puffins landed on his roof and covered the grassy banks nearby. He had been many things before arriving on Skomer: a policeman, a miner, an art student and he had worked at a bird observatory in Canada. He loved Skomer, but was worried, for the peace and sanctity of island life is an illusion as the seabirds and their ancient

Puffin

cliffs are threatened by the activities and the carelessness of man. He was on the island on October 12th, 1978: "It was a beautiful, clear, sunny day, with a flat calm and visibility of twenty miles, when the Greek tanker *Christos Bitas* ran aground." Over 2,500 birds are known to have died as the island's bays, including North Haven, filled with oil. Michael Alexander is a big, strong man: "One of the delights of Skomer is to watch the seals and I had grown very attached to one. I had seen it grow up, but I saw it drown in oil as its mother tried to save it. I was helpless. I could do nothing and just sat down and cried." From a drawer he produced colour transparencies of North Haven covered in oil, together with oiled seals, pathetic, bewildered, and eyes full of fear. It seemed a savage price to pay for internal combustion and uncomfortable nylon shirts.

Although many birds died, Skomer was lucky since its summer population of auks had left and the casualties were from other areas. If such an accident had happened in mid-summer, Skomer would have died. The dangers could be lessened with early-warning systems, booms to keep out oil, and aerial spraying for faster cleaning but, in Britain, time is wasted while local authorities and government departments argue over who is to pay for clean-up operations, and priority is given to holiday beaches rather than wildlife refuges. In the event, while the others argued, B.P. moved in to play the major part in cleaning Skomer, at a cost of over £200,000; it can only be hoped that their action resulted from genuine concern, rather than the need for good public relations. The *Christos Bitas* was carrying 35,000 tons of heavy Iranian crude oil, and it has been estimated that between 2,000 and 3,000 tons were lost. To combat the threat over 80,000 gallons of dispersants were used. If ever a super-tanker runs aground in June, the results will be horrific.

Numbers of auks in Southern Britain have almost stabilised after years of steady decline, but now Michael Alexander sees another threat to the Skomer birds: "An area like Skomer and the islands around should be classified as a Marine National Park, just like a National Park on the mainland. But we get boats and fishermen disturbing the birds and we get disturbance too from divers who go too near the breeding colonies and who take shells and interfere with the local fishermen. The British Sub Aqua Club increased from 5,500 to 22,000 members between 1964 and 1974, which hasn't helped."

He obviously cared for his island and was eager that visitors should feel the same way. I decided to stay on a few more days and Michael promised to try to persuade a local fisherman to take me for a closer view of Grassholm. During the night the wind increased and by morning rain was driving down in drenching sheets – Grassholm had disappeared from view. The deputy warden knocked on my door: "Force nine gales are expected. If the boat gets through, all visitors have got to leave as you could be stuck out here for days." We waited, dripping, in the warden's bungalow, possessions covered in large plastic bags. The wind was gradually increasing and the grey sea was flecked with white. Late, the boat dipped and rolled to the landing station: "Hurry up," the boatman shouted. "We've got to run for harbour as soon as we've dropped you lot." Three gannets flew easily by in the wind and rain, completely at home surrounded by the spray, mist and black walls of rock.

At Marloes, the Lobster Pot was warm, with a gas stove creating a comfortable fug as clothes dried. Even chips, peas and rubber-like sausages seemed to be a meal of rare quality, washed down with beer and coffee. Later the boatman arrived to warm up and dry out after taking his boat to the nearby harbour of Dale: "You've had Grassholm," he said gloomily. "There's no chance of getting there for days." In addition to his boat he owned a small farm, just fourteen acres, which he let for grazing at £75 an acre for eleven months of the year. He used his boat for lobster fishing and taking visitors to Skomer: "Fishing's a good life, but it's impossible to make a living now, as all the fish in the bay are so small."

Once, fishing in the area had been good and taken for granted; now, with a gale blowing, a rough sea, and oil-tankers close at hand, it seemed likely that one day Skomer's wildlife would also be mentioned in the past tense.

The effect of oil is not just limited to a few offshore islands and notorious incidents. Tankers wash out their tanks illegally, while at sea, to save time and money, and fuel and waste engine oil are spilt by ordinary vessels as they go about their business. Consequently oiled birds can appear at any time of the year, and several people have set up "bird hospitals" to try to cope with the problem, and to alleviate suffering. Some say that such activities are a waste of time and effort, and that the oiled birds should be destroyed, but often the birds are so pitiful that action is taken to save them. One of the problems is the treatment itself, for in using detergents to clean the birds, the oil in the feathers is destroyed, the natural waterproofing is ruined and the birds would become waterlogged, and die, if returned to the sea.

While in Devon I came across a private bird hospital, the Redgate Bird Sanctuary at Exmouth. The owner was a tall bespectacled lady wearing a scarf and wellington boots, who had started her work in 1959 with a solitary sparrow; since then she has converted her large house and overgrown garden into a bird refuge. Birds, from a tatty parrot to pigeons, occupied almost every room and it was obvious that she found it difficult to make ends meet financially. In the garden there were more birds and cages, and as we spoke a small French-man approached for instructions. He was wearing boots and overalls and I assumed he was the gardener; he turned out to be the hard-working husband.

Some enclosures contained gulls that had been injured by fishing lines, hooks and plastic beer can containers, and another held guillemots and razorbills, which had been oiled and cleaned. Some looked fit, but others had obviously lost their waterproofing, and one razorbill had lost most of its feathers as well, making it look like a small, disconsolate vulture. Astonishingly, some of the guillemots were sitting on eggs; large blue-green eggs, heavily tapered at one end to prevent them from rolling off rocky ledges; "You must have seen eggs on ledges before," she said with pride, "but never in an English garden." They have been laying since 1968 and every year chicks hatch and die. There appeared to be no salt water and they seemed a sad, forlorn little collection: "Each year I get problems with prolapses. It's almost as if they say it's time to start laying, whether they are ready or not, and they strain away. When that happens I have to give them a sedative and tape up their bottoms."

Back at the house, two guillemots, apparently in fine condition, were brought into the living room, and a blackbird sang loudly from an adjoining room. My hostess appeared with a bottle of wine: "It's orange and malt; we can make it in three weeks." Her husband nodded knowingly: "You English make wine from anything." It was a disgusting liquid, with a tart chemical taste, that I drank with difficulty. Before I could decline I received a generous refill; I thanked her kindly and made it last until it was time to leave. As I drove away I could not help but admire her dedication, yet I wondered whether it was really kindness to keep birds alive that could never be returned to the wild.

As I headed towards home, I passed through Somerset and Little Creech, where John Hughes runs a wildlife unit for the Royal Society for the Prevention of Cruelty to Animals, and he too takes in guillemots and razorbills. Some of the Society's activites seem rather strange, but his unit was well run and does a worthwhile job. A red deer hind, just changing into her summer coat, greeted me and nuzzled into John's side. She was called Blossom and had been saved from drowning in floods when a fawn. Elsewhere, in pens, were buzzards, kestrels, a little owl and a row of tired fledgling tawnies, who could barely keep their eyes open on a warm day. They had been cut out of a dead elm and would be returned to the wild when able to fend for themselves.

John Hughes's main work is with guillemots and razorbills, and he has a special block of buildings where they are hosed down, cleaned, and then put in pools to check their waterproofing: "Sea birds can only be returned to the sea as long as they have attained a hundred per cent buoyancy and they are fit. Until comparatively recently there was no evidence of long-term survival, but we have developed our techniques and we are getting success. One of our released birds was picked up again on the Dutch coast, six months later, with a damaged wing. Another one was recovered dead, twenty-five months later off the Yorkshire coast at Bampton, and a guillemot released on December 22nd, 1977 was found re-oiled at Cork on April 5th, 1980. With a large oiling incident of over a hundred birds we expect to release about fifty per cent, and from a small incident, a hundred per cent. Those that do not recover are humanely destroyed. We received 430 birds from the *Christos Bitas* incident; 315 were able to undergo treatment and 142 were released. They do not suffer from stress when we clean them, as they are not the most intelligent of birds. Within a few minutes of new conditions they seem to regard them as normal, whether they are riding in a lorry or eating sprats out of a dish." He keeps two tons of sprats free of charge in a local cold store in case of emergency. He does not agree with the theory that if the money was not spent on de-oiling it would be spent on prevention. More importantly, he thinks his work keeps birds away from the kitchen sinks of ordinary well-meaning people, who in fact can cause long-term harm. He commended their compassion, but some of the results worried him.

A mild, pleasant man, with a beard and a soft Geordie accent, his work and methods could one day become vital as sea birds face an increasing threat: "It's terrible," he said. "The birds have been happy for centuries just pattering about on their ledges and doing their own thing, and then we have to do this to them. At the moment I think it's a toss-up as to which runs out first, the auks or the oil."

9

Marshes and Madness

To Cobbett, London was the "great wen", and to Thomas Bewick it was no better:

> I would rather be herding sheep on Mickley bank top than remain in London, although for doing so I was to be made Premier of England . . . I was quite overpowered by the coldness and selfishness of everything I witnessed . . . I never saw a single recognition of acquaintanceship or friendship in the streets . . . In London life is cheap; the hearts of even good men get hardened; and that mutual regard and sympathy, which are the real balsams of life, are seldom tasted. I was delighted beyond measure when I turned my back on the place.

Times do not change and London remains for me a depressing, claustrophobic city. Its centre is pretentious and shallow, feeding on glittering lights and expense accounts, surrounded by a wilderness of bricks without feeling or soul. It holds out the rewards of prestige and status; superficial and ephemeral gains. To many, work in London is a sign of success, but often, once they succeed, the emptiness and harshness falls into clearer focus and they yearn to move away. I visit London as infrequently as possible, but when I do, I drive to the East End, leave my car, and take public transport to the centre.

Bethnal Green and Bow, the home of Cockneys and street markets, are dismal areas, where in recent years high-rise flats and open-plan estates have ripped apart old street communities and destroyed any character they once had. "Wogs go Home" and "National Front – Nazi Front" decorate walls in bitter graffiti; small children roam the streets at night while parents drink in pubs, and the people, like their surroundings, seem vacuous. Some of the high-rise lifts reek of human urine, uniformity and conformity press down, and loneliness is commonly found in the middle of crowded living.

Off the main through road, a red-bricked Victorian building provides a strange link with East Anglia. It looks like an old workhouse, but until recently it was used as a factory, making matches from English poplar trees grown in plantations close to the Norfolk–Suffolk border. Now it simply distributes matches that are made elsewhere, from the wood of cheaper foreign trees. The enterprise was "rationalised" and the plantations were sold to the pension fund of a large London bank.

The A11 (M11) road strikes north from London, linking the East End to where the remaining poplar trees stand. I drove away from the city on a Friday afternoon, the start of the Spring Bank Holiday. Cars were pouring out in a steady stream and I could understand people's need to get away. The motorway cut straight through fertile farmland and bluebell woods, and to the right I could see the low buildings and aeroplanes of Stansted Airport. Just before Cambridge a branch of the motorway swings westwards, linking London and the airport with the Midlands. Twenty years ago surveyors informed a few local people that: "If the road comes, Stansted will be London's third airport." Such long-term plans were not made public, and when the case for the motorway was made its link with the airport was not mentioned by those presenting the plans. Yet despite public enquiries and two refusals, the planners are still fighting to increase the airport's size. It is another example of how government in Britain is not as "open" as the politicians suggest, and the findings of public enquiries seem to be expensive irrelevances.

Through Cambridgeshire and into Suffolk, the volume of traffic increased, with cars pulling caravans and boats, heading for the coast and the Norfolk Broads. The Breckland with its pine trees and sandy soil is an appealing region, but from a long traffic jam, where the road divided, there was little to see.

I turned off the main road to pass through villages, close to an American air force base. The fields were small with black soil, like the Fens. Over a river bridge a lorry stood in a lay-by loaded with lengths of recently-cut poplar, and then came a rutted farm roadway awash with puddles. Through trees a heap of roots and trunks smouldered where land had been cleared and new drainage ditches were being dug by a mechanical digger. Soon the once wet, marshy ground would be in full production, providing cash-crops for London.

The track turned left past woodland; the air was fresh, cool and damp. Tall, straight poplars covered land to the west, their leaves rustling in the light breeze. They seemed to magnify the clear, fluid notes of songbirds. Comfrey was on flower and new grasses and greenery bent over with the weight of retained rain. Hawthorn and willow were fresh with spring foliage and when the sun briefly shone it became a dripping green of translucent leaves. In just a few minutes I had entered a new world and the queues of traffic were already forgotten.

From deep inside the plantation came new melodic notes of liquid beauty; bell-like yet flowing, the like of which I had never heard in England before, reminding me of far-off tropical forests. To my left, over a recently-sown field came a more familiar sound, that of a snipe "drumming". It is a strange bleating noise, which forms part of the bird's courtship display. The snipe flies high, before gliding in a fast downward curve, and the rush of air through its tail feathers causes the peculiar "drumming" effect. For years no one knew how the noise was produced. Gilbert White wrote: "In breeding-time snipes play over the moors, piping and humming; they always hum as they are descending. Is not their hum ventriloquous like that of a turkey? Some suspect it is made by their wings."

The track continued over a railway line, with more poplars on one side and a large area of marsh on the other. From a high bank of nettles and brambles the whole area of marshland could be seen; new green reeds among the tasselled heads of the old, and a variety of willows, from small clumps, to large mature trees. The call of a female cuckoo chuckled out as it flew from the poplars towards the marsh, sounding at first almost like the bubbling of a curlew. Small birds mobbed her as she flew and it was easy to understand how cuckoos and sparrowhawks were commonly mistaken in earlier times. Two males followed, flying into the willows, calling "cuckoo". Pochard were feeding in the reeds and a pair of Canada geese had a brood of newly-hatched young. Moorhens fed, their tails flicking, and coots called. From the undergrowth, whitethroats and warblers sang and a roding woodcock flew slowly over my head making a croaking call.★ All around, signs of courtship and springtime were in full swing, amid the wealth of varied wildlife in this small area of marsh and damp woodland.

Golden oriole

From well within the poplars the bell-like song began again, clear and piping. It drew me along the railway line to look deeper into the trees, when suddenly a bird flew in undulating flight across the track: of brilliant golden yellow plumage streaked with black, in seconds it had disappeared high into the treetops. It was a male golden oriole, a bird that had also puzzled earlier writers. Gilbert White gave them the charming name of "golden thrushes" and Richard Kearton wrote:

> This bird, although a somewhat rare and accidental visitor to our shores, has, according to some authorities, bred in several parts of England. There are, however, sceptics who

★The courtship display of the woodcock.

doubt this, and adduce, as a reason, that there is not a collector who can boast the possession of a British laid specimen. Be this as it may, it is doubtful whether the bird will ever succeed in breeding in this country, on account of the eagerness with which the collector seeks after the skin of the male, whose attractive colours excite his cupidity.

Now several pairs breed in these plantations, as they do in other areas of Southern Britain, but the places they favour are rapidly becoming more rare than the birds. The poplar plantations were of course planted by men, since the trees are an ideal crop for wet fenland, but they give the appearance of being damp and wild.

The new owners say that some of the trees will be retained, but already felling and draining is creating land fit only for carrots, potatoes and cereals. It is more than a local problem, for all over Britain the remaining wet places are increasingly threatened; a threat to both wildlife and people, for their attraction and quality cannot be replaced. Some of the wetlands of East Anglia are among the best in the land, but already, for many of them, it may be too late.

The cuckoos still called as dusk approached and a long triangle of sunlight cut deep into the darkness beneath the trees. Returning to my car I met a small party of birdwatchers walking along the track, equipped with binoculars, tripods, thorn-proof coats and woolly hats. The leader eagerly asked me: "What's about? Are there any orioles?"

"On the marsh there are some Canada geese with young," I replied with enthusiasm.

He looked at me incredulously: "Canada geese?" He could hardly believe my ignorance and was not interested.

They were a group of "twitchers", a comparatively new breed, who comb the country far and wide in search of rare species. In places, their activities pose almost as great a threat to struggling birdlife as drainage schemes and development.

Darkness fell as I followed winding roads to the village of Melton Constable, in Norfolk, and the home of Roger Tidman. He had been a successful optician, who had sold up and moved to North Norfolk with his wife and dog to take up wildlife photography. He had tired of eyes and lenses and wanted to spend more time doing what he considered to be more important and fulfilling. For him Norfolk held more appeal than other areas being rural, coastal, on the main bird migration routes and with a variety of wetlands and heath.

The next morning the land was wet, as grey skies had brought rain: "Don't worry, the toads will still be there," he said, as we drove along roads lined with cow parsley and alexanders, a Mediterranean herb once cultivated in monastery gardens but now growing wild in many coastal areas. We passed through the villages of Great and Little Snoring to a minor road with gorse and broom in full and dazzling bloom. We stopped at heathland, an area of hummocks and hollows with short grass, brambles, bracken, sandy soil and a number of small stagnant pools. The pools seemed almost lifeless apart from the occasional beetle, but then, at a larger one, with long grasses and clumps of rush, a toad, a golden line running along its back and golden eyes crazed with black, sat half hidden, before running for total cover. Next to an empty Watneys beer can sat another, lighter, and even more striking, as if made from mottled marble. They were natterjacks, rare toads of heaths, dunes and brackish water, that in Britain are getting rarer as their habitat is gradually drained and irrevocably altered. Roger was pleased to have found them: "In Norfolk we have three kinds of toads, the walking, running and hopping varieties. They are really the common toad, the natterjack and the common frog." The local names give quite an accurate description, and even "jumping toad" is more exact than "common frog", since in many areas of Britain the frog is no longer common. As we left, an old man walked by with a boisterous little boy and an uncontrollable terrier; both were running into the water and through the clumps of rushes. After their passage the toads may have become even rarer.

We proceeded to the coast, to Cley-next-the-Sea, for Roger wanted to take me to a sandy hilltop where adders breed, overlooking the low-lying marshes. To him the area and its rich birdlife was paradise and gave him an opportunity to try a new way of earning a living. The rain had stopped by the time we climbed the hill, almost treading on a slow worm as we went; it was soft, smooth and perfectly formed as it quietly slithered away. Sure enough, we came across an adder lying under a gorse bush, but on seeing us it slid into the under-growth; although adders are feared because of their poisonous fangs, they are in fact very shy creatures.

Also overlooking the area of lagoons, reed beds and water meadows was a hut run by the Norfolk Ornithologists' Association. Inside, bird photographs and conservation pro-jects were on display; outside, stood another group dressed in oiled cotton coats and woollen hats, trailing tripods, tele-scopes and binoculars – more "twitchers". Their dark cloth-ing was like a uniform, and they looked down on those birdwatchers who wore brightly-coloured anoraks: "They belong to the R.S.P.B.: they are not proper bird-watchers; how could they be, wearing conspicuous stuff like that?"

Their greeting was almost the same as the previous day's: "What's about then?" The talk was of a purple heron, Tem-minck's stints and dotterels. To them, bird-watching seemed to involve only exotic species and rarities. One had seen the purple heron in a ditch; another had also wanted to see it but "dipped out", as some over-enthusiastic pursuers had fol-lowed it along the ditch and flushed it. Accordingly, they were not "twitchers" but "bloody flushers".

Among the marshes the Norfolk Naturalists' Trust had a number of wooden hides, but we decided to walk close to a high drainage bank overlooking damp meadows. There, too, small groups of twitchers were searching for Temminck's stints. One asked as usual: "What's about then?" accompanied by a genuine nervous twitch. They are called "twitchers" because when they see a bird they "twitch" as an automatic reflex; then if it is a bird they have not seen before, they "tick" it off on their European list. We saw another, more advanced twitcher, looking through his telescope; he was a postman with a double-first university degree, who preferred to deliver letters and watch birds in his spare time, than move to a birdless area for academic or business benefits. In fact there seemed to be more twitchers in the area than birds.

Back in the village of Cley it was time for tea, and we made for the end house of a small row of flint-walled terraced cottages. Above the window a sign proclaimed: "Teas, Coffees, Sandwiches and Snacks", while in the window itself the wares were advertised more poetically:

Bric à Brac
Soup and Snacks.

We had come to Nancy's tea room, known throughout the "twitching" world. Inside the door lay a heap of packs, bags and binoculars, while on the phone a bearded man was talking about the purple heron. The warm small room was crammed full of uniformed twitchers having tea, and Ethel served us with beans on toast (no chips). The talk was of blue-headed wagtails and Roger was asked if he had seen any Savi's warblers at Hickling Broad. A book was passed around; inside were messages of sitings and locations, one signed by "Punk Steve". Somebody had seen a great reed warbler at the Ouse Washes and there were messages about birds in Dorset and Dungeness. Someone, eating a scone, was complaining about the "flushers" who had made the heron disappear: "That's nothing," another replied. "On Shetland someone threw a rock at the albatross to make it fly and killed a gannet."

"An albatross?" I asked.

"Of course. It goes there every year. Everybody goes to tick it, haven't you?"

From the conversation it was clear that the territory of the twitchers ranged from the Scilly Isles to Shetland, and any rarity in between would be instantly pursued. One wore a jumper enscribed with "Hunt Saboteurs' Association"; he obviously could not see that by rushing all over the country he was actually helping to sabotage birds. At regular intervals the telephone rang and the nearest person answered to give news of the Cley rarities; twitchers phone Nancy's from all over Britain. They had even developed their own language; the purple heron was referred to as the "purple frank", great skuas on Shetland were "bonxies"; a grasshopper warbler became a "gropper"; a sparrowhawk a "sprawk"; a meadow pipit a "mipit", and a rare red-breasted flycatcher was an "r-b flicker". When seen for the first time the bird became "a life tick", then there were "yearly ticks" and "monthly ticks". When I mentioned that earlier in the year I had seen my first European hoopoe, my sighting was greeted with disdain – "a boy's tick". By their activities and rivalry, the twitchers had managed to turn bird-watching into a competitive sport.

Nancy herself was in the kitchen, a friendly motherly lady surrounded by beans, scones and her speciality, bread and butter pudding. She started selling refreshments sixteen years earlier after some visitors had leant over the wall to ask where they could get teas. She saw a demand, obtained planning permission, and started serving teas in her front room. Bird-watchers began to call, the place gradually built up a "birding" clientele, and few of the telephone calls are now for her. She likes them: "They come and go as they please and they are a happy crowd, even in the worst weather." Appropriately Nancy's married name is Mrs. Gull; better still her husband is Mr. J. C. Gull, and one lady bird-watcher always upsets her children by calling them "little black-headed gulls".

Norfolk is most noted for its Broads, a series of large inland lakes and lagoons, linked by 129 miles of navigable waterways, most of which probably originated from old peat diggings when the whole area was undrained. Then it was a haven for waterfowl, wading birds and marsh plants, but now the Broads, or "water spaces" as the planners call them, attract people rather than wildlife and each year in excess of 250,000 visitors use them for boating and fishing.

On the Sunday morning the roads were busy with trippers,★ but we did not follow them to one of the 110 boatyards; instead we went to Hickling Broad, a National Nature Reserve run by the Norfolk Naturalists' Trust, where a battle is being waged, albeit a losing one, to preserve part of old Broadland. Hickling itself covers nearly 1,400 acres, but unlike the surrounding area it receives only authorised visitors, numbering some 2,000 a year, although, absurdly, a public footpath and a right of way for "stink boats" pass through the reserve. The warden, Stewart Linsell, refers to all the hire-craft as "stink boats": "At one time they were driven

★One estimate put the number of visitors to the area over the Bank Holiday weekend at 150,000.

by petrol and any spilt or discharged fuel evaporated away. Now they are driven by diesel, which spreads all over the water." He had not been looking forward to the holiday: "I always seem to get a rarity during the Spring Bank Holiday and that brings in the twitchers. Last year a black-winged stilt turned up, and eighty people wanting to get a tick arrived on the bank where there is a public footpath. The year before at the same time a great white heron arrived. I've even had twitchers walking through the reed-beds like beaters, trying to flush the birds. As if that was not enough we get egg collectors, armed with planks to get over the dykes, as we've got the only inland nesting site of little terns in the country. Then we get butterfly collectors after swallowtails; the butter-flies are not endangered by them, but they cause a lot of disturbance to nests."

Like so many others involved with wildlife, Stewart was a quiet, calm man, as if care and concern had mellowed his features and sharpened his understanding. With light blue eyes, grey hair, and windburnt cheeks he seemed out of place in his office surrounded by pictures and books for sale to visitors, and administrative papers, which unfortunately, just as in any other job, have their place.

His interest in natural history, especially the 3b's – birds, butterflies and botany – started while at school, where James Fisher was the biology master. Stewart wanted to be a vet, but war broke out and on his nineteenth birthday he was called up, in error, two years early. Throughout the war while on active service with the navy, he sent James Fisher information on the fulmars he saw. After his discharge he worked in the family business, a rambling shop at Felstead: "It sold everything from cosmetics to paraffin, rat traps to butter." At the same time he became a voluntary counter for the Wildfowl Trust, and in 1967, when the family shop was sold, he was appointed a warden for the Essex Naturalists' Trust, finally arriving at Hickling in 1975.

Despite his efforts to safeguard the reserve he was pessi-mistic about the future: "This year* we have no bitterns at

*1981.

Hickling, the first time since 1911. It's very sad, not a single boomer. I think it's the food; neither the bitterns nor the herons can feed inside the Broad as the water gets so mucky that they cannot see their food. The problem is the 'turbidity' of the water; it gets like Campbell's condensed green pea soup. It's caused by agricultural fertilisers being washed in, phosphates and nitrates. Also phosphates from sewerage treatment works, for the treated water is very high in phosphates. The whole area is so bad it cannot really get worse. There are a quarter of a million black-headed gulls dropping phosphates in too. In the old days it wasn't churned up, now boats are churning it up all the time. Over the last twelve years Hickling's water lilies and mares' tails have gone. Marsh harriers are doing badly too; the males lose interest and go and the females can't manage on their own. However, the bearded tits are doing well and the swallowtails are safe for the time being as there is plenty of milk parsley, their foodplant.

"Holiday-makers are a problem, pumping out their bilges and even canoeists cause trouble going up the small channels and frightening the nesting birds. Then there are the fishermen. I dread June 16th ever year, when the coarse fishing season starts. They get everywhere, leaving line, lead weights and hooks, and cutting down reeds with sickles and leaving the banks open to erosion. They are worse than coypu; I have become rather fond of coypu and would hate to see them go completely."

We left Stewart working and moved on to the reserve, through managed reed beds that are harvested each year, making 20,000 bundles of Norfolk reed and 4,000 bundles of sedge. Hickling itself was superficially most attractive, its large areas of water fringed with reeds; many boats were on the water, some moored to a reinforced bank; one sailor was relieving himself, a dog was running wild and a brackish lagoon was covered with a skin of diesel. From a hide we looked out on to a man-made shingle scrape. Two men with northern accents were already inside studying the area through telescopes; there were little terns, common terns, shellducks and a redshank with unusually red legs.

Returning, we visited the old shooting lodge where King

George V often stayed, and from its roof gained a wide, watery view of reeds, channels, open water and islands, including the small island where Emma Turner, the pioneer bird photographer, lived for several years around 1902. Back at the car park Stewart arrived; he had been warned of egg collectors in the area and was checking for known collectors' car numbers to try to protect his little terns.

Lunch was attempted at the nearby Pleasure Boat Inn, crammed with people looking uniformly miserable in safari suits, sailor hats, bright anoraks, Tony Jacklin trousers, shiny leather shoes and plimsolls. Several children whiled away the time by throwing bread to three friendly swans, trying to get them close in to the bank. Inside there were queues for beer and plates of chips, peas, scampi, and variations on the theme.

It was impossible to eat or drink in comfort among the mass of intrepid travellers, and so we quickly left. Returning towards Melton Constable, we meandered slowly through the countryside; in one parish all the field edges had been sprayed to kill the "weeds", thus killing all the wildflowers too. I stopped to ask the old farmer why he thought such drastic action was necessary. He wore a cap over his eyes, but beneath the peak they sparkled with pride. He answered in a broad Norfolk accent: "It keeps the outside of the crop clean, then we don't get any rubbish in the combine. A lot of our neighbours are copying us now." Around his fields there were no places for butterflies to feed, or young partridges to find insects; I did not ask him why, he simply would not have understood.

At the village of Sparham an old red-brick house stood in the remnants of an ancient orchard, where several swans preened, and outside was parked a red estate-car bearing the inscription "Swan Rescue Service". We stopped again; who would want to rescue swans and for what? Len Baker, a man in his forties, came to the door looking pale and tired: "You'll have to excuse me, but we had a breakdown when coming back with a swan last night and I've only had two and a half hours' sleep." His wife Sheila, however, was very much awake and soon made coffee. They were an unusual couple; Len had been a motorcycle racer, then, after several serious accidents he became a businessman and a traveller, before becoming involved with swans. He and Sheila had lived with Aborigines in Australia, and spent some time with the Hopi Indians in New Mexico, who made a great impression on them: "They are beautiful people, ruined by civilisation," Len said sadly. "They taught me all I know about birds, looking after feathers and using feathers as splints. When I was with them I was interested in eagles but they told me that in the future I would not work with the bird of the bent beak, but the bird of the great white wing. I thought they meant seagulls. Then in 1977 I found a swan tangled in fishing line at the bottom of a boat yard at Horning; we called her Ella; that was 615 swans ago and we have released 497 back into the wild. Normally a swan will live for fifty to sixty years in captivity; in the wild the average life span is three years two months.

"Last year [1980], we studied the breeding success of ten pairs of swans. Sixty-five cygnets were hatched; fifty-two were killed. Thirty-eight died because of fishing hooks and lines; three were shot; nine died as a result of boating accidents, five of which were intentional; two were killed by stoning and thirteen survived. Fishing is the big problem; at this time of year visitors throw bread to swans; then in three weeks' time June 16th arrives and the swans swim up to nice friendly fishermen who don't want them around. Some of the injuries are caused quite deliberately."

His stories were heart-rending and horrific. His worst case was in 1979 when he found Ella again. She had been crucified

Mute swan

on a tree with three crossbow bolts, two through her wings and one through her chest: "She died in my arms as I took her down; it was the first time I ever shed a tear over a swan. Some are hit by oars; one had boiling treacle poured over her, aftering being lured in with bread. She survived but we had to chip the treacle off her. Some are hooked with coathangers over their necks and dragged along for fun and a duck was plucked alive and put back on the water. In 1979 it seemed that a pair of otters were trying to establish themselves in the Broads again; they had bottles and beer cans thrown at them from passing boats as well as a fire bomb made from a Cherry Blossom boot polish tin, filled with lighter fuel and a wick inserted.

"Plastic can containers can get over a swan's neck and if they get their heads through the handle of a plastic bag and the bag fills with water, they get pulled under. Then of course forty-one per cent of the swans are suffering from lead ingestion, after swallowing lead weights left by anglers and retaining them in the gizzard. There's still more; stuffed swans make £575 in Saudi Arabia and people get swan feathers for greetings cards. For this some swans are lured close with bread and get their tail feathers pulled out. It's terrible and we are the only people who seem to be working for them. Swans are not alone; last year thirteen coots were found with beer can rings over their beaks – they had starved to death. It is thought that the rings look like vole holes to coots, and as they are often good places for dropped seeds, they peck inside."

Around the room were photographs and paintings of swans, together with a Red Indian prophecy: "When the earth is sick, the animals will begin to disappear. When that happens, the warriors of the rainbow will come to save them."

Len showed us around the pens in his garden where he still had sixteen swans to care for and to treat; he picked one up and opened out her soft white wings; the feathers felt like a delicate tapestry of pure silk. One still had a hook imbedded in a vertebra and another had a broken neck but appeared to be comfortable. Len carries out numerous operations to remove hooks, repair damage and amputate limbs; these he performs in a caravan fitted out as an operating theatre with help and advice from Steve Cooke, a Berkshire vet. One of his successes was swimming on a small artificial pool: "She had her bottom bill completely severed by nylon fishing line, but we managed to fit her out with a new fibreglass replacement. We are quiet now; as soon as the fishing and holiday seasons really get into full swing the orchard will be full of swans."*

Len writes poetry and recently wrote a poem to celebrate the best day of the year, in November when the Broads have emptied of people and he can return the swans to the wild. "Release day is wonderful, tempered only by the knowledge that some of the swans will be back next year, injured or poisoned again, and some will die." He called it the Release Poem:

> And you will fly again
> On mended wings,
> Our thanks being your release to freedom
> And to fit back into the scheme of things.
> So until, through the folly of man,
> We meet again
> Go with our blessings,
> And our thanks
> For your trust.

Damage to swans on such a large scale came as a complete surprise, as did the deep concern of Len and Sheila Baker who were using much of their own limited money to pay for the suffering inflicted by others. They even treated lead ingestion, combating the poison with injections of sodium edetale, and the impacting of the oesophagus, by kneading the obstruction away, a long and arduous process.

The problem has been increased by the use of nylon fishing equipment, and the "throw-away mentality" of some of the fishermen. Because of the ease with which new hooks and weights can be fitted, the old tackle is often discarded at the end of the day's angling, leaving an estimated 250 tons of lead weights every year in our rivers, streams and waterways. In

*During June, July and August 1981 the Bakers took in 165 swans.

1978 a mute swan census was carried out by the British Trust for Ornithology; it showed that although overall numbers had not fallen alarmingly since other surveys in 1955–6 and 1961, significant changes in distribution occurred due to pollution and disturbance. It was calculated that the population of the mute swan in 1955–6 was about 21,000; in 1978 it had fallen to about 19,000. Taking all the mathematical variations in making a census, it was estimated that the number of swans had decreased by between eight and fifteen per cent.

In the Broads the decrease has been more alarming: "Whereas, in 1961, Hickling Broad alone held a herd of 320 non-breeders, in 1978 the entire Broads accounted for only sixty-nine, of which a mere twenty-two were at their former stronghold. Breeding pairs throughout Broadland showed a similar decline – on the Broads from twenty-four to twelve pairs, and on the Rivers Bure and Yare, from twenty to six and from eighteen to four respectively."*

Mute swans are elegant, peaceful birds, but despite their name they are not entirely quiet, having a wide range of almost conversational calls; and as they fly the soughing sibilations of their wingbeats add beauty to the grace of their movements. There is a long-held belief that swans sing before they die – hence "swan song". If that is true then in Norfolk there are many singing swans.

There was drama at Roger's "local" in the evening; it had been Rogation Sunday with "beating the bounds". A boy had been turned upside down at the four corners of the parish and his head banged on the ground for fifty pence a time. Bill, one of the church wardens, a farmworker approaching retirement age and dressed in his best Sunday suit was pleased the old tradition had been maintained. Another old man announced that they had beaten the bounds in the wrong place: "Fancy doing that." He spoke in a series of surly grunts and from his size it was clear that he obtained spiritual refreshment entirely from the pub.

A ruddy faced gamekeeper was intrigued by the golden

---

*From the "Norfolk Bird and Mammal Report" by Moss Taylor for the Norfolk Naturalist Trust.

orioles: "I knew a landowner once who named all his children after birds; Wigeon, Peregrine and Spurgeon. Well, a spurgeon isn't a bird, he must have meant sturgeon, though that's a fish."★ He then told a story about an Irish pigeon shooter who shot a hang-glider, with Murphy saying: "I was only trying to make that big bird drop the man."

"Well, mine's a true story," another elderly man, wearing a cap, interjected. "I've had a big bill from the Anglian Water Authority. It's wrong and I'm not going to pay it. I've told them what they can do with it."

"They'll cut you off."

"They can try. My cottage is in a row of four; if they cut me off the other three will dry up as well."

Their broad local accents and independent minds showed that at least some aspects of Norfolk life had not died.

Rain greeted the Bank Holiday as I made for Ludham Bridge intending to take a boat. The Broads Authority, in a report, states: "Congestion may be defined as situations where the free flow of boats is seriously impeded." At the narrow bridge signs of "congestion" were already evident, caused by inexperienced boatmen; some were reversing to make way for others, one steered into the bank and they were all getting very wet. The rain became even heavier; I headed for home, my journey incomplete.

I returned to the Broads at the end of July hoping to see swallowtail butterflies. Stewart was pleased to see me: "You've come at a good time; we'll go by boat." He had been right, the water was a thick pea green, visibility reaching only two or three inches below the surface, and apart from the beds of reeds there were no water plants. From the small motor boat he pointed things out: "Over there fishermen cut down the reeds and the bank is eroding away. We even had people fishing on the evening of June 15th this year – they just could not wait a few more hours. That hole was caused by a boat steering into the reeds because they couldn't be bothered to moor properly for the night."

★More likely the child was called Spurgeon after Charles Hadden Spurgeon, the nineteenth-century preacher and evangelist.

We moored and walked along a bank built by Cornelius Vermuyden who drained the fens and created the Ouse Washes. Over the bank, out of the Broad, the water in ditches was clear, supporting pond life and aquatic plants. There, too, at the side of the path were the delicate lace-like leaves and small white flowers of white climbing fumitory, a scarce flower of marshland. We moved into oakwood, and climbed ladders sixty feet to the top of a tall tree, from where we had a fine view looking beyond the foliage to the long wedge of Broadland with its many cruisers, fishermen and acres of reed beds. Even at that height, and despite the breeze, numerous insects flew around us: "On a warm day in a good year you will even see swallowtails up here, but it's been a bad year for them; too cold and too damp, and to make matters worse the little terns have been flooded out."

Chugging back to the old shooting lodge through the lapping water and the sheltering fringe of reeds was relaxing. But the holiday boats and pea green water made it obvious that Hickling was almost dead. It was also clear that since boat hiring and visitors bring over £16 million into the area each year, things will not change; money still talks more loudly than reason.

East Anglia is noted for another wetland area, Minsmere in Suffolk, a reserve managed by the Royal Society for the Protection of Birds. The journey through rural Norfolk and Suffolk was pleasant, and a marked difference between the two counties is obvious, but difficult to define. I enjoyed Norfolk, its people, its birds and its villages, especially the small hamlet of Heydon, built at the end of a by-road, with a blacksmith, a well, a village green and a row of cottages, half hidden behind rambling roses and thriving vegetable gardens. In general, however, Norfolk seems a colder place, being flatter, with slightly larger fields, more severely cut roadside verges, and houses of bare brick. Suffolk, on the other hand, leaves an impression of trees and hedgerows, pink-painted cottages, thatched roofs and hollyhocks in gardens; altogether softer and more picturesque.

From Hickling I drove along winding roads bordered by villages and fields of arable; the winter barley was golden, almost ready for harvest, but in most of the fields the wheat was still green. Suddenly the landscape changed to that of fen, rather like the Ouse Washes or even Holland. Grass grew in small fields, there were grazing cattle, ditches choked with reeds, and windmills. I had reached the Yare valley, a low pastoral place, for which, inevitably, there is a plan to transform the meadows into arable fields.

There is no road bridge across the River Yare between Yarmouth and Norwich, but at the village of Reedham a primitive car ferry operates. I rang the bell and the ferryman appeared from the nearby pub. A pleasure boat cruised by with sunbathing bodies on top and a large wash behind, tossing a family of ducks, and thudding into the banks on both sides. It was easy to see how banks are eroded and nests destroyed. The ferryman angrily waved at them, for they were going much too fast; but the holidaymaker at the wheel, complete with sailor's cap, ignored him.

The small ferry was towed over by a diesel engine, pulleys and a long chain, reminding me of the Camargue, which came as a delightful surprise. One of the attractions of travelling in Britain is that, with time, wandering at random, one can still come across the unexpected. Further along the road at Earsham, near Bungay, by the river, Philip Wayre has managed to breed European otters in captivity for re-introduction into the wild. Then, at an old farmhouse, along back lanes, I met a craftsman and his Japanese wife who made replica bygones, such as sand glasses, bobbin stands, and hand-painted china thimbles. Two fields away, in a small farmworker's cottage, worked Emily Mayer, an attractive girl from London, with large, brown, doe-like eyes. She had already achieved her life's ambition of getting her own workshop in the country to carry out taxidermy. Her pet fox was kept on a lead outside and inside were a collection of lifelike stuffed owls, jackdaws and small birds; most of them restored perfectly after being hit by cars. In her bathroom sat a flourishing young tawny owl, befriended following a fall from its nest. After my earlier experiences with holidaymakers and twitchers, I was reassured to see such individuality.

The Suffolk villages were worth passing through just for

their names: Fressingfield, Pixey Green and Monk Soham. At Badingham I stopped at the White Horse, where an old farm cart was parked on the lawn. Ancient wooden benches furnished the public bar and an old stockman, wearing his brown working coat, sat drinking with his wife. I asked him what the unusual village name meant: "I don't know that, all I know is what the villages are like:

> Yoxford rich,
> Sibton poor,
> Peasenhall pretty girls
> Badingham whores."

It is amazing how many country areas have similar rhymes about their villages, a mixture of flattery and insult. "If you want something really Suffolk," he continued, "you should try a John Turner – gin with mild beer in it – that'll make your hair curl." He finished his drink, but on hearing that I was going to Minsmere he stayed for another: "I've got a poem just right for bird-watchers:

> There was a little bird, sat on a bough.
> If he's not gone, he's still there now."

The final approach to Minsmere led through heathland and forest; gorse, then pine with lush bracken, taller than I had ever seen before. Some must have been well over six feet high and gave the appearance of genuine jungle. Then came the reserve itself, over 1,500 acres owned by the R.S.P.B., which has had an interest in the area since 1945.

The reserve is an appealing place, for there is something strangely haunting about low-lying marshland; a combination of wide skies, the sound of wind in the reeds, and the cries of wading birds and wildfowl, that is evocative of freedom and our distant past. Even in comparatively small areas of reed-bed, marsh and wetland, distance becomes magnified, time seems suspended, isolation is intensified and feelings stir that usually lie dormant.

That much of the character of Minsmere has been retained is

due to the work of Jeremy Sorensen, the warden, another of those who opted out of a routine job, selling wallpaper, to follow his interests and convictions. He is a quietly spoken man, whose accent still betrays his northern background. He is a good friend with a fine sense of humour, but because of the damage done by man he gives the impression of liking birds more than people. Around his bungalow bantams and wild pheasants scratch contentedly for food and a robin will take food from his hand.

The day was perfect with a hot sun and a light, warm breeze. As I walked towards the Island Mere I passed through the dappled light of oak woodland where butterflies danced over flowering brambles. There I saw gatekeepers absorbing warmth through open wings, and a comma, its tattered wings giving surprisingly strong flight and copper-coloured brilliance. The path led on to grassland where stalks of ragwort had been chewed bare by millions of the black and yellow

Gatekeeper on blackberry

striped caterpillars of the cinnabar moth. Most lay dead, having eaten themselves out of their food supply. Close to a dyke was another scattering of white climbing fumitory and beside it a small frog hopped into clear water. Among the faintly whispering reeds grew rosebay willow herb, a mixture of soft pink flowers and bursting seed-pods of white down.

On the mere itself, dazzling water in a sea of reeds, were ducks, coots, moorhens and a white spoonbill scything its long-ladled bill through the water as it fed. A family of bearded tits appeared in the reeds just in front of the hide, golden and bronze; one almost did the splits as each foot gripped a separate reed. A kingfisher flashed by, in a streak of turquoise blue, and a coypu nibbled contentedly at rushes. Across the water a bittern moved slowly into flight, to be "mobbed" by a solitary tern, and a female marsh harrier, with fanning tail and long yellow legs, dropped down to its nest in the reeds. It was one of those days, rich and varied, that showed the wealth of an area where the water was still clean and the people were controlled.

Elsewhere, the slender tendrils of tufted vetch supported the plants to make them look like small blue flowering bushes, and clumps of marsh mallow gave flowers of fading pink among their soft silken leaves. Adult avocets, graceful black and white birds with curved, upturned beaks, were defending their large chicks as they chased off young shellducks that ventured too close, and two mute swans swam alongside their four cygnets with dignity and pride. There were dunlin, redshank, ringed plovers and black-tailed godwits, their rich rufous plumage complementing the pale blue of the water. Oystercatchers called noisily, their scarlet eyes matching their beaks. One visitor, at Minsmere, on seeing an oystercatcher fly, is claimed to have pointed and said: "Look, there goes a puffin with a carrot in its beak."

Little terns stood on the shingle beach while others fished over the calm sea, hovering and diving to catch food for their young, making it easy to see why they are called sea swallows and shrimp catchers. Further along was the great concrete mass of Sizewell nuclear power station.

Back at the bungalow the top of the power station could still be seen: "Look at it," Jeremy commented. "What a wasted opportunity. They should have put ledges on the sea-facing wall for kittiwakes." His eyes brightened as he saw a group of people approaching: "Look again, twitchers. They've already heard that there's been a marsh sandpiper seen. As long as there's not too many of them, we let them in, but we get them each to pay 75p first.'

I felt ill at ease visiting Sizewell after hearing about the dangers of nuclear power from the propaganda of pressure groups. The site covers 245 acres and is dominated by the reactor building and the turbine hall, where I was shown round by the manager. The turbines were noisy, but else-where was clean and quiet, with no smell; the control rooms were a maze of science-fiction panels, showing monitors, lights, buttons and bells. People demand power and energy, and after the dirt, dust and noise of the South Leicestershire Colliery, it made a fascinating contrast. The manager had worked there for several years: "It's quite a simple process really. We've got 465 men employed on the power station. Do you think they would work here if it was dangerous?" He had hit on one of the dilemmas: physically, the production of nuclear power is much more attractive than coal, but then radioactivity cannot be seen or smelt, and men have always been willing to undertake dangerous work, assuming that disasters only overtake others. It is argued that nuclear power is safe and attractive – as was the *Titanic*. Their ultimate safety depends on whether technological advance can cope with the unseen, the unexpected, and, most dangerous of all, human error.

After Sizewell I travelled a few miles along the coast to Aldeburgh, the home of Sir Laurens van der Post. He is a most remarkable man; a writer, traveller, philosopher, and conser-vationist. Born into an Afrikaaner family in South Africa he was one of the first Afrikaaners to speak out against apartheid; he was captured by the Japanese during the war; made epic journeys into Bushmanland researching for his books, *The Lost World of the Kalahari* and *The Heart of the Hunter*, and also became a personal friend of Carl Gustav Jung. I was intrigued

to know why a man of such wide experience should choose to
live in Suffolk.

Aldeburgh is an agreeable, clean little town of red bricks and
sea air. Fishermen with open boats cleaned their nets on the
shore and tourists filled the pavements. By six thirty p.m. a
long queue had already formed outside a fish and chip shop
and on the shingle beach a couple played cricket with their two
children.

I found Laurens van der Post in a small house overlooking
the sea. He opened the door looking very fit and well for a man
in his mid-seventies, with light blue, clear eyes and an air of
tranquillity. As we ate home-made cake and drank coffee,
looking out to sea, a tern flew along the beach. His voice was
quiet and calm and his sentences flowed, complete and considered, without the usual need for qualification.

His reason for living most of the time in Britain was simple:
"In South Africa I get drawn into local conflicts and so when I
am here I can pull out and get on with my work, because if you
are a writer and your mind is taken away you have nothing to
write with." The proximity of Sizewell presented no distrac-
tion or problem: "You cannot suppress what is known, or
pretend that it has not happened. We must go forward and find
a way of using nuclear energy that is not radioactive – it is
possible.★ Nuclear power is like a drink; drink in itself is not
wrong; it is the way we misuse it. The whole history of man
shows that he is compelled to discover; but what we must do is
to heighten our own responsibility to what we have discovered. To ignore what we know is the ultimate evasion."

He enjoys Suffolk and its people, but the way in which they
are changing concerns him, making conservation of both the
land and the human spirit so important: "The need for conservation can be seen here at Aldeburgh; just a few years ago
behind the town there were marshes, but now many of them
have been drained and ploughed. In the old days I could hear
the larks sing and as recently as three years ago I saw otters –
but there is a steady erosion. Now with arable crops the
farmers burn the stubble and by so doing they often destroy

★Based on "fusion", not "fission".

the nature of the upper soil. I have even seen dust storms during the autumn in East Anglia, something that was unknown. Hedges have been cut down too, and a whole ecological system has been destroyed.

"Our relationship with the land is now wrong, as the old understanding has gone; unless we get back in touch with the natural, physical and the spiritual we have had it. We are increasingly governed by people with a town mind; their sense of nature is a window box; in fact it is the industrial town mind. They do not see the relevance of the seasons – growing, flowering and harvest – how things need time; they want immediate solutions. Consequently we human beings are our own destroyers; we must stop ourselves and we must go and learn again from nature. If given the chance it will come back. I remember coming back to London after years away during the war; seeing the rubble and the bomb sites and seeing how the buttercups and dandelions were taking over. It will come back if given the opportunity.

"We need re-educating away from scientific rational values. We need to learn about loving and caring. That is why nature is always portrayed as a woman – for she is a great mother who gives, but she also needs love and care. Because of this I am involved with the World Wilderness Foundation, to take people from towns back to nature, and we are taking parties of townspeople to Scotland and Kenya.

"None of our problems are going to be solved by destroying land. We are going to run out of coal one day and we are going to have to find an alternative. We cannot find an alternative for valleys and woods, yet people seriously want to dig up coal from the Vale of Belvoir. We live in a cash-crop civilisation; what pays now is important, but the sanctuary provided by nature is beyond price, for it influences the spirit of man. Man was open to the influences of nature until the sudden development of the Industrial Revolution; that is why our greatest poets and artists came before it. We must change the imagination of human beings, to see their role in nature in a new light – the old way. We must listen to nature; the hills and mountains, and even small areas can help us."

I could have listened for hours, but Laurens had to leave, to visit a friend. He was so calm, peaceful and intellectual; I left feeling that I had been in the presence of a most exceptional person. As I headed west I passed the first combined fields of barley, and then, on the skyline, smoke began to billow upwards; burning stubble showed that another harvest had really begun.

10

Horses and Harness

The countryside has changed in many ways since the end of
the Second World War, and not only have those changes
influenced the people living in it, but they have also affected
those who at one time travelled through it, along traditional
routes. During my childhood the sight of authentic gypsies on
the move was common; horses, vardos (the hand-painted,
horse-drawn gypsy caravans), and swarms of dark curly-haired
children, whose numbers confirmed my belief that gypsies
stole children. The women would sell pegs, charms and tell
fortunes, while the men found seasonal land work, hoeing
sugar beet and picking fruit. It was a way of life that, with one
or two minor adjustments, had existed for many generations.
In earlier times Richard Jefferies had also met them:

> Not far from where the track crossed a lonely road was a
> gypsy encampment; that swarthy people are ever about
> when anything is going on, and the reapers were busy in the
> corn. The dead dry thorns of the hedge answered very well
> to boil their pot with. Their tents, formed by thrusting the
> ends of long bent rods like half-loops into the turf, looked
> dark like the canvas of a barge . . . The men wore golden
> ear-rings, and bought 'Black Sally', a withy that has a dark
> bark, for pegs, and 'bots' of osier for basket-making . . .
> Though the women tell fortunes, and mix the 'dark man'
> and the 'light man', the 'journey' and the 'letter' to perfec-
> tion, till the ladies half believe, I doubt if they know much of
> true palmistry.

Since then, the genuine gypsy has almost disappeared; landwork relies on machinery rather than casual labour and few

driftways and hedgerows remain where the gypsy can set up camp for caravans and horses. Travellers still exist, but in the main they have become a collection of roadside didecoys; car breakers and scrap metal merchants carrying out their trades illicitly in roadside squalor.

Despite this, and the pressures to change, a few gypsies still manage to retain their old ways and values. Others live in houses, running a variety of successful businesses; even so, they retain their links with the past by keeping horses, for wheeling and dealing, and simply for the pleasure of seeing them graze in paddock or field. Traditional ways are sustained, too, by a number of gypsy fairs which still flourish, the most famous being the Appleby Horse Fair, held in the Pennines every year, starting on the second Wednesday of June. So it was to Appleby I travelled, to see whether it really was an authentic gypsy gathering, or simply a collection of didecoys buying worn-out nags to sell to pet-food manufacturers.

The drive up the A1 was a long haul during which I was again amazed at the ugliness of the slag heaps near Doncaster, and amused by the Alpine Inn beyond Weatherby – a pub designed to look like an Alpine chalet, and which seems to grow in absurdity every time I pass it. Somehow I managed to overshoot Scotch Corner, from where the main road leads to the Pennines and the Lake District; a remarkable feat, and so I had to take minor roads. Immediately away from the motorway the countryside was quiet and rural, with hedges, flowers and the sound of curlews. I stopped; the air was cool and clear, the sun showing the cloud patterns over the fields in patches and pools of bright and dark green. The two curlews had young, or a nest, and dive-bombed a crow so effectively that they physically knocked it from the top of a hedge. Driving on into the Pennines I passed stone walls, arched bridges over streams, and small meadows golden with buttercups, all in a countryside awash with the fresh greens of leaves and grasses, hedgerows and fields. Sorrels and plantains were flowering in the verges and meadows, while beyond, where grasses merged with heather, farm fields became moorland. The country was beautiful but, from the size of the small stone farmsteads, it obviously yielded its living reluctantly.

I saw the first horse-drawn caravan on dual carriage-way, dwarfed by the container lorries speeding past, and closer to Appleby several more joined from the side roads. Appleby itself is a pleasant little market town, straddling the River Eden; on its outskirts is an Eden Vale factory, making "Cheddar cheese" in Cumbria. A predominantly rural, quiet, unspoilt and unhurried town, during the ten days of the fair its population increases from 6,000 to 12,000.

On the arched stone bridge in the town centre a crowd had already gathered, watching horses and ponies being ridden into the river by young gypsy boys and girls. The water was peaty brown and fast flowing from heavy rain up in the hills. One larger youth was thrown and briefly disappeared; he enjoyed it: "I nearly half drownded," he laughed, as his jacket and trousers streamed with water.

Some washed their mounts with Fairy Liquid, and others rode them in a wide arc to reach deeper water where the horses could swim; there the children, all riding bareback, hung on to manes amid swirling, deeper water, but most had total control and a natural affinity with their horses. It was a view of the romantic past and the free spirit; an attractive combination. Beyond the bridge were overhanging boughs, swallows feeding close to the surface of the water, trout rising, and a spotted flycatcher fluttering after flies before returning to its perch.

The small square was busy with shoppers and drinkers, although three pubs were shut for the duration of the fair, evidence that things were not always peaceful, one even being boarded up completely to save its windows. A shopkeeper was doing brisk business: "I don't really mind the fair; it's just the funny smells I can't stand." Police were in ample evidence, over a hundred having been drafted in from other areas in order to quell any trouble. According to one, even working twelve-hour shifts was no hardship: "It's the same as a holiday and we get overtime as well." Like the pubs, the church, a mainly fourteenth-century building with a weathered stone arch over the churchyard gate, was locked. In the porch a computerised rota of church duties brought it well into the twentieth century.

Along the road out of the town was a continuous two-way stream of gypsies and didecoys on foot, in horse-drawn carts and spilling over from Ford transit vans and Toyotas; a mass of protruding arms and legs, they were reminiscent of over-loaded lorries in Africa. In normal times they would have been stopped, but the police turned a blind eye, as they did to children standing on tow-bars and to the absence of tax discs: "It's harder to get away with it now," an unshaven driver of a rusting van said dolefully. "At one time we would put a beer bottle label in the window, as that was the same shape and colour as the tax disc." The sound of horses' hooves on metalled roads, mingling with the harsher sounds of internal combustion, formed a strange combination.

The site of the fair itself, on Fair Hill, was a sea of mud and ruts, where 750 caravans were parked. They were a complete mixture, some chrome-covered and large, with gaudy glass and china in the windows, others small and grubby with sticky children spilling from the doors and on to the rubbish-strewn ground. Horse-drawn carts were inhabited by latter-day hip-pies, and there were vardos, some to be sold as garden ornaments and holiday homes, but a few were still lived in the whole year through. With ponies, clapped-out Fords, Mer-cedes and Rolls Royces, the site represented a complete cross-section of gypsy society; dealers, didecoys, and hangers-on, as well as a few whose distinctive features betrayed their pure Romany stock. They are proud, handsome people with ebony hair, skin the colour of tanned hide, and penetrating blue eyes. Their ancestors originally came from Northern India many centuries ago; the old women in particular, with their swarthy complexions, shawls, wizened faces and gold teeth, looked distinctly Indian. It seemed that for a short period in June Appleby had become the holiday centre for Britain's gypsies and would-be gypsies, where for a few days they could lead the type of life that they really wanted.

Outside some vans were tethered horses, goats, working terriers and lurchers, as well as boxes containing gamecocks. An old man from Hereford kept various kinds of animals, and had arrived to do a "bit of dealing". His Yorkshire terriers were far different from their pampered, shampooed cousins often found in suburbia: "Aye, I put them in after foxes; they are good little devils. The lurcher's good too; he belongs to me son; he turned down £150 for him yesterday. He'll take a hare with no trouble and he jumps a five-bar gate as if it wasn't there. I like the fair. There was some cock-fighting going on over the way just a minute ago and bare knuckle fighting yesterday. There's a lot of dirty people too; they spoil it." His wife had the look of a true gypsy with dark hair falling down to her shoulders in ringlets and real sovereigns in her gold rings and chains. On a chain around her neck hung a genuine Queen Victoria £2 piece; she had no idea of its value.

Elsewhere, cheap-jack traders were selling imitation sovereigns, "Sovereign re-strikes", for £2, as well as rings, ear-rings and necklaces, but real gold seemed just as plentiful. Other stalls were selling hamburgers, tea cloths, harness, melons and china. The china covered a wide range of quality, prices and tastes; one stallholder from West Bromwich had over £60,000 of stock: Capo di Monte from Italy, depicting gypsy scenes, "reduced" to £1,250; Crown Derby and Royal Worcester, including an ice bucket for £3,000. In one breath an elegant soup tureen cost £2,000; in the next it had risen to £3,000. Looking at the large container, a potential customer asked: "What do you call that?"

"If you pay £3,000 for it, sir, you can call it what you like. But make sure you only use it for Baxter's duck and orange, and not Campbell's and common stuff like that."

Clairvoyants were doing good trade, with their various claims and achievements proclaimed on boards outside their caravans: "Madame Smith – She is known all over the travelled world." Gypsy Rose Lee on the other hand made do with a window sticker: "Epsom Grand Stand Association 1981" and an assurance that she was "patronised by all classes". A woman in her sixties, wrinkled, with a confident, understanding manner, she charged £3 for one hand, £5 for two and £7 for the crystal ball. From the lines on my left hand she surprised me; she told me I was a writer; I had been travelling abroad a lot, and I would probably do so again later in the year, all of which were true. She then strayed on to more conventional ground; September was my lucky month; I was on the verge of marriage; I would father between three and five children, and I would live until I was ninety – a truly frightening thought.

At £2.50 for one hand Madame Smith was less impressive. She simply asked questions and then said: "I thought so", until faced with a negative.

"You work with figures."

"No, I write."

"There you are, I was right, I can't read or write, so words and figures are all the same to me."

"You are going to get married."

"Really, who to? On your board you claim to give names."

"Oh no, sir, that's for a £5.50 reading, you only wanted £2.50, so I can't tell you that. You've been the cause of a marriage breaking up."

"No."

"You don't take opportunities when they present themselves."

"No, that's not right."

"Well, you are going to travel abroad where there are a lot of coloured people, your lucky month is August and you will be the father of two children. I can't tell you any more for £2.50."

So my left hand told two different tales; undoubtedly some fortune-tellers are complete charlatans, but Gypsy Rose Lee seemed to have some degree of insight. But was she really Gypsy Rose Lee? When I passed her caravan again, an even older lady was gazing into the crystal ball. Like the police they were obviously working shifts.

The roadway to the horse sales was crowded with many people and vehicles, and Japanese models had clearly replaced much of the market once dominated by the Land Rover. Surprisingly, however, the horse is still the main attraction of the fair, made so successful by the gypsy's flair for trading. A queue had formed at a blacksmith's forge, where he charged £7 a horse. From the state of the hooves it seemed that many of the horses were only shod once a year, at the fair. It was strange to smell again singed hoof and hear the metallic ring of hammer on shoe and anvil, things I had not experienced since the days when I wore short trousers and watched the village smith; yet immediately I noticed them, distant memory stirred and the sights, sounds and distinctive tangs seemed familiar once more.

One old dealer, seeing a hoof trimmed and the trimmings thrown away, commented: "When I was a boy you wouldn't do that. We'd get the frog★ and sell it to ladies for a tanner to give to their dogs. It would get us into the pictures and the dogs loved them. They chew it and when they get tired you can put it away and bring it out another day. I run a riding stables in Cromer; we let people ride for £2 an hour – better than working, isn't it?"

Midway through shoeing one horse the blacksmith stopped to do a deal. He bought a pony for £75 for his son, giving £1 back as "luck money". All along the road by Fair Hill the horse dealing was in full swing; like their owners the horses were all shapes and sizes – skewbald, piebald, black, brown and white, for riding, trotting and working. Bodies scattered when shouts of: "Oi, oi, oi", warned of a horse being ridden or led at a brisk trot along the road, to impress potential customers. Standing around could be dangerous and some carts missed bystanders by only inches. Knowing eyes quickly assessed the merits and faults of each animal: "Nice filly that, Nathan."

"That old nag blows a bit hard."

A tight crowd gathered as a deal was done.

"How much do you want for her?"

"Three and a half [£350]."

"£300."

"No."

"Come on, £300."

"Nothing doing."

Supporters of each man began shouting encouragement.

"Raise it a tenner."

"Meet him halfway."

As the prices closed, so the advice grew louder.

"Only ten difference."

"Go on, split it."

★The elastic horny substance in the horse's sole.

"Give him the horse."

"Give him the money."

Finally the men grasped hands with a loud slap and the deal was done for £330. Such a deal is as binding as any contract and a thick wad of notes appeared from the buyer's trouser pocket. Thousands of pounds must have changed hands in cash during the course of the fair. One deal broke up in pandemonium as a frisky stallion tried to mount another, sending hooves flying and people stumbling, but order and decency were soon restored. In the age of the horse, injuries to animals and people must have been as common as nowadays with cars.

Back in the town there were queues in the two cafés; the traditional gypsy food of stews and stolen potatoes had evidently given way to chips with everything, convenience foods and sauce bottles.

Gypsy horse

As evening approached, locals and gypsies streamed away from Fair Hill to meadows by the river. There, in a great natural arena, with a high bank overlooking grassland, the "trotting" races were held. Thousands of people attended as well as fifty-one "bookies", some from as far away as Scotland, with ideal bookmaking names such as Artie Wood, Harry Marlow, Scottie Wilson and Tom Berry.

A local farmer had a pony of his own: "The sport comes from the gypsies, probably because the gypsies encouraged trotting for their caravans and carts. It is also possible to spot a good animal from a broken-winded horse after a trot. There's a lot of money in it. We all give 'luck money' up here; it's 5p for a sheep, £1 for bullocks and fat cattle, £10 for a horse and a shilling in the pound for dairy cattle. That is too much, for a good cow can be worth five or six hundred pounds. If you want a really good sport, then the best one round here's hound trailing. It goes on all through the summer."

Back in Appleby the two functioning pubs were packed. By the door of one, a blonde girl and a leather-jacketed youth were locked in peroxide passion; inside, beer glasses were being drained at higher than usual prices to cover breakages. There was drinking, talking, much laughter and friendliness too; someone seemed to recognise me: "Hallo, you're Mary Smith's son, aren't you? I saw you here last year." Whether Mary Smith was the same as Madame Smith I had no idea.

The mistake was made by a buxom Scottish lady, who was wearing gold and enjoying herself: "That's the trouble these days; you can't tell the difference between gypsies and non-travelling folk. It's because gypsy life is changing. So many young gypsies are marrying country people; that's making the fair change, too. It's getting more of a country flavour than a pure gypsy one." The old grandmother was unconcerned by this: "I've been coming ever since I was a child, and I'll be here again as long as I keep getting my social security."

A hotel in the square was open to "residents only", but security was not good and I walked straight in. Eleven people, an over-manned television crew and its "star", were drinking before dinner, while a group of fishermen from Barnsley sat in the corner. The fattest fisherman was not impressed: "Look at her over there. Dyed hair and tan out of a bottle. She looks proper rough, more lines on her face than a road map. She looks better on television – in black and white."

They were on a trout fishing holiday to fill in the few days before the start of the coarse fishing season. Including equipment and travel they all reckoned to spend well over ten pounds a week for their sport. They had arrived unaware of the fair, but did not object to the gypsies: "We don't mind coloured people either – mainly because we haven't got any in Barnsley. Anyway we are like the schoolmaster in Brixton who told his class: 'I'm not a racialist, I don't care what colour people are, black, white, mauve or red. Well, today you can all be green; I'll have the light green over here and the dark green over there.'"

The light still lingered as I set up camp in a small grass field. Across the valley the distant lights of the encampment stood out brightly. Beyond lay the Pennines and the hills of Teesdale, and to one side the Lake District. The field was splashed with buttercups; a stream murmured between banks covered with campion and butterbur, and a curlew bubbled as it flew in a series of high undulations, calling and gliding as if marking out its territory at the end of the day.

In the morning the horses and ponies were in the river once more, as several television crews tripped over each other trying to get the best shots. Selling on the hill was already in full swing, again a fusion of faces, eyes, voices, hooves, and the smell of horses. A lot of the men still wore grease on their hair, and many pairs of "best" trousers, usually baggy, with turn-ups, were enjoying their annual airing. The children seemed to get the most out of gypsy life, wandering by the river and resting in flower-filled meadows. One gang of small boys, on seeing a moorhen, immediately made off to find its nest, while others tried to creep up on a goat to squeeze milk from its pendulous udder. A group with wind-tousled hair and ruddy cheeks just sat in the sun; boys and girls on the brink of maturity, talking, chewing grass and taking in themselves and their surroundings. These things were once the basic elements of many childhoods, but now they are limited to the lucky few.

During the evening camp fires were lit, more Romany features were evident with gold teeth and smiles, amid the smoke and dirt, and a farmer earned extra cash by pulling out vehicles at £5 a time after the heavy rain. In an age of increasing conformity it would be sad if Appleby ever tired of its fair.

From Appleby I took the Penrith road to the Lake District in the hope of seeing some hound-trailing. This is an unusual form of racing; a circular trail of scent is laid using a mixture of aniseed and paraffin, with the start and finish being almost in the same place. The hounds are slipped, and the first one back wins. It probably began well over a hundred years ago when fox skins were dragged over the fells to encourage young hounds to follow scent. Since then it has developed into a sport in its own right and breeding has turned the trail hound into a lighter, faster dog than the fox hound.

From Penrith the scenery changed dramatically; the Lake District looking dark and rugged, like another land. Suddenly crags, valleys and forests appeared with the tops of the mountains enveloped in cloud. Although higher, the features were gentler to the eye than those of the Peak District; perhaps the combination of water and wildness gives "Lakeland" a softer visual unity.

Wordsworth found the mountains of "The Lakes" irresistible:

Their forms are endlessly diversified, sweeping easily or boldly in simple majesty, abrupt and precipitous, or soft and elegant. In magnitude and grandeur they are individually inferior to the most celebrated of those in some other parts of the island; but in the combinations which they make, towering above each other, or lifting themselves like the waves of a tumultuous sea, and in the beauty and variety of their surfaces and colours, they are surpassed by none.

The roads wound through wide valleys and by lakes fringed with trees, which formed new and unfamiliar landscapes, with overhanging leaves, the flowers of mountain ash, grass fields, bracken and fell. In places rhododendrons mixed with ash trees, mosses covered the walls, sheep wandered on the roads, herb robert and meadow cranesbill grew among the grasses, and everywhere water seeped and dripped.

Patches of pine forest near Lake Bassenthwaite were made darker by rolling clouds, heavy with rain, and already cars and showers were turning the grass of the trail field into a quagmire. Wearing a raincoat and cap, the farmer at the gate was not worried by the weather: "It doesn't matter, we need some rain to fill the lake up for the tourists." In the meadow across the road, shouting, waving and whistling greeted the arrival of some hounds, while more dogs streamed into the car park field. I assumed there had been two races. I was wrong; half the hounds had completed the course, but the others had somehow lost their way and returned following the scent backwards, to finish at the start. After retrieving his dog, one owner was amused: "Good, isn't it, you pay once for two finishes." Others could not see the joke and blamed it on those laying the trail: "Two blokes are supposed to meet in the hills, then one drags his soaked rag in a half circle to the start, and the other goes in a half circle to the finish. The fools must have left a gap in the middle, where they parted. The trail for puppies is run over five miles and takes about eighteen minutes; the older dogs go ten miles and it takes thirty-two minutes."

Hounds running

Refreshment vans and tents for officials, and twenty-five bookies were arranged in a large circle; some of the bookies made sure of increased takings by accepting bets on televised horseracing; everybody looked cold. The loudspeaker announced the next trail: "The start is down the bottom of the field by the telegraph pole." Sixty owners lined up with their hounds and each dog was colour marked on its head, to prevent a new dog from being introduced halfway round. Soon a local youth wandered in from the hills dragging a soaked rag; when he was close the hounds were slipped and all set off eagerly, in full cry. They streamed over fields, through a wood and then ran in a line, silhouetted along a ridge, on to higher ground and out of sight. An old man watched with a knowledgeable eye, leaning on a shepherd's crook; he was not a farmer, but had been a collier for forty-seven and a half years until his retirement several years earlier: "We miners love the country, and the hounds. Trailing's been in our blood for years." He was joined by a shepherd of equal antiquity: "Everybody likes it round here. Why, some of the people who work at Windscale even put their hands where they shouldn't. They get a radio-active reaction and have to stay away from work; then they can work with their hounds and pigeons. Most visitors think we are just a load of country Johnnies; so what, we enjoy it."

The hounds appeared again, strung out along the skyline, then down into a valley, along a gulley, over a stone wall and up into moorland until they were again lost from view. Bets were still being taken, binoculars were raised and owners began lining up at the finish. When the leading dogs appeared over a ridge, bedlam broke loose, with men, women and children shouting, whistling and waving handkerchiefs to attract and encourage their dogs. The hounds ran into grass fields, through marsh, under a fence, stretching for home. The shouting grew louder, bowls of food were put down as the final inducement, and as each dog arrived it dived for its dish, tail wagging. The winner collected £100 as his prize but as he had moved towards his dog in excitement before it had crossed the winning line, he was fined £25. It scarcely mattered to him, however, as he had put £40 on the result and so relieved the bookies of £640.

Two successful trails were run before the final race ended in chaos. Half the hounds returned to the start, others took a short cut on seeing the leaders far ahead, some came in from the side, leaping high over a stone wall then through wire and the remainder got lost. Complaints naturally followed; owners claiming that their dogs had completed the course, others arguing that short cuts had been taken. To an impartial observer it was extremely amusing, but a punter was full of gloom: "I suppose it would be funny if I hadn't put so much money on it." To add to the problems, most of the cars became stuck in the gateway and had to be pushed out of the field.

The hound trailing had been entertaining, and after it had finished, with no particular plan in mind, I drove towards Ullswater, stopping at the small village of Glenridding, a collection of stone cottages around the large Glenridding Hotel. I decided to eat at the Fairlight, a house converted into a restaurant, where I expected to find cheap tourist snacks. Instead I found food of the highest quality, with good wine, at prices only slightly higher than at a transport café. It was run by a buxom, smiling woman, who looked as if she had personally tasted all the dishes, and her Swiss husband, an expert chef. I selected Cumberland sausage, which is still found extensively throughout the Lakes: it is meatier and coarser than a normal sausage, and depends on its seasoning for its distinctive taste.

Cumberland sauce also improves sausages, but it is best served with cold pies or any rich cold food and is easy to make:

Cumberland Sauce

¼ lb red currant jelly
2 large tbs port wine
2 peeled oranges, sliced and blanched
1 small shallot, chopped and blanched

Mix all the ingredients together and boil with a touch of cinnamon until the liquids blend together.

The Ratcher Bar of the Glenridding Hotel was more predictable, the young blue-eyed barmaid being its most attractive feature. She came from the nearby village of Hartsop, a collection of thirty people and twenty-five houses, including nine holiday homes. Her father ran a small farm, and when she was a girl only four children lived in the entire village. Most young people have to move reluctantly away for work, and she was simply filling in time, as well as beer mugs, before taking a course of "recreation business studies". Certainly serving drinks was not her vocation: "I hate tourists. They come here from the towns without understanding the countryside or those who work in it."

The bar had large "wooden" beams that made a loud hollow sound when tapped, and some of the customers seemed almost as artificial. A folk group consisting of two teachers, a nuclear power worker, a retired photographer, a forester and a repairer of dry-stone walls burst into song. A group of youths was clustered around a Space-Invaders machine and alongside, a visitor with one ear-ring and a studded leather jacket was working the one-armed bandit; it can only be a matter of time before they too become part of the English folk tradition.

Since it was by now getting late I was directed to the home of a shepherd in the broad sweeping valley of Grizedale for bed and breakfast. To reach the farm I went along a small winding track, past the kennels of the Ullswater Foxhounds, through a gate and over a cattle grid from where I had a view of meadows, buttercups, stone walls, tumbling streams, crags, rock faces and sheep. The small stone house and farm buildings were well up the valley, over a humped bridge, and in the twilight I again heard the bubbling of both water and curlews. Dogs, and Dennis the shepherd, greeted me; a ham was hanging from the ceiling, lino was on the floor, terriers were asleep on the chairs, and a collection of thumb sticks and shepherds' crooks stood in the corner. A basic, "lived-in" house, it was nonetheless comfortable and warm, with a bright log fire combating the wind and rain outside; although it was almost the middle of June, a fire was still necessary so high up the valley.

Dennis had 2,400 sheep in his care, roaming over 5,000 acres, and he enjoyed his work as he loved working with dogs. He had six collies, a fox hound "walking out" for the summer and three terriers: "We need terriers because of the foxes. I let them go down badger setts too. The badger is master and so it makes them stand off for foxes."

The high valley sides prevented television reception; this presented no problem, for Dennis's wife was an avid reader, his children could do their homework in peace, and he made crooks and sticks, using blackthorn or hazel, to which he attached handles of ram's horn or red deer antler: "I boil the horn to straighten it, then fix it between two clamps, and then carve it." The finished articles were well made and fetched good prices in the summer.

Wind and showers greeted the morning and Dennis was up early seeing to his Swaledale sheep, ear-marking the lambs and marking the ewes with dye. He was helped by the kennelman from the hunt; every summer most of the hounds are "walked out" on local farms during the non-hunting months and so he is free to assist with the sheep during the busiest time of the year: "We've got forty-four hounds and last year they killed over eighty foxes. We don't follow on horseback, we go up into the fells on foot. You have to be fit."

The sun had won through as I arrived at Hartsop, a sad modern-day hamlet – a mixture of tradition and holiday homes. It presented a picture-book scene with houses built into the valley side along a tributary stream, and dry-stone cottages with balconies and climbing roses. There were no street lights or kerb stones and it seemed tragic that such a place should be changing into a summer residence for city dwellers rather than remaining a living village. At a farm gate, I met Mrs. Wear and her son Alan accompanied by border collies and a fox hound. She still worked her farm and enjoyed her way of life but was not entirely happy: "We are gradually being taken over by people who move in and do not understand country life. The tourists are bad too; they let their dogs upset sheep and roll stones from the walls, and if challenged they say: 'This is a national park, we can do what we like and go where we like.' They forget that we work here and get our livings from the land. The conservationists are the same; they blame us, but they want to look elsewhere for the cause of the changes in the Lake District." She was a sincere and concerned woman, who cared for both the Lake District and the traditional forms of farming that went on within it.

After a pot of tea, her son Alan, who managed a neighbouring farm, took me outside: "It's funny, really," he laughed. "At this time of year newcomers spend all their time cutting the grass and we spend all our time trying to get it to grow." He was proud of his Lakeland origins: "The family has been farming in the Hartsop area since 1850. But the village is changing – dying – and gradually becoming a place for old people. When you drive home in the dark of winter you see few lights. Even the Planning Board don't seem to think we ought to live here. If we want to turn a barn into a house, they object; why should people who live here not be allowed to build here? They are worried about us making money, yet accountants and doctors and people like that move in, they have little trouble and manage to keep hold of a bob or two."

At the back of the farm he showed me a small building, the only corn drying kiln in the country made entirely from stone, including the beams. In the shed next door were four trailhounds: "I started a few years ago; it's addictive. My first one was always in the lead, but then on seeing me at the finish she would slow down, wag her tail, and get overtaken. She's outside; she's pupped twice, both on February 29th; I want her to make it three in a row." Strangely, he is involved entirely because of the dogs, and rarely bets: "I get very attached to them. Recently I sold one to Ireland for £500; it was quite a wrench. It's tremendous when you see your dog coming home in the lead."

When the season ends the hounds follow him around the fells during the winter with the sheep dogs, and he feeds them mainly on beef, rabbits and hens: "I think hound-trailing started when cockfighting stopped and the locals had nothing to do. We use our own recipe to make the dogs run fast and keep them in good condition. I make 'cock loaf' which the old sportsmen used to bake, to make the cocks fight better." It is a mixture of Guinness, raisins, brown bread or brown flour, rock sugar and washed liver which he bakes like a cake and which has a very nutty smell. "I also give them plenty of meat, cabbages and leeks. Honey is good for them too. I never give them glucose, like some people; it makes them go to water and with a belly full of water you can't run. At the back-end [autumn] I let them eat blackberries – foxes eat them and they've got plenty of stamina."

He has problems with foxes from time to time: "Crows are bad as well, they take the lambs' eyes and tongues. There are eagles back now; I love to see them." Two years ago he had a problem with a fox taking two or three lambs each night: "So we got some hounds and followed them up to the den. It was near the eagles and so the R.S.P.B. people came swarming over and warned us off. Shortly after that I saw some people stealing peregrines so I didn't tell the bird people. If they don't care about my livelihood I don't care about their birds. Actually I've mellowed since then and would tell them now, but I wish they would make more effort to understand us."

It is a fact that many country people are misunderstood, with visitors and newcomers equating rural accents and old working clothes with ignorance. Alan wanted to show me his valley so we drove up it, followed by three galloping collies and a fox hound, to look at old lead workings by the stream. He was in his shepherding clothes, and I was wearing my wellington boots and old coat which usually see duty in Cambridgeshire. A group of tourists looked at us with what seemed to be a mixture of suspicion and superiority: "You get used to it," Alan said. "People just regard us as country yokels, so I play the part for them. One day someone asked me if I knew what the weather was going to be from the signs. I had heard the forecast on the radio, so I told him it was going to rain because I had noticed little flies flying upside down to keep their heads dry. They went away trying to look at flies and it rained soon afterwards, so I suppose they were impressed. Lambing time is worst, we have to put notices up asking people to keep their dogs on leads. When they see them, miners will put their dogs back in their cars: it's always teachers and solicitors who cause the trouble. They think they are a cut above you. Anyway, they'll do away with farms soon and have us all as paid park keepers instead."

A heap of stones and rotting timber, overgrown with grass and bracken, showed where the lead workings had been. Many small greenish beetles clung to the bracken fronds: "We call them 'bracken clocks'. When they used to appear it was always good for trout fishing and I would take a week off, but the trout seem to have gone. In any case I've only had two days' holiday in four years." The dogs had caught up with us, as we stood in a peaceful spot beside the stream, boulders and grassy slopes. Yet according to Alan even here things had changed: "On the bank over there a red primrose appeared a few years ago and quite a patch grew up. Last year they were all dug up; I suppose they are now growing on somebody's suburban rockery."

The life of a hill shepherd is still one of the more traditional farming activities, where lambing, shearing, and tupping, dominate the shepherd's year. Although changes in arable agriculture have brought expensive equipment and technology, the shepherd's most valuable tools remain his dogs and his crook or thumb stick. I was pleased when Dennis invited me to go with him one morning to check his sheep. The sun was bright, the wind was fresh, and the dogs were keen to go. We set off with two sheep dogs, Sam, three years old and experienced, and Meg, sixteen months and inexperienced, a young terrier, Tiny, and finally a foxhound, Lord Tramper, on the farm for the summer. They made an unlikely collection, with the collies interested in sheep, the terrier in rabbits, and Lord Tramper taking an academic interest in everything. We crossed the water meadows to follow a sheep walk along the far side of the valley. Above us the valley wall rose to nearly 3,000 feet, a mixture of crags, grassy slopes, rock faces and scree. As we walked, Dennis sent Sam off to move sheep along, to work his dog. The collie ran eagerly upwards, taking the easiest paths to get over scree and above rock faces, and immediately a small group of sheep began to move. He kept them walking steadily and carefully. He stopped briefly high above, standing on a small pinnacle of rock, his outline cutting perfectly into the bright sky, ears eager and enquiring as he waited for a new command. Soon Dennis shouted: "That'll do, Sam, that'll do," and the dog returned reluctantly to his master. Meg then went off quickly, anxious to work, up over rocks, sometimes out of view, until she was several hundred feet above us. A small group of sheep were behind her but she would not go back for them. An impetuous animal, she ignored Dennis's calls of "Get back, Meg, get back", and refused to go back, preferring to approach sheep ahead of her. Dennis whistled, but she could not, or would not hear. Sam was anxious to join in, but stayed obediently to heel. Tiny and Lord Tramper still followed, totally uninterested in sheep.

"Get back, Meg. GET BACK," Dennis shouted again. "You need a dog to go back after them, otherwise you have to go up after them yourself when you really want them."

"It must be very frustrating when that happens," I mused.

"I wouldn't call it frustrating, it's bloody hard work."

As the grassy slopes fell steeply below us it was easy to understand why a shepherd uses a thumb stick, not as an ornament but as an essential aid to balance.

Ahead the broad sweep of the valley ascended, smooth and rounded, gouged and moulded by ancient ice. The floor was lush and green with Grizedale Beck flowing in gentle meanders, tree-lined, through pastureland. Beyond, towered Striding Edge and Helvelyn; ridges, rocks, fells, granite, tumbling streams, scree, and vivid blue sky. Dennis saw such scenes every day but he paused: "It's beautiful; every few feet you get a different picture of greens, rocks, bracken and crags. Over there is Eagle's Crag – that proves that there were eagles here once." A buzzard flew from an isolated ash tree and wheeled over the valley: "I like to see them; they don't harm us. I like eagles too, they are back across the ridge. I wonder if they will ever return to the crag? They should be left alone; if everybody shot at them they would soon be extinct."

He let Sam go, for often an experienced dog will improve a young dog, just by example. Across the valley the first line of distant ramblers with their bright anoraks were heading for the summit of Helvelyn. As we began to descend over a large area of ice-shattered rocks, Dennis glanced upwards and saw an ewe caught in the scree upside down, its lamb waiting anxiously at its side. "She's wrong end up in a rock bed," he said with concern. She must have stumbled and been unable to right herself; he released her, but she was very unsteady and could not stand after her ordeal. She continued to stagger and sway, the scree making it difficult for her to balance, so Dennis bent down, hoisted her over his shoulders and carried her down to the flat grassland by the stream, where she was rejoined by her lamb.

As we strolled back towards the farm, along a stony track, another group of ramblers passed. Dennis was not impressed: "They look on me as a country bumpkin. They go up there in all weathers, but if they had to do it for a living, like us, they would go on strike." We walked through a meadow full of pignut, a small cow parsley-like plant with clusters of white flowers on long green stems. Dennis bent down and cut off a tuber from beneath the soil: "I used to eat them when I was a child. Badgers love them and sometimes you'll come to a whole field where they have been rooted up." He gave me a piece to taste, and I found it rather like watery coconut. Sycamores and ashes grew by the beck, as well as a few dogwoods (or was it buckthorn?) with cocoons of fine silk thread in the leaves, full of caterpillars. Along a small tributary stream, brooklime, marsh marigolds and cuckoo flowers were in full bloom. We had completed a wide circuit of several miles, and met one of his daughters returning from church as we arrived at the farm. Dennis did not share her enthusiasm for church: "The vicar doesn't help me with my job, so I don't help him with his."

The return of golden eagles to the Lake District and the attitudes of Alan and Dennis towards them demonstrated a remarkable change, for it was persecution, particularly from shepherds, that led to the bird's original demise in England and Wales. There is no doubt that golden eagles do take live lambs, and although a good ewe will go to the aid of its offspring, inevitably some are lost. An adult eagle eats about 180 lbs of food in a year, including carrion, rabbits, hares, and birds, and its range will be over at least 4,500 acres. The number of lambs lost on a single farm is therefore quite small, but, even so, the anger of a shepherd when he sees a lamb taken is easy to understand.

In a small bungalow at a village close to where the eagles nested five temporary wardens of the R.S.P.B. were employed to watch the eagle's eyrie, as well as those of peregrine falcons. Indeed a telescope in the garden was trained on a distant crag, where it picked out a white fluffy peregrine chick.

The wardens were a happy but frustrated group; they were all doing what they wanted to do, work with wildlife, but could only find employment during the summer. In winter, one sold furniture, another drove a van, and an ex-civil servant went on the dole; he had had enough of tea breaks, annual increments, index-linked pensions and a tedious job filling in forms.

Despite the telescope it had not been a good year. Of sixty peregrine eyries in the Lakes, twenty had been robbed by falconers and egg collectors, and twenty had been destroyed by bad weather. In addition ordinary walkers and climbers had caused problems: "Teachers are the worst; they are mostly just educated idiots. We get people go by here in rough old clothes in mist and rain, and they come back safely; then on a fine day we get teachers in new anoraks and boots, with all the gear, and they get lost. The worst last year were two lecturers who climbed near a peregrine's nest and then shouted abuse when asked to move. Climbers are causing a lot of trouble during the nesting season; "gardening" is now very fashionable; they remove all the vegetation from ledges, to make it better for them and so ruin many good potential nest sites. Without the vegetation the eggs would roll off. They even clean the ledges with wire brushes.

"The eagles have been disappointing too, because of the cold spring. They hatched a chick but it died. Another pair nested as well; they got snowed out. They returned in 1969 but the male was shot in the winter of 1975–6. The female got a new mate straight away, as odd single eagles do appear from time to time. They have reared six young so far."

On our way to see the eagles we went through a picnic area and car park in mid-afternoon, where most of the cars were full of people reading papers and drinking tea. Why do people go on holiday to read a newspaper in a car park? The driver of one car with an R.S.P.B. sticker in the rear window was trying to get a chaffinch to feed from his hand. "Look at that," observed one of the wardens. "A bird watcher facing the wrong way and playing with bread crumbs, when he's got a family of peregrines on the crag directly behind him. You'd be amazed at the ignorance of some people. The other day we had a telephone call from a lady who wanted advice. She said 'I've got a nest box with ten young blue tits inside. They've got out nine times already and I've put them back each time. What must I do? I've blocked the hole up with Sellotape now.' We had to explain to her that growing birds did actually leave the nest and learn to fly."

The path took us over grass and rock, through bracken, past old ash and oak trees. We arrived in a broad side valley of stone walls and grazing sheep, which gradually rose into a great natural amphitheatre of scree, cascading streams and sheer cliffs of rock. In the glistening green of the damp, coarse grass, clumps of bird's-eye primrose grew, delicate pink flowers with a touch of yellow in the centre giving the name "bird's-eye". Gerard the old herbalist wrote: "In the middle of every small flower appeereth a little yellowe spot, resembling the eie of a bird, which hath mooved the people of the north parts (where it aboundeth) to call it Birds eine." Butterwort was plentiful too; its alternative name of bog violet now seems more appropriate, however, since to most people the origins of its name have been obscured by time; it was once rubbed into the udders of cows to improve the milk and butter; the leaves were used to thicken milk and the whole plant was associated with the medicine and magic of cattle.

The wardens had a small wooden hut in the valley where we sat out of the wind drinking tea, to wait for the eagles. Sheep walked towards us without fear and several ring ouzels, like white-chested mountain blackbirds, searched for insects and worms. Normally they are regarded as shy birds, but around the hut they seemed quite unafraid. Gilbert White was at first puzzled by their appearance and disappearance, until he eventually realised that they were just summer visitors.

Without warning, the female eagle broke the skyline as she glided over the distant ridge and planed down to the "frustration" eyrie, built after the death of the chick. Soon the male appeared and joined her; she was dark and large; he was lighter in both weight and colour, being more golden. They briefly flew, planing on wide-fingered wings, before again perching on a far-off crag. The walk and wait had been worthwhile, simply to see wild golden eagles in England.

Returning towards the bungalow, we stopped again by the peregrine eyrie. The valley side was wild and windy with the backs of the leaves showing silvery, a warning of rain. Oak, birch and sycamore grew from the slopes and ledges of the

Peregrine

crag. Black clouds swept across the deep blue of the sky, and outlined against this wildness the female peregrine, the falcon, flew. Her wings were curved, cutting through the wind as she came in to perch on a dead branch overlooking her chick. A gull headed laboriously into the rising gale. Suddenly the smaller male peregrine, the tiercel, appeared above; he folded in his wings and stooped towards the gull. The gap between the two narrowed until the gull veered and flapped in disarray. The peregrine pulled out of his dive without making contact and cruised to perch along the rock face. He had simply been threatening, or playing, but for a few seconds he had combined potential savagery with mastery of the air, to give a display of deep and primitive beauty. This call of the wild and reminder of the past, in addition to the element of co-operation with man, gives the ancient sport of falconry its appeal, and explains why so many eggs and chicks are illegally and regrettably stolen.

As darkness crept over the land I was told to walk through bracken to watch an area of excavated, light soil in a hollow of grass and rocks. I stood by a gnarled oak; it gave no protection from the cold wind that distorted the calls of sheep, curlews and yellowhammers. Suddenly a black and white striped head appeared; a badger, emerging from its sett. It began to grub around, before sniffing the air, looking towards me, and hurrying underground. It was clear that the eddies of turbulent air had betrayed me. Twice more the same thing happened; whether I saw one badger three times or three badgers once I do not know, but it rounded off a memorable day.

My last morning in the Lakes started warm and bright; Ullswater was still and crystal clear, giving a perfect reflection of the surrounding fields, woods and hills. I left the main roads to drive over Wrynose Pass and Hard Nott Pass, in places climbing at 1' in 3' to a land of crags, streams, waterfalls and rough grass. Wheatears flew and pipits parachuted down in spiralling display. The road fell into gentler pasture land, lush and fertile, and I followed it round into Wasdale. It was another "different picture", with Wast Water, long and blue next to the road. Across the water a massive ridge of rock formed a great barrier, with streams of scree flowing towards the surface of the lake. Wasdale is said to have the deepest lake, the highest mountain, the smallest church and the biggest liar in the whole of England. Some go further and say it has the biggest liar in the world, and each year at the Bridge Inn, Santon Bridge, the most notorious liars of the area compete for that prestigious title.

The road ended at Wasdale Head, a small hamlet of farms and fields locked in on three sides by towering crags, where a "television personality" was complaining that a footpath had disappeared into a farmyard. In fact he had wandered away from the path and the farmer found life hard enough without having people walking through his yard. The farmer had several days' stubble on his chin, and clogs with leather boot tops on his feet. He was finding things difficult: "We have Herdwicks, the local Lake District sheep here – they are the poor man's sheep. They don't make any money when you sell them these days. It even takes a gallon of petrol to fetch a gallon of petrol living up here." It was liquid of a different sort that worried him and his wife most: "The Lake's beautiful and it's a good life really – but Windscale wants to take more water out. One day they will turn the lake into a dam."

Windscale and the Calder Hall Nuclear Power Station appeared as a silhouette of towers, a silver dome, pylons and steam against the blue sea. After the Lakes, with shepherds and hound trailing it looked mysterious, even ominous, like moving from one age into another. Wire fences and security men were at the gates and I was ushered into the Information Manager's office; he was a former B.B.C. man with a staff of fifteen: "My job's necessary because people fail to separate nuclear weapons from the peaceful uses of nuclear fuel. We probably have more PhD's to the acre than anywhere else in Britain. Do you think they would work here if there was any danger? They only feel threatened when they are driving to work. Opposition to Windscale is commensurate with the distance you live away from it. The other day a woman phoned to ask if it was safe to swim in the sea along here; she was told, 'The raw sewage in the sea will kill you before we do'. We employ 8,000 people in an area of high unemployment. Half a million pounds are paid in wages each week and eighty-five per cent of the workforce are local, living within a radius of twelve miles."

The telephone interrupted him; a boat had left Dounreay Prototype Fast Reactor in Caithness, carrying plutonium nitrate for reprocessing at Windscale. Environmentalists would meet it, as would the media, and would he be there to answer questions on safety?

He explained the function of Windscale: to process fuel; to generate power; to recycle spent fuel and to engage in research and development: "We get waste, of course, but after twenty-eight years of operating we only have enough dangerous waste to go into two semi-detached houses. The really high waste is stored on site and the medium waste is dropped in steel drums into the sea. Some highly-active waste, such as gloves, is buried along the coast. Windscale is safe; we get isolated incidents, but even they are minor. Most of the milk produced by the cows outside – and milk is a good monitor of radiation levels – remains fit for human consumption."

I was handed over to a colleague to be shown around the site; he was a local politician who described his political activities as his "hobby", a description of politics I had never heard before. Is that why so many people without creative, healthy interests turn to politics? If so it would help to explain the reason for so many politicians being colourless, tedious and interfering.

The atmosphere of the place reminded one of Orwell's *1984*; regimented, monitored and sterile, with fences, warning devices, and people uniformly dressed in white coats or overalls, with special socks and shoes. All around were computers, thick concrete walls, flashing lights, deep green water with underwater arms, lights and cameras, where fuel was stored, huge cranes and technology at a most advanced level. It was science fiction actually earthbound and working; an example of technology overtaking the understanding of the ordinary man in the street, and leaving him well behind. That is why most discussions on nuclear energy are futile, for so few people have the knowledge and judgment to consider objectively all the advantages, risks and options.

On adjoining land more processing plants were under construction, with many men working on huge concrete walls, creating formidable safety barriers: "It's good," my companion informed me. "All this expansion is creating work."

It made an interesting point from which to leave the Lakes, and I was grateful that normally I lived over 250 miles away from it.

11

Fish, Firewater, Forests and Fur

After looking briefly into the future, I wanted to see the present more clearly and had arranged with B.P. to visit an oil rig, from Aberdeen. Almost inevitably, however, the past reappeared; following a leisurely drive through lowland Scotland and Edinburgh, I stopped for the night at a small house overlooking the River Earn, close to where it flows into the Tay. At a nearby pub a local ordered beer in an accent so broad that it was almost like a foreign language: "A pint of heavy [bitter], Freddy." I had previously thought that such a request was a music-hall joke, not part of a living dialect. Several old men sat drinking whisky and beer in the corner, talking about salmon fishing. One with a long coat and canvas bag looked the complete poacher, but claimed to be netting legally from a boat later that night: "That is if the boss doesn't smell my breath; if he throws me off I shan't go home. I can't stand the wife any more." They were all worried by the numbers of salmon: "It's not like it used to be, and disease is everywhere except in this river." A small, dark man with greasy hair and tattooed arms, of didecoy appearance, was unconcerned: "I still get all I want. I gaff them in the pools. I took forty-seven pounds of fish the other night, but then had to walk nineteen miles cross-country because the police were waiting by my car."

Back at the cottage, the owner, Brian, also a salmon fisherman, said he would be going out later that evening to fish. Although making a living from salmon, he respected them, was fascinated by their life cycle, but was concerned by their decline: "It's over-fishing at sea and in the estuaries that's causing the problem. Seals do a lot of damage too; they know where they come and they follow them right up the river.

Sometimes they will take them from the net. The wee otter does no harm, he's not big enough."

It was dark as we left the cottage to walk down to an artificial pebble beach where his seventy-five-year-old father had already untied the rowing boat. One end of the net was secured to the bank and the other to the boat; then the old man, wearing waders, rowed in a wide circle back towards the bank. Almost immediately, there was splashing and the net was winched in; it held a fourteen-pound salmon, large, silver and streamlined, in peak condition. The old man was pleased: "In the old days we would get several fish like that every time." They caught three more smaller salmon and two sea-trout, which at £3 a pound was not a bad evening's work: "You never see sea-trout on a menu, do you? They sell it all as salmon." Across the river, by a small green bothy [hut], more fishermen worked, but they did not meet with the same success; from the noise and commotion it sounded as if one had been drinking.

Breakfast could have been genuine Scottish porridge, but I declined; instead I sampled Aberdeen "butteries", or "rowies", a type of salty roll, best served warm and buttered. It is not a dish prepared especially for tourists but part of everyday fare. Cobbett, however, was not impressed with northern food, believing it to be based on potatoes, "Ireland's lazy root", and oatmeal:

> I see very few of Ireland's lazy root [he observed on one of his journeys], and never in this country will people be base enough to lie down and expire from starvation under the operation of the extreme unction: Nothing but a potatoe-eater will ever do that . . . Now, this I know, that, in the North, the 'enlightened' people eat sowens, burgoo, porridge, and potatoes: that is to say, oatmeal and water, or the root of extreme unction. If this be the effect of their light, give me the darkness, 'o' tha Sooth'.

As I approached Aberdeen, I saw a fishing trawler ploughing through a heavy sea; a flock of gulls followed in its wake and a rainbow curved overhead beneath heavy black clouds. Aberdeen had the appearance of a boom town; new factories, garages with unsightly advertising bunting and a general air of affluence. The town centre with wide streets and turreted granite buildings had an air of permanence not matched by the ephemera of oil money.

For some years it has been possible to send messages from earth to distant space craft; unfortunately B.P. had not succeeded in communicating between London and Aberdeen and as a result my trip to an oil rig was lost in a bureaucratic wall of confusion and unhelpfulness. I moved on, wanting to see some of the old Highland forests.

Graffiti on a wall proclaimed "It's Scotland's Oil", and a longer railway bridge had room for "End English Misrule Now". The village of Jericho was an anachronism; a biblical name in a land overflowing with distilleries and transport cafés, although in attractive countryside; undulating, with patches of moorland, forest and field, their edges marked in golden boundaries of blazing broom.

Elgin was once an interesting town, before planners converted it into a gigantic traffic roundabout and car park. Nonetheless bed and breakfast was easy to find at £5 a night with supper included – chips, peas and white pudding, another Scottish dish that would have appalled Cobbett:

White Pudding

2 lbs oatmeal
1–1½ lbs good beef suet
3–4 large onions, finely chopped
1 tbsp salt
½ tbsp pepper
tripe skins

The ingredients are mixed up and put into tripe skins. They should be boiled for an hour, pricking them to prevent them from bursting. They can be dried and used when needed – fried or put in stews.

I enjoyed it, however, and afterwards Jock was eager to show me "real Scottish life". "Shall we have a wee dram? No, we'll go to the club." He took me to the British Legion Club where he and his friends proceeded to down beers in quick succession, each accompanied by a whisky. I made no effort to keep up, or compete with their remarkable capacities. His friends were all working men – electricians, builders and carpenters; they were also Freemasons; working-class freemasons are almost unknown in England, but commonplace in Scotland.

Returning towards the house at eleven p.m. we stopped at the bakery, which had just opened. The huge white-clad assistant, from whom Jock bought fresh bean and potato pies, looked as if he ate far more than he sold. The evening ended not with a question, but a statement: "Now for a dram." Jock opened a cupboard and took out an orange squash bottle full of a very dark liquid. He poured some into a glass: "Taste that – it's the real McCoy." It was the hottest whisky I had ever tasted; real firewater which burnt all the way from my lips to my stomach. Top quality malt whisky, it was darker and richer than that sold in pubs: "It's 120% proof; it's the stuff we distill and mix with grain whisky to make the ordinary blended brand names. It would be at least £40 a bottle to buy, but it's so strong they won't allow it to be sold." To prove his point he poured some into an ash tray and flicked in a match; it burst into blue flame. "It's like gold," he said. "I can barter whatever I want with it in this town." He was proud of his haul; he stored bottles in cupboards, under the stairs and in the garden shed. Under the incinerator at the bottom of the garden was a concrete lid; inside the miniature cellar were yet more bottles – squash, lemonade, beer and milk – all full of whisky; the whole house was literally awash with the stuff, worth many hundreds of pounds. He had some "clearic" too, the colourless whisky freshly distilled: "But that's much harder to get." As I should have guessed, he worked in a Speyside distillery. "Look at these," he said, producing pipes that could be dropped down his trouser legs, and a large flat, curved can that fitted under his shirt and round his rib cage. "We all go to work looking very thin and come oot very fat."

I was amazed: "Don't you get frisked?"

"Och nay, they wouldna' do thart, the union wouldna' let them."

He consumed three tumblers full, on top of his beer, without any visible ill effects. I could not even take a second sip.

Without a hangover, he was up early and arranged for me to visit a distillery in the Spey valley at Cromdale. There, the old farm buildings still stood among the larger warehouse-like buildings now used. Originally it had been farmed by a MacGregor who ran an illicit still. In 1824, so the story goes, the excise men arrived and said: "Isn't it time you had a licence for your neep [turnip] shed, John?" He took their advice and whisky has been distilled there ever since.

The water comes from a tributary of the Spey and only Scottish barley is used in producing the whisky. The barley dust is sent off to make cosmetics and talcum powder; dead mink and barley dust – what an exciting combination. After the malting process the barley is dried with two oil heaters and two peat heaters, the peat being shovelled by hand; the peat smoke is said to give Scotch whisky its distinctive flavour. Certainly the smell of malting barley and peat made a pleasant combination. The liquid was fermented in large oak containers and finished in copper stills. Much of the equipment was old and carefully locked, access being restricted, in theory, to the excise men. The clear whisky was finally poured into second-hand sherry barrels to mature and to get its distinctive colour and taste.

At one time the distillery workers were "drammed" each day with the "real McCoy", but according to the manager: "It was not good news. In the old days with much more physical work the men could work it off, but it was causing problems and even the union pushed for it to be stopped. It is the cream of the barley though, but to drink it regularly is mad; it's bordering on poison, a real liver killer."

I returned to Elgin through Forres, another small town, where after an unusual meal of chips and haggis wrapped in plastic, I was directed to a stone-built house where an old fishmonger still smoked his own fish, including thirty to forty salmon each year for his friends. "Aye, I only smoke fish now as my doctor's just stopped me smoking cigarettes, but I still have a crafty puff now and again." His smoking shed, small with black tar-covered walls, was at the bottom of the garden. Inside hung rows of filleted haddocks: "We call them finnans, or Moray Firths, but further along the coast they become Aberdeen haddies. There are two ways of smoking salmon; leave it with dry salt on it, or put it in pickle – salt and water – for six hours, before giving it one smoking to dry it. Then cover it with a mixture of whisky and soft brown sugar – you open it up like a kipper, using three-quarters of a gill of whisky. Some people use rum which is the proper way, but I prefer whisky." As he spoke he pointed to a bottle with a squash label, but filled with dark brown liquid: "I can't always get it, but it's the best malt. You smoke it four or five times to get it right – when it begins to lose its redness – but it mustn't get too crusty. I make the fire from shavings with fine sawdust on top to make it smoulder away like peat. I use sawdust from oak or silver birch. Birch is best; the smoke is sweeter and it gives added flavour."

Sawdust is easy to obtain for there are forests in many parts of the Spey and Findhorn valleys. Close to Forres the Forestry Commission has its largest nursery in the country, eighty-five acres supplying between eight to ten million small trees each year, both hard and soft woods. Towards the sea lies one of the most unusual wooded areas in Britain – Culbin Forest, part of the 17,000-acre Laigh of Moray Forest. What makes it even more remarkable is the fact that it is run by foresters with a deep interest in its natural history.

The forest covers undulating land, but it has no soil, for below the surface vegetation of heather, moss, lichens and pine needles is fine sand. Forty years ago it was an area of shifting dunes, a genuine desert, but then it was "thatched" with pine branchwood, birch and broom; trees were planted and the forest thrived. Ironically it has been designated an S.S.S.I. (a Site of Special Scientific Interest), since sand dunes all around our coast, unique areas with their own wildlife and vegetation, are rapidly contracting through development and tourism. Culbin was one of the best, but the "cash-crop" mentality triumphed once more and it was planted. Fortunately the forest is more attractive than factories, estates and nuclear power stations, but a feature of very special character has been lost. The ranger was proud of his forest and pointed out badger setts among the trees. When we were deep within the plantations he stopped the van. "Follow me," he said mysteriously, walking along a narrow track through dense pines. He signalled caution, moving carefully towards a tall dead tree with a large, dishevelled stick nest in its upper skeletal branches. High-pitched calls came from above and a large brown and white bird, with talons and hooked beak, landed by its sitting mate; an osprey. Both briefly flew around the nest, before the female resumed incubation. We left quiet- ly, anxious to cause no disturbance. Willie was pleased, since he had found the nest earlier by accident, but it showed how successful the osprey's comeback to Scotland has been.

The forest was alive, with more signs of badgers, a wood- cock roding, capercaillie droppings, a buzzard sitting in a tree, the small white flowers of wintergreen, and several glimpses of deer; roe, dainty and delicate, peering through trees, their eyes and noses etched in dark perfection, as their ears showed the direction of their interest and concern. Ducks flew over marsh as did red-breasted mergansers with frenetic wingbeats. In the forest, an ex-German prisoner of war with the broadest Scottish accent I had heard waved Willie down. He spoke of finding a deer with its bottom jaw shattered by a .22 bullet. It was standing blind, deaf and starving; he had shot it to end its misery, and had been disgusted and angered. He suspected a poacher; perhaps a fisherman who claimed to own a gun to use against seals.

Next we came to the estuary where the Findhorn river, clear and smooth, flowed through wide banks of sand into the sea. White surf and ice-blue water showed where land ceased and salmon ended their ocean journey. It was a wild, beautiful place. A group of men with two rowing boats were fishing with sweep nets and winches and they had several large fish. "In conditions like this they can see the fish coming," Willie commented. "We get other fishermen too — there are usually several ospreys fishing over the estuary."

Back in the forest we looked for capercaillie, or "great grouse", without success. "It's peculiar, the birds will always be about the forest, then at this time of year they just vanish.

It's probably when they've got young." We stopped again at a low-lying area of open, marshy ground: "Look," he said, pointing to a small, pale flower. "A one-flowered wintergreen, one of the rarest plants in Britain." Over a ridge lay the open sea: pale sand littered with dead trees where dunes were being washed away by large white breakers; there were no footprints on the beach, just precious isolation.

Dabchick

From the Findhorn I travelled to the Spey, stopping as I went by a small loch surrounded by pines, birch wood and rhododendrons. A dabchick dived, while high above an osprey flew slowly by, uninterested in food. A few trout fishermen were casting from rowing boats and an irritable bailiff was checking his clients: "That osprey again. We have to tolerate them because of the conservationists, but we don't stock the loch with trout for the benefit of ospreys."

In evening light the Spey was compelling; wide, fast-flowing, with pools and rocks. I stopped to walk by it, through woods and water meadows. At a bridge grew forget-me-nots, cuckoo flowers and large, melancholy thistles, so aptly named, for when the flower heads first form, they hang down in sadness. There were large boulders where pied wagtails perched, appropriately described by John Clare as "little trotty wagtail". Some were feeding their fully-fledged young, flitting over the water after moths and flies, sometimes climbing vertically in pursuit, with blurred wings and tails;

trout were rising and gulls were gliding in the gentle currents of air above the water. Beyond were woods, meadows, pools of mist and mountains flecked with lingering snow. Six pochard burst into flight and a roe deer quietly grazed. As I watched the river a gleaming silver fish arched into the air, with sparkling droplets cascading from its glistening, plunging body. It was a salmon, still free; it had run the gauntlet of trawlers, seals, nets and rods to reach this part of the river. The romantic cycle of the salmon adds to the visual beauty of the Spey; a cycle that starts and ends among the streams of the forests, fields and mountains at the river's source.

At a bend in the river sand martins were feeding over the water, with more adults falling from their nest holes to spring into aerial artistry. Wild roses showed pale and pink, foxgloves hummed with bees, birches rustled in the breeze, and a flock of curlews called, high and flying north; two fishermen began to cast their flies.

Further along the Spey I slept in woods close to Loch Garten where ospreys have nested for several years. The return of the remarkable osprey is an encouraging story. Visually it is reminiscent of the African fish eagle, an appropriate resemblance, for those nesting in Scotland migrate to Africa each winter, travelling down to Senegal. Every spring they return, and the force that drives them is so precise that they usually arrive on Speyside within a day or two of April 3rd. The osprey is unique; the group of birds to which it belongs is divided into two families; on one side there are 218 species, including hawks, eagles, and vultures, while on the other there is just the osprey. It lives by fishing, ninety-nine per cent of its diet consisting of live fish, which it seizes in its talons by plunging into the water. As a result, it is the only bird of prey to have a reversible outer toe, for fishing, and nostrils that can be closed at will. Its fishing has also given it the name of fish hawk and eagle fisher. Indeed its success rate is so high that early writers and naturalists believed that it held some strange power or attraction over fish to draw them to the surface. Thus in 1594 George Peele wrote:

I will provide thee of a princely osprey,
That, as he flieth over fish in pools,
The fish shall turn their glistening bellies up,
And thou shalt take thy liberal choice of all.

The sixteenth-century naturalist William Turner commented:

When the Osprey hovers in the air whatever fishes be below turn up and show their whitish bellies. The Osprey is a bird much better known today to Englishmen than many who keep fish in stews would wish: for within a short time it bears off every fish.

Its liking for remote places makes it impossible to say precisely when the last ospreys bred in Scotland before their reappearance, but it is thought to have been in the early years of this century, possibly as late as 1916. Trout fishermen did not welcome the birds, but the main culprits of their decline were oologists (egg collectors), as the eggs are particularly attractive, being blotched and variable in colour, and whole clutches were taken.

Similiary the date of the ospreys' return cannot be given with complete assurance, but it is thought that a pair bred successfully in the early 1950s. Several breeding attempts followed and the R.S.P.B. made efforts to protect the site at Loch Garten on Speyside. Overcoming problems caused by egg collectors, gales and hooligans, who tried to fell the tree, the ospreys have now successfully raised young for several years and hundreds of thousands of visitors have seen them through telescopes mounted in a public hide concealed among pines.

It is a fine site close to the loch, in an area of ancient Caledonian pine forest. The forest itself is possibly now more threatened than the ospreys; although the whole area is a Site of Special Scientific Interest, some of it is owned by commercial forestry operations and "clear felling" has taken place. The owners plan to replant with quick-growing commercial timber, and there is no way of preventing this.

I awoke to a bright and clear dawn; three roe deer were grazing quietly by my car and red squirrels were involved in a frantic, dizzy chase around the trunk of a large Scots pine. Over the loch an osprey called. The deer moved slowly away; far off a doe barked, as if she had a small kid hidden in the undergrowth. This was the best time to see capercaillie, I had been told, but again the forest tracks were empty of large birds.

Mid-morning in a warm sun, and many cars were already parked by the loch close to the entrance of the public hide. Women walked along the stony track in high-heeled shoes, accompanied by holidaymaking husbands with their now familiar caps, like out-of-work sea captains. Others with instamatic cameras and smouldering cigarettes seemed on edge and worried, as if they were out of their natural element; as indeed they were.

The large stick nest was in a tall pine next to the original tree; each year more twigs are added and nests can become as large as a double bed and up to three feet deep. The female was standing, pulling at a fish to feed to her chicks, their fluffy heads just visible above the edge of the nest. The Loch Garten nest has been protected since 1958; in 1975 a fresh male chased the old one away and in 1980 a new pair moved in, the female being a chick that was hatched and ringed in 1976. The birds are still at risk and a dozen part-time wardens work in shifts to watch over them. ★

The wardens were housed in a camp on a nearby croft; it was a typical Scottish house, yet with a corrugated iron roof, surrounded by small fields and forest. Outside was a fenced garden, with plum and apple trees, currant bushes and vegetables. It was run by the crofter, eighty-one-year-old Isabel MacDonald, who moved there at the age of fourteen. Her family had been farming since the Crimean War and her father had taught her how to work a dog, fire a gun and use ferrets. On her twenty-two acres she grew oats, barley and potatoes,

---

★The summer of 1981 proved to be the best since the ospreys returned; with twenty-four known pairs on territory, twenty successful nests and forty-three young reared.

Osprey

as well as rearing eight cows, fifty hens, a few ducks, some guinea fowl and three hives of bees. She could do little of the work herself because of arthritis, but over the years she has looked after more than thirty foster children and, like the ospreys, they return regularly to help her out.

She has enjoyed her life and work at the croft and thinks that more and more people want to get back on the land. At one time she used to be self-sufficient: "I would shoot with a twelve bore and a .22 for rabbits. It was the rabbits that kept people going during the First World War. I used to shoot roe deer too, but stopped after I had reared one; they are such beautiful and friendly animals. I had a doe until quite recently, but it left last Tuesday and has not been back." She was a contented, selfless old lady: as I left a roe deer was walking cautiously through oats towards the house. It must have been hers, for a truly wild deer would not have ventured out at midday.

Evening at Loch Garten and the ospreys were again calling; the loch held the rippled images of mauve mountains and trees merging into rushes. The woodlands were scented with pine and the light shone a brittle orange between the trunks, illuminating and magnifying light and shade. A great spotted woodpecker called and flew on its undulating way, the sun catching patches of crimson. It landed on the copper trunk of an old Scots pine, probing and penetrating the peeling bark with its bill. It dislodged an oak leaf of autumn that gently rocked its way downwards, bronze in the summer sun. The woodpecker moved on to a nearby tree where it fed an almost full-grown young bird. All evening parents and three or four youngsters fed in the trees. From the edge of the loch a common sandpiper called in warning and flew to perch in an overhanging birch tree – the first time I had seen one land above the ground. Then more movement in the tops of pines as two crested tits fed among cones; below them, a roe buck, with small, fine antlers, was held in frozen movement as we surprised each other by our presence, before he bounded away. The old self-seeded forests were rich in timber and woodland life; sadly, today that is no longer enough.

Aviemore is the tourist centre of Speyside, full of shops, hotels and hostels. At the Happy Haggis a queue of hikers had formed for a "fish and chips take away". But it offered much more than fish and chips: "Take away a great British Tradition – also beefburgers, pizzas and do-nuts." Such take aways sold in Scotland, served by Asian immigrants, described as a British tradition; what would William Cobbett have made of such a combination?

At Inverdruie I came across evidence of a more sophisticated palate – a fishery producing fifty tons of fresh trout every year. The fish farm consisted of a number of pools containing 400,000 trout of different sizes, fed on fish pellets. Several feet above, miles of red twine covered the whole site. The young, bearded manager explained that before the twine the ospreys were regular callers: "When they had young they were taking six trout a day, ranging usually from half a pound to a pound. They preferred fish between four ounces and half a pound. If they got larger ones of up to three pounds they had problems taking off in the limited space. Often they would drop them, ripping out great pieces of flesh. The twine has done the trick and we get no more problems; in fact we like seeing the birds about. Black-headed gulls were the biggest pest, but we get no more bother from them either. We have dogs and a fence to keep otters out and that has worked well. If you are sensible you can rear fish and tolerate wildlife."

Close to Inverdruie another unusual form of farming was taking place. The road led through pine forests, past Loch Morlich, to the Cairngorm mountains and Reindeer House, a bungalow just off the road, which forms the centre of an experiment to rear reindeer. The project was started in 1952 by Mickel Utsi, a Lapp, and was being continued by his widow, Dr. Ethel Lindgren. Although at first it might seem eccentric to breed reindeer in Scotland, in fact they are native animals of Britain, and were hunted to extinction in the twelfth century. They thrive on the mosses and lichens of tundra conditions, which the Cairngorms possess, like an arctic intrusion. The area has more than the vegetation of tundra, for its dotterels, snow buntings and ptarmigan are all birds of colder arctic climes.

Alan Smith, the reindeer keeper, invited me to see the herd. He was tall, young, and if it had not been for the reindeer he would have been a ghillie like his father. He obviously enjoyed being Britain's only reindeer keeper; his other claim to fame was achieving second place in a haggis-throwing competition, wearing plus-fours and wellington boots.

He collected the morning's group of visitors and led the way to the 1,000-acre reindeer enclosure, over a rock-strewn gully to the fenced-off mountainside with rough grasses and boggy soil. Some of the visitors were dressed as if they were going shopping at Marks and Spencers, and soon they were cleaning black gleaming mud from their ankles; one lost his smart leather shoe completely, and it was only recovered with the aid of a stick. Alan called loudly: "Low, low . . . Come on", and soon the deer appeared over the brow of a hill, some with bells clanging. As they ran, with a wide, stiff gait, a peculiar clicking noise came from their hooves. They are ungainly deer without the elegance and daintiness of roe; they were moulting, too, which did not help their appearance. Both the cows and bulls had large antlers and there were several small, attractive calves, carrying out conversations with their mothers in short, deep moos. Alan fed them with oatmeal and Ryvita, and even those people with wet feet seemed satisfied.

He guided the trippers back to the road and we then took the chairlift to the summit, as Alan wanted to fetch five bulls, living free on the higher slopes, back to the herd. A pamphlet posed the question: "What is a chairlift?" It also supplied the answer: "It is a novel and exciting way to travel to points usually inaccessible to the normal traveller."

"Such as what?"

"Such as a restaurant and viewpoint on one of Scotland's highest mountains." The restaurant proved something of a disappointment, serving tea from polystyrene cups.

The view from the "novel and exciting way to travel" was attractive – forests, lakes and mountains. Directly beneath, however, it was disturbing, with the small gulleys and gorges of soil erosion, caused by too many feet and skis having worn away the protective surface vegetation. In places it was so damaged that it looked like a builder's tip, and a stream had been made to flow through a straight, man-made bed; it seemed incredible that remedial work should be carried out to a mountain. Once off the chairlift, steps had been made to the summit: what next? Perhaps a Cairngorm escalator; then it would be possible to get to "one of Britain's most inaccessible places" without actually moving.

From the top, the whole area of the reindeer enclosure, and beyond, could be seen, including Lurcher's Gulley where the deer often shelter during the rut. Inevitably it was the subject of a public enquiry, for approval had been given by the Highland and Islands Development Board to extend the area of ski slopes and snow fences. With damage already obvious it seemed that the Development Board ought to consider a new name – the Highland Demolition Company.

Most of the chairlift travellers climbed the steps, one listening to Radio One as he went. We walked beyond the summit and soon were quite alone. It was quiet and hot; Alan called, but there were no signs of the deer. We sat in the sun with a wide view in front of us, of valleys, corries and a small tarn, blue, turquoise and crystal-clear. Behind, a pair of ptarmigan moved from a rocky ledge, mottled and lined like the lichens and grasses that normally concealed them. The cock had white wings and a red eye-stripe; he seemed, too, as if he was wearing plus-fours, with feathers down to the knees, which in winter spread right down to the feet.

Across the valley small specks moved; through binoculars we could see they were not reindeer, but red deer, five hinds and two small calves. We abandoned the search and returned downwards. As we went we passed a botanist working on a deserted slope. He was counting and measuring plants in a small square for his PhD. What would his study show? Quite simple really; that in areas of people and shade there were fewer plants than elsewhere. Education is a wonderful thing!

In the evening Alan promised to show me both blackcock and capercaillie: "Capercaillie are fine birds, but when you eat them it's like going out and licking pine trees." We passed through old pine woods, and again they possessed the combination of elements that make ancient forests so rich and attractive; tall trees, deep silence, reflected light, the fragrance of fallen pine needles, the fresh melting green of larch fronds, heather, regeneration and the chance of seeing deer. A tawny owl, dark and mottled, merged perfectly with shadow as its head swivelled to watch us, and there, too, in a clearing, were grazing roe. As the sun fell, glowing crimson, the mountains again absorbed mauve light; but the capercaillies remained well hidden.

After a long day, we made for the Forester's Bar, but there were no foresters inside, only more hollow beams, fitted carpets, gassy beer and tourists. The enjoyment of conversation was shattered by the arrival of a live group with guitars,

Roe deer

amplifiers and microphones. Their music was flat, devoid of any obvious talent and loud; so loud that it was impossible to talk. Every few minutes the female singer would run her fingers through her long hair; either self-infatuation or a scalp irritation.

A few months before my visit, a truly unusual animal had arrived on Speyside – a puma "caught" near Inverness and taken to the Highland Wildlife Park at Kincraig. For years there had been rumours in the Highlands of a puma loose in the mountains and forests, and some claimed that the capture proved the stories to be true.

The Wildlife Park was founded to show tourists the wildlife of Scotland. When most visitors are present in July and August, the deer are away in the hills and wildlife watching is at its worst, so consequently this collection of British birds and animals was started. It is a fine, well-planned park and ideal for introducing children to their native fauna. Earlier in the summer a teacher had tried to do exactly that; she had arrived at the pine marten enclosure, but all the martens had been inside their boxes. Not to be discouraged she explained: "Well, children, there are three types of martins in Britain – house martins, sand martins and pine martens."

The director took me to see the puma. Instead of the spitting, angry wild animal I had expected, it was a quiet, friendly female, like a great contented domestic cat. It came up to the side of its cage and Eddie stroked it through the bars; it rolled over purring. While being transferred from the trap to its cage it had tucked its tail between its legs as if it had done it before: "The whole thing is strange," he said. "The trap was not by a hedge or gate as I would have expected, and from the start the animal seemed well fed and contented."

It was a mystery. Were there really pumas living wild in Scotland? If so, how did they get there? Was someone trying to introduce them as a new species, or was it simply that people had released unwanted circus or zoo animals that had become too much trouble? Either way it seemed undesirable for such an alien animal to be released into the countryside, for something as large as a puma could cause considerable damage to both wildlife and domestic animals.

The puma had been caught at Cannich, a village not far from Loch Ness, a remote, sparsely populated country, with forests, sheep farms and a few isolated settlements. In places red deer roamed close to the road, and a stag with antlers in velvet fled at the approach of my small green van, splashing through a stream as it went. There seemed little doubt that a wild carnivore could live on sheep and deer quite easily and unobtrusively in such country. But if tame pumas had been released, would they have managed to kill and survive? The experience of George Adamson in the African bush shows that captive-bred big cats have to be taught how to kill, otherwise they starve.

The farmer who had caught the puma could not be roused. The farmyard was untidy, with a collection of dogs, ducks, geese, hens and guinea fowl, but no signs of human activity. Eventually a man came to the door of a caravan: "Oh they won't be up in the bungalows before afternoon as they went to the Royal Highland Show at Edinburgh yesterday."

Opinions in the village varied: "There have been pumas seen round here, but they've been dark. Ted caught a light one."

"There's no pumas here; somebody's been playing tricks on the old man."

"If there aren't pumas, what was one doing in the trap?"

"Forest workers have seen them, and a botanist who has collected birch seeds in the forest for many years came face to face with one in a clearing. It was black; he turned and ran."

I was advised to go to a farm on the other side of the village: "He's reliable and a good farmer."

Mr. MacDonald's wife was at home: "I don't know if my husband saw a puma," she said, "but he saw something strange about a year ago. He was checking the sheep in the evening when he saw a large cat-like animal with a long tail. It was darker than the puma in the trap. He had seen many foxes and wild cats, but it was neither of those. At that time too we had several lambs taken; they were skinned before being eaten. A fox doesn't do that. This year it's been quiet. When we've had lambs die my husband has left them out for the foxes, so they don't take live ones, and even they have not been taken.

The only thing stolen now are eggs, by pine martens. They are lovely animals. I saw one the other night with a white spot on its chest running along a stone wall towards the farm. The hens lay out and I usually collect the eggs. We had a nest in the rushes and I put a china egg there to encourage them to lay; the eggs were taken, and the china egg as well. The hens were all right because we shut them up at night."

Outside the village, hidden from the road and approached by a rough track, were three crofters' cottages. Two were in disrepair, the other well maintained with a blaze of flowering lupins in the small garden, surrounded by marshy ground and forest. A small lady came to the door, an "unclaimed treasure", living alone with her garden and her wild animals: "It's almost perfect here," she said. "People have lived in this valley for generations. All the menfolk from these three crofts went to fight at Culloden; none returned." Around the walls of her living room were her own pictures, a leaping salmon and a puma, coloured and childlike, surrounded by decorative patterns and flowers: "It was wonderful for animals here once, but so many of the deer have gone. The wild animals are clearing out the natural animals. Once the roe deer would hide their young in the heather and bog myrtle out there, but I never see them now. I loved the puma before it was caught; it lived in the cottage next door for four years."

She led me down through the bog where the leaves of the myrtle smelt sweet: "I pick it and put it with my clothes to keep the moths away." The trap that caught the puma was shut and unbaited. It was large, with a weighted trap-door, string, wire and corrugated iron, similar to a home-made fox trap I had once seen in the Fens. Inside the cottage where the puma had lived was rubble and dust, but no signs of a large wild animal.

As I left, the little lady was admiring the flowers in her garden. It was warm and tranquil: "You must come again," she smiled. "They haven't caught all the wild animals in the wood yet. The other day I saw a tiger cub."

12

Eagles and Eyries

From Cannich to Loch Ness I saw no tigers or pumas, and driving beside the loch towards Fort William I saw no monsters either. At a remote lake-filled valley I spent a morning looking for the chequered skipper butterfly, but even in its last stronghold I met with no success. Earlier, too, I had been disappointed not to have seen capercaillie in the Speyside pine woods. It is said to be an impressive bird, with the cock indulging in a spectacular display during the "lek", and also an important bird, for it shows that threatened or locally extinct species can be successfully re-introduced.

During the eighteenth century capercaillie became extinct in Britain through the disappearance of natural pine forests and the activities of sportsmen. But in 1837 fifty-five Swedish birds were released in Perthshire, and the capercaillie has thrived in Scotland ever since.

The ever-present threat from pesticides, pollution and disturbance means that similar re-introduction may be vital in the future. Birds, animals and butterflies could all be restored, either by transporting wild creatures from an area of abundance to one of scarcity, or by releasing captive-bred species back into the wild.

In view of the importance of such work I headed for the "Road to the Isles", and the island of Rhum, to see an experiment in progress to re-introduce the sea eagle, also known as the white-tailed eagle, or white-tailed sea eagle. The sea eagle is a magnificent bird with an eight-foot wing span, a large, hooked beak, and golden eyes that give it its Gaelic name of Iolair Shuil na-greine – the eagle with the sunlit eye. It is slightly larger than the golden eagle and when it soars and glides, its wings take on a vulturine aspect; long and horizontal with finger-like feathers at the ends.

Just a hundred years ago the eagle was commonly found in Western Scotland, the Scottish Islands and Ireland. But then, like so many birds of prey, it was persecuted ruthlessly by gamekeepers, shepherds and egg collectors, and it slipped quietly into extinction. The last known nest was on Skye in 1916 and the last two sea eagles on Rhum were shot by a gamekeeper in 1907. The eagles lived mainly on a diet of fish, sea birds and carrion. Yet because the occasional deer calf and lamb were also taken, the presence of eagles was not tolerated. Again, although a shepherd's anger is understandable when he sees a lamb carried off, or if he finds the remains of lambs at an eyrie, in fact sea eagles are naturally lazy birds, and carrion, including many dead lambs, forms a major part of their diet.

In normal circumstances, 1916 would have seen the last of the sea eagle in Britain. Unlike the osprey, it does not migrate and the chances of a pair wandering from Scandinavia to establish themselves in Scotland are remote. Yet sea eagles can again be seen in the Scottish Islands thanks to a long-term project run by the Nature Conservancy Council (N.C.C.). Originally the Royal Society for the Protection of Birds tried to re-introduce the bird by releasing four young eagles on Fair Isle in 1968. It was not a success. Fair Isle was too remote, there were too few birds, and the fulmar population was too high. When threatened, fulmars spit out an unpleasant oily substance at their enemies, and at least one of the four eaglets died as a result. Consequently, the N.C.C. chose Rhum for its experiment as it seemed the perfect location. A National Nature Reserve, it was the centre of the bird's old range, and with sea birds and deer there was a plentiful supply of food. In addition, it was an adequate size, being six miles wide and eight miles long, covering 26,400 acres. The first four eaglets were brought in from Norway in June 1975 and a young zoology graduate from Aberdeen University, John Love, was employed "for five or six weeks", to look after them until they were old enough to be released. John Love has been working with the eagles on Rhum ever since, and each year he has received between four and ten eaglets, obtained with help from the Norwegian government. Thirty-seven birds have now been released and the programme is continuing to ensure a wide range of mature and young birds.

As I drove beyond Fort William I came to a great sea loch, held in a cradle of mountains, rugged and remote. I stopped briefly at a salmon farm, where cages held thousands of salmon; they were surrounded by wire to protect them against seals, cormorants and shags. It is strange how broiler houses and factory farms arouse hostility and emotion, but fish farms provoke little criticism.

In hot sun the winding road to Mallaig gave new sights and memories with every rise and bend. The hills looked greener and older than those that had gone before, with flooded valleys of glittering water, islands with pines, ancient rocks, clarity and distance. It was a land of breathtaking beauty, a country of ballads and poetry; the further one travels from London, the closer reality seems to become. It was more than the historical reality of the Western Highlands, for that was harsh – feuds, persecution, dampness and toil – but something deeper and more profound. For when you travel physically through an old landscape, the feelings go beyond the sound of the sea, the texture of rocks and the call of the curlew, to even more distant and powerful forces, that can still enter and uplift the spirit of man. Unfortunately, in modern city living it has been stifled, killed and discarded.

Of the Downs, Richard Jefferies wrote:

Broad are the downs and open the aspect – gather the breadth and largeness of view. Never can that view be wide enough and large enough; there will always be room to aim higher. As the air of the hills enriches the blood, so let the presence of these beautiful things enrich the inner sense.

What would he have written on the road to Mallaig?

From a high bend overlooking the sea the islands appeared; Skye, with its pale, lunar landscape of grey mountains; Rhum, with its mysterious line of pyramidal peaks, and Eigg, a plateau of green raised above the white-topped waves. Mallaig was quiet and peaceful; a mid-summer football match was in progress, high wire netting preventing the ball from reaching the sea. A fishing boat chugged into harbour.

Five a.m. was grey and overcast, with the sea the colour of ink; a fisherman was standing up in his rowing boat, paddling across to a small trawler. The inter-island ferry left at six a.m. with just three passengers, each paying £3.20, outnumbered two to one by the crew. It was cold even below deck, and since there were so few passengers no early morning tea was brewed.

Halfway across the fifteen-mile stretch of open water guillemots and razorbills could be seen fishing and washing, and then small rafts of dark, less familiar birds appeared. Large numbers were flying with long, narrow black wings, planing just above the water, gliding into the troughs between the waves, then rising briefly, wheeling right, then left, before falling again. They were Manx shearwaters and their easy control in wind and spray made a total contrast to those grounded birds, flopping and scrambling after dark on Skomer. An estimated 130,000 pairs nest on Rhum, forming Britain's largest breeding colony. Strangely, all the nests are found above 2,000 feet, possibly because of better drainage.

Early Viking seafarers had not heard of Manx shearwaters or "cups of cocoa" and they certainly did not use the word "onomatopoeic". To them the ghostly night-time calls of summer were made by island trolls, and so one of Rhum's peaks was called Trollaval, a name it retains today. If they had known the Latin name to be imposed on the Manx shearwater at a later date, they would have been even more surprised, for although scientists claim to use Latin to avoid confusion, the Manx shearwater is known as *"puffinus puffinus"*; the poor puffin is apparently a *"fratercula arctica"*.

Before arriving at Rhum, the boat stopped briefly alongside the small quay at Canna; it seemed a delightful little island, low and lush green, with a church, a small group of cottages, and "the big house" overlooking the bay. A group of islanders, not wardens or naturalists, hoisted bulky sacks of fleeces aboard, and a deep-freeze in a large cardboard box was manhandled from the boat to the back of a Land Rover. A group of eider ducks floated nearby and a seal lifted its head out of the water to get a better view of the proceedings.

The boat backed away from the quay to make the short crossing to Loch Scresort and Rhum. It was still cool as we cruised gently into the wide bay where Kinloch was clearly visible as a row of white houses and a castle, another impressive folly, built in red sandstone, looking completely out of place, rather like a large Victorian waterworks. The village was surprsingly wooded, some of the neighbouring hillsides being planted with young deciduous trees; away from the settlement the landscape grew into wild hills and peaks.

A motor boat full of students and researchers on their way back to the mainland met us and unloaded its passengers on to the ferry; we were in turn transferred and taken to the shore. Peter Duncan, the young summer-warden, directed me to a small house, the home of the MacIvers, a friendly Scottish couple, to deposit my bags and binoculars. Wyn worked in the castle, and John, with a happy toothless smile, worked on the estate. Whereas the scientists and conservationists went about their business along the stony tracks by Land Rover, he commuted to and from the farm on his tractor.

The chief warden, on temporary duty from the Hebrides, lived in a large white house. At one time he had been a dairy farmer, but had not liked the direction farming was taking and as a result obtained a job with the N.C.C., who sent him to the islands. He fitted in well, for fishermen and farmers have much in common, enabling him to understand their problems, as well as help smooth over the conflicts between fishing and natural history.

He was a contented, amusing old cynic, mixing perception with wit. His philosophy of life was summed up perfectly by a poem hanging behind his desk:

> Out of the gloom
> A voice said to me,
> "Smile and be happy,
> Things could be worse."

So I smiled
And was happy
And behold,
Things did get worse.

He had a year to go before retirement, if his cigarettes and smoker's cough did not finish him first: "But there's nothing you can say that will stop me smoking, for human beings are funny things and there are some things people will not accept. For instance, a man will accept that his wife is committing adultery, but he will not believe that he can't drive his car, or train his dog. I will not accept that cigarettes harm me and if they do it's too bad."

He liked his occasional stints on Rhum: "But we get too many scientists studying the back left legs of green beetles and other important subjects like that. Then we have geologists behind every other rock. We call them 'stonechats', because the noise they make with their little hammers against a rock is just like a stonechat. I have the complete answer to the conservation problem; every species with a population of under 50,000 should be killed off, then there would be nothing to worry about – the trouble is, there would still be geologists, as their world population must be higher than 50,000. But Rhum is a fine island, with deer, otters, and of course, the sea eagles."

I had landed on Rhum just after another batch of five eagles had arrived from Norway. Single eaglets had been taken from eyries containing two chicks in Northern Norway and flown by the R.A.F. to Kinloss. They were then carried by road and sea, arriving on Rhum within twelve hours of being taken from their nests.

A quiet and patient man, John Love was ideal for dealing with the young birds and he showed me two of the chicks close to his bungalow. They were only five weeks old, beautiful and still with their fluffy brown down. They were unable to stand and had deeply hooked beaks and brown eyes, which only become "sunlit" with maturity. He fed them fish from his freezer and it was clear that they already regarded him as "mother".

To prevent "imprinting" he always handles the young eaglets as little as possible, and to emphasise the point he took me to see the three ten-week-old birds that were already fully feathered. To reach their cages we drove across the island along a rough, winding road past mountains, groups of red deer, and lochans where red-throated divers breed. The eagles were large and in excellent condition; he intended to keep them caged or tethered for a few weeks, and then to release them, putting out dumps to ensure a supply of food until they had learnt to look after themselves. Their diet in captivity consisted of frozen fish, gulls, crows and fresh mackerel.

The attempt at re-introduction will only be successful if the young eagles survive long enough to breed in the wild. For three days I saw no sign of wild birds, but on the fourth day I crossed the island with Peter Duncan, passing two stonechats (both birds and geologists) on the way.

It was hot and cloudless as we left the Land Rover by a lochan, where a stag had been cooling itself waist deep in water. Around the water were dragonflies with wings golden in the sunlight and damsel flies glowing brilliant red and blue, while beneath the surface were beetles and palmate newts. For two hours we walked along the rugged coast, on deer paths and trackless grass, stopping only to drink in a clear, cool stream. From high up, the shimmering Atlantic spread before us, the islands mapped out perfectly – Tiree, Muck, Eigg and to the north, the Hebrides. With cliffs and points the landscape was ideal for sea eagles and not unlike their native land. There were deer, a wild goat on a rocky ledge and pipits. Flowers shone through the grasses: orchids, eyebright, wild thyme, devil's bit scabious, lousewort, milkwort and delicately petal-led bog asphodel. Unhindered by the breeze butterflies flitted too: common blues, fritillaries, small heaths, large heaths and a solitary grayling. Only an occasional "cleg" (horse fly) ruined perfection.

We stopped by a loch, with rounded hills, scree and rock faces behind us; kittiwakes called and a red-breasted mer-ganser swam with her six new chicks. I lay in the grass, near anthills covered with flowering wild thyme. A common blue landed on pink flower heads, its deep, vivid wings held open, the same depth of colour as the sky. Conditions seemed ideal for the large blue; for many years rumours have persisted that the large blue butterfly is to be found on Rhum, and on such a day, when butterflies from a small colony could have been flying, it seemed a distinct possibility. We were the only two out on the island not studying rocks, and in such a remote place, for just a few days each year, it could be that the large blue still lives.

Sea eagle

My thoughts were interrupted when Peter called: "Eagle." High and wheeling in the clear blue sky was the unmistakable outline of an eagle, a fully mature sea eagle with large wings and a white wedge-shaped tail. Soon it was joined by another, before they glided away over a headland. Being mature birds, they had obviously been living free for several years and were completely wild. It was a wonderful place, and to add to it, a golden eagle flew by.★

On our return we found John Love had been fishing; he had caught twenty-four fresh mackerel for the eaglets. He was pleased, as the fish had arrived in the sea-loch a month earlier than the previous year. It had been a good day for everybody, except the mackerel.

★During the summer of 1981 the R.S.P.B. carried out a survey which revealed between twenty-four to twenty-six sea eagles living wild in the mainland and the Western Isles of Scotland.

Although it took me over three days to get just a brief glimpse of the sea eagles, my time on Rhum was not wasted, for it is a fascinating island. The permanent community numbers about twenty, involved in various conservation projects and in running the estate, which keeps Highland cattle and the unique Rhum pony, as well as having a tree nursery, for extensive tree planting is taking place.

Each week a few visitors arrive on day trips to see the castle and walk along nature trails. A doctor on the neighbouring island of Eigg visits when necessary, wearing a kilt; the dentist arrives twice a year, and the vicar steps ashore to take a service once a month, not on a Sunday, but a Wednesday. Occasionally even the Jehovah's Witnesses turn up to visit door to door.

The castle is a tribute to a bygone age. Sir John Betjeman wrote: "There can be few examples surviving in Great Britain of Edwardian splendour equal to the interior of Kinloch Castle. In time to come the castle will be a place of pilgrimage for all those who want to see how people lived in good King Edward's days." It was built in 1901–2 by Sir George Bullough, a wealthy Lancashire mill owner. His father, born in 1799, was sent to work in the mills at the age of seven, before making his fortune by inventing and manufacturing new spindles. Sir George inherited his father's empire and his main desire in life was to become a Scottish laird. So keen was he, that he offered the castle builders, over 300 of them, a bonus of 2d a day to wear kilts – an extremely draughty proposition. Once completed, he employed a piper to play the bagpipes along the terrace, in addition to his staff of forty-four.

The inside of the castle was just as unusual as the outside, for it was the most advanced house of its time, with marble-topped radiators supplying central heating, electricity, air-conditioning, and also double-glazing. Sir George, at the age of twenty-one, sailed round the world in his own boat, *Rhouma*, which he loaned to the government during the Boer War and the First World War to use as a hospital ship. A professional photographer travelled with him, and bound photograph albums record the journey. The castle's interior reflects the trip, with furnishings and decorations from Japan, China and India. On the floors lie animal skins, and in addition to the exotic, there are Chippendale chairs and four-poster beds. A library contains leather-bound books on travel, sport and wildlife, while the ballroom's elegance is enhanced by chandeliers, a minstrels' gallery and flashing lights, rather like an opulent early disco. To complete the comfort and entertainment of guests are a billiard table with instructions for "pool", a Steinway grand piano, and an orchestrion, built in 1902, and one of only two. The other was owned by Queen Victoria and is now in the London Piano Museum. Sir George remains on the island he loved, in a mausoleum in the southwest, overlooking the sea; he lived with style and went out with style, in a building resembling an ancient Greek temple.

Time seems suspended when the northern sun shines, as it wanders almost aimlessly across the sky, giving a long day. One warm, windy morning I walked along the southern side of Loch Scresort. In a plantation of larch, birch, chestnut and pine I met a Yorkshireman returning to the village. He was fat, sweating profusely and, even on Rhum, wearing a seafarer's cap: "It's great here, mate, ain't it? They tell me the boat's in this afternoon, the *Shearwater*. They say it's got a bar aboard; must get over there for a couple of pints. See you." He trundled on. I moved through a carpet of wood sorrel with white flowers and large clover-like leaves. The grassland had flowers and butterflies and the pebbles on the beach gave a brittle sound to the breaking waves. Small cliffs with horizontal grooves of softer rock were littered with shells, and screaming oystercatchers mobbed me. In Gaelic part of the southern shore is known as "Carn-an-Dobhrain Bhig" – cairn of the little otter. There were no otters to be seen, but the name carried the warm feeling that most people hold for the shy creature. It was an area of bogs and flowering cotton grass where the smell of new growth mingled with sea. Another blue butterfly landed on thyme, closed its wings and took in nectar; a family of small wrens burst from a clump of bracken. Gorges and waterfalls made passage difficult and the streams flowed out over white sand and into a clean, rich sea. A heron circled very high to avoid mobbing by gulls and close to the shore a seal rolled over in lethargy; its drowsiness spread as I sat surrounded by foxgloves and warm air.

Common blue on thyme

Another journey into the heart of Rhum took me to where the Manx shearwaters nest. As I walked through the wooded grounds of the castle a late cuckoo called, but the small hydro-electric turbine in a stream was almost silent. It supplied direct current to run the island's lights without dirt, smoke, noise or radio-active waste. The power was not sufficient for washing machines and vacuum cleaners, but it did allow battery television sets to be recharged through the light sockets during the night.

High up by a stream a dipper flew; I had not realised that they lived so high. The valleys were wide and green, with deer, pipits and orchids. Higher still I came to a raised, rock-strewn valley, where two "stonechats" worked with their metallic hammers. Only a few hundred feet below the summit I still had not seen a shearwater's burrow, and assumed that I was in the wrong area. I began to climb the final peak of Hallival, rising to 2,500 feet above sea level. Then, on the final steep slopes, the holes began; thousands of them, hollowed beneath rocks and scraped out in shale. Unlike Skomer, there were no rabbits, and all the burrows had been excavated by the birds themselves. As a result the holes were shorter than on Skomer and the incubating shearwaters could be seen inside. It was a marvellous place to have a nest, one day giving a view of valleys, lochs, the open sea, and the scent of flowering thyme; the next enveloped in mist.

Some visitors to Rhum are not lucky with the weather and the island is known for its dampness and high rainfall. It was on a wet afternoon that I had an experience to match the view of the eagles. Heavy clouds had closed in for the day and the neighbouring islands had been lost in sheets of rain. Walking on the wet rocks and through saturated long grass next to the beach, on the northern side of the loch, was difficult: I was soaked and to add to my discomfort midges were biting hungrily. The tide was falling, leaving pools and boulders brown with seaweed. I glanced up at movement that merged with the browns of the shore to see an animal with a long tail heading for the sea. The otter had not seen me as it splashed into the water, to swim along the surface to floating weed; there it dived, emerging seconds later to shake the water from its head. Swimming slowly on it dived again. Each time it dived the ripples spread and faded; it really was "the little otter", unhurried, wild and free. The midges and dampness went unnoticed as I watched; at last I had seen the animal that had remained elusive for so long. For me it was the end of a personal quest and I was not disappointed by what I felt and

Otter

saw. The otter worked its way slowly round a headland and then I walked back to the house; curlews were feeding at the low water mark and a male eider flew. I felt sorrow that such an attractive creature should have been driven from lowland Britain by pollution, disturbance and lack of concern.

Despite its position, Rhum has not avoided graffiti, and much of it reflected the isolation and the weather:

> Are you allowed to kill midges
> On a National Nature Reserve?
>
> Midges are like Space Invaders
> The more you kill the more they attack.
>
> If you hate sex and booze and a decent night's
> sleep then this is the place for you.
>
> Think yourself lucky
> Some people live here all the year round.

Underneath "Dump nuclear waste on Rhum", a more perceptive visitor had written: "I'm afraid I disagree, I like Rhum." To me, after eagles and the otter, Rhum will always be a very special place.

On board below deck, returning to Mallaig, in rain and a rough sea, a little old lady was drinking coffee. She had been staying at the castle: "It was wonderful, I have wanted to visit it for years. My father worked for Sir George Bullough. He was a good employer and provided a lot of work. I don't begrudge him a penny." She was quickly brought back to twentieth-century standards – the only spoon with which to stir her coffee was plastic and lying in a dirty ashtray.

13

Islands and Oil

On my return to Aberdeen, the faceless men at the end of telephones still could not fulfil the hopes raised by B.P. in London for a visit to an oil rig. Instead, I caught the P&O car ferry, an expensive exercise, to the Shetlands. Over many years the islands have had a romantic attraction for me, and I wanted to see how traditional island life had come to terms with the advent of oil. Roger Tidman and his camera had already arrived at the docks, having obtained a lift in a long-distance lorry from Norfolk.

The M.V. *St. Clair* was larger than expected, to cope with the gales and high seas that often sweep the vast area of open sea where the Atlantic Ocean meets the Norwegian and North Seas. The passengers were oilmen, Shetlanders returning home, a few holidaymakers and a handful of "twitchers". The sea was calm, and as we moved steadily along the coast, oil rigs and platforms could be seen still under construction. Schoolchildren crowded around the space invaders machines and one-armed-bandits, pushing money in at a startling rate, and corpulent, beer-swilling Scotsmen, the type that seems to wear half-hitched trousers specifically designed for stomachs to hang over, were much in evidence. A punk rocker, already out of fashion, sported tight tartan trousers and a leather jacket bearing the contradiction "Anarchy and Peace". He had a safety pin through his cheek, evidently an optional extra, for occasionally he would remove it for reasons that were not obvious, unless such appendages get metal-fatigue. There were respectable ladies in flat shoes and tweeds, and a man in sunglasses, the lenses of which were so dark that every time he looked out of the window he had to lift them to his forehead.

As soon as land had disappeared the "twitchers" were busy

scanning the sea for signs of bird life. An exception sat close by, like me staking his claim for a night's rest on the seats, rather than pay still more for a cabin. He was an apprentice from Leicester on his way north hoping to see the albatross and various other rarities, for a good "twitch". On his way back he intended to visit a stretch of coast near Aberdeen to see king eiders and Steller's eiders: "Then I'll nip down to Cley to see what's about. [He was a frequenter of Nancy's tea room.] It'll take about a week and then I'll be back at work Monday morning." Apart from the ferry he was hitching lifts and living rough: "Earlier I went with some mates to the Hebrides to see corncrakes. We heard one in a field, so we moved in from three sides and managed to flush it." He did not regard the Rhum sea eagles as an authentic "tick": "They're Norwegian; you can't count them. You can't have a sea eagle with a ring on it, so if they breed you can forget their young as well." I asked him how he would react if he saw a sea eagle that was too far away for a ring to be visible. This presented him with a major personal crisis and he claimed not to know what he would do. I suspect he would seize his pen, and by "sea eagle" enter "√".

To accompany the Scotsmen's heavy drinking, a "cabaret" was provided in the form of two rather bored looking musicians. Things improved when a pair of buskers were invited to perform; they were on their way to spend the rest of the summer on the islands, one with a guitar and the other with a tin whistle and a mandolin. They played together very well although they had only recently teamed up. One came from Northern Ireland where he had tired of working in a car factory, and the other, with fair hair and sad eyes, had just obtained a university degree, but did not want to use it.

We passed Fair Isle, bare and bleak; it seemed incredible that the first bustard taken from Porton Down should have arrived at such a desolate place. At dawn a few "twitchers" were already active. Fulmars were following the boat and gradually other birds were seen; gannets, guillemots and finally great skuas, known in the world of competitive birdwatching as "bonxies". The first islands appeared, low, green and bathed in mist. Fulmars were everywhere, more common than gulls.

As we approached Lerwick, islands lay on both sides of the ship, the more distant having towering cliffs and great caverns, arches and pillars of rock, facing the variable moods of the sea.

Lerwick was a small town, with grey stone houses and slate roofs, that looked distinctly Scandinavian against the low hills. The islands were owned by Norway and Denmark for hundreds of years, passing into Scottish hands in about 1468 when Christian I of Denmark gave them to James III of Scotland as a pledge for the unpaid dowry of his daughter. Little did he know that he was giving away millions of gallons of oil at the same time, so that Britain's oil wealth is a total historical accident.

The people, too, had a definite Scandinavian air, and their accents were much softer than on mainland Scotland. It was cool and overcast for early July, and on the quay most people wore warm Shetland jumpers. Fishing boats were unloading their catches in the harbour; I expected to see large fish such as cod, haddock and mackerel. Instead they had been catching small sand eels for a local factory to convert into fish meal. One trawler was emptying its haul into a large boat from Norway which wanted 1,000 tons for Norwegian mink farms. It seemed an appalling waste.

A larger trawler was preparing to leave in search of white fish. In a thick, patterned jumper, a crewman was checking crates of beer: "We'll be gone about ten days. Fish stocks have dropped right down in recent years – it's the Common Market that's to blame for the state of fishing. British fishermen are checked and made to keep to their quotas – the French ignore them and nothing's done. Recently large shoals of herring were back. They are banned,* but French trawlers were going in to their home ports overloaded. One local fisherman caught some by 'mistake' – he took them to Denmark. The authorities were going to 'do' him, but there was a foreign trawler around that looked just like him and they didn't get the

---

*A few weeks later the ban on herring was lifted and a quota system implemented. It did not alter the belief in Shetland that foreign boats fish illegally and ignore quotas.

number. He's made between £50,000 and £80,000 – good luck to him. If the French get away with it why can't he?" Such feelings were not surprising, for in the referendum on the Common Market in 1975 the Shetlanders voted to leave.

Away from the harbour Lerwick was an attractive town, with a population of over 7,000, by far the largest of the islands' settlements. An officer at the Seaman's Mission had noticed change: "A few years ago the only shops in Lerwick sold groceries and Shetland crafts; now they have videos, hi-fis and all mod-cons. In Lerwick too, you pay Lerwick prices like in all capitals."

A schoolmaster in the town, Jim Tate, was vice-chairman of the growing Shetland Movement, an organisation that cut across normal political boundaries. He welcomed me into his comfortable semi-detached house, and almost before I had sat down he said: "Have a wee dram", but that was the only thing he had in common with Scotland. He was middle-aged, informed and concerned over the future: "Shetlanders are a proud, independent people. We want our islands to retain their identities, but we also want greater autonomy. We don't intend to make a unilateral declaration of independence, we want to stay British, but we do want more control over our affairs such as oil and fishing. And, of course, it's not Scotland's oil. For if they say it's not British oil, then it's Shetland's oil. When Shetland became Scottish the landowners became Scots and the folk memories of the people are still clear. Some had grandmothers evicted. Then they sent ministers of the Church over who were dour and hard; as if that was not bad enough there were real cultural and class differences. People still say: 'We never got anything from Scotland except bad meal and greedy ministers.' That's why they want nothing to do with the Scottish National Party or regional government with Scotland.

"There are few links with Scandinavia and the Faroes these days, but we do feel different from the rest of Britain and we retain an emotional attachment to Scandinavia. We like our individuality, and it has not changed because of oil. Only the prices have changed and people are better off.

"But we must get adequate returns from oil, and our fishing

must be protected. Fishing has always attracted the locals, including many of my contemporaries, because it contains elements of gambling and adventure. We should have larger fishing limits and tighter controls. The Norwegians started the problems using purse nets and everybody else followed suit, with echo meters – they work like huge vacuum cleaners. We must be able to look after our little patch as part of a bigger world. The whole can not be healthy if the parts are unhealthy."

On the outskirts of the town were yards full of pipes as well as much new development, all linked to the oil companies. Then came open country, a gently rolling landscape of deep lochs and parallel ridges of land. The grass was green, a vivid green, for during the summer it photosynthesises twenty-three hours a day. The colour only faded on the higher moors where heather and peat dominated. In the valleys were crofts and small fields divided by stone walls and wire fences. A large inland loch had a life and rhythm all of its own; buttercups growing in profusion around its edge and yellow irises with bright fresh "flags"; terns calling, seagulls crying, ducks and divers feeding, and a merganser swimming with her new brood.

All the islands, it seemed, were washed in mist and moisture-laden air, helping to maintain the lush green. Yet it was somehow a barren landscape, which I found more desolate than anything I had seen before, from Dartmoor to the Western Isles, and even including desert in Africa. An impression resulting from the lack of trees; the cool wind; the wild cries of the birds, with not a song bird to be heard, and the higher land with rows of dark peats and peat diggings, giving the land the wrinkled, wizened look of extreme old age.

Using the ferries to get from the main island of Shetland – Mainland – to the islands cost just 70p a time, for the car and two passengers. The ferryman could not understand it: "The prices keep going up and the fares keep going down." It was one of the advantages brought by oil revenue. Yell was the first island, followed by Fetlar with even smaller islands, seals and black guillemots in the blue wind-whipped water in between. Fetlar is just fifteen square miles, with a population of nearly 1,200, but it has sights and a feeling that cannot be forgotten: two red-throated divers feeding fish to their young; a snowy owl taking to the air on large white wings; birds appeared from nowhere, to harass it in flight – curlews, whimbrels, oystercatchers, lapwings and angry arctic skuas. At a large loch surrounded by flowers and small rushes, red-necked phalaropes fed surrounded by flecks of white foam from the waves. They were such pretty, dainty little birds, yet so close and unafraid, picking tiny black insects from rushes and a beetle from a buttercup. We were only three or four yards from them as they worked their way along the shore. Further out an eider duck and two young floated on the choppy water, the ducklings diving to feed. In marked contrast to the phalaropes, a wheatear with young called in agitation from a stone wall.

The next day was calm and still as we walked along a sandy bay towards a heather-covered ridge. A great skua was flying above the moorland when a small, determined bird of prey, a fraction of its size, flew up to drive it away. It was a merlin, streamlined and apparently fearless. High-pitched calling behind us signalled the arrival of the male, even smaller, about the size of a blackbird, and carrying a kill. She flew towards him and their talons touched as he passed the dead pipit to her before they both dropped down into heather where they must have had young.

At the side of the bay high cliffs overlooked small coves; in one, on a rock table exposed by the tide, and dripping with

Common seal

seaweed, lay three common seals and two pups, one nuzzling its mother for milk. The young were almost black, giving them the local name of black seals. The middle cow was dappled black and grey; she saw me high above and anxiety filled her dark, soft eyes. As she snorted they plunged into the sea; ripples and a trail of bubbles diving deep into the blue-green water were all that remained. Fulmars were nesting on grassy cliffside ledges and the carcass of a Manx shearwater lay discarded on the path. "*Puffinus puffinus*" had reached Shetland too.

A bearded fisherman with a soft, warm accent invited us into his cottage, where his wife and daughter made Shetland jumpers, his wife using needles and his daughter a machine. He and his daughter claimed to be "Shetlanders", but his wife thought they were both dreamers and was proud to be "British". He fished and farmed, his hundred acres producing grass, neeps and black tatties (potatoes with a dark mauve skin); he kept ponies, sheep, and a house cow, cut peat and salted fish, strings of which were drying above the stove. They were virtually self-sufficient.

Living off the land and from the sea, he was a good naturalist, calling the birds by their Shetland names: the puffin became a tammy norie, the great skua a bonxie, and the Manx shearwater, not a *puffinus puffinus*, but a "cockasootie"; at last the perfect onomatopoeic name and a more accurate sound than "cup o' cocoa". In fact the name was even more local than Shetland, being a Fetlar name.

He often saw otters and heard them whistle, and one night a cub moved so close to him that he picked it up. Years ago he trapped them with gins and could get £2.10sh. a skin, but he could not kill them now. He thought there were too many seals, but they did little harm: "What I can't stand are the bonxies. If an eider duck has eleven ducklings the bonxies will take them one by one, leaving just one or two. I've even seen them take a full-grown duck. They drown them, flying over them, making them dive until they are exhausted and they can get on their backs. I shoot them sometimes, even if they are protected. I have to shoot sheep too, if they get stuck down 'cloughs' [inaccessible parts of cliffs]. They get badly bruised when they fall and we have to feed them to the dogs." We were offered tea, cakes, and admired a variety of jumpers and sheep skins. At eleven p.m. more visitors arrived; snipe were still drumming at midnight and by five a.m. the sun was already well up and warm.

Yell is a much larger island, eighty-three square miles, but that, too, had its appeal; more red-throated divers with young, seals fighting, and a flock of golden plovers. In a rough sea, close to the beach, the whiskered head of an otter emerged looking straight at me before diving again out of view. The village stores were large, selling a wide range of goods from sugarlumps to toothbrushes and tins of paint. One evening villagers packed into a local hall where a group of Faroese singers, musicians, and dancers performed, the fiddlers getting a knowing response from the audience as the girls, with long skirts, shawls and ready smiles, danced; sadly, since it was Sunday, the audience was not allowed to join in.

Bobby Tulloch was one of the organisers, the Shetland representative of the R.S.P.B.. He was a stocky, bearded man with blue eyes, whose appearance confirmed his island ancestry. Originally he had been a baker, until it became cheaper to import mass-produced loaves from Scotland. Because of his knowledge of the islands' wildlife he then began his work with birds. Many of his schoolfriends went whaling or became merchant seamen, and even he would like to have joined a whaling ship for a year just to see the Antarctic.

His understanding and contacts enable him to give an overall view of what is happening throughout the islands: "Eider ducks are experiencing a bad crash at the moment. They receive a hard time from the skuas. It is difficult to know what to do, for it is a protected bird against a protected bird. I'm inclined to let nature take its course. The trouble is it's always difficult to ascertain man's influence. This year there are warnings from the Lofoten Islands off Northern Norway, for puffins have been found dead and starving, with chicks dead in the burrows. It could be the fishing of sand eels. Previously the big fish had been over-fished resulting in more sand eels, as their predators had gone. So puffins had never had it so good. Now sand eels are being caught. Here, some are sent to Denmark and returned as fish-flavoured bacon. We could be facing a serious turning point. There has to be a more scientific approach to all this with more controls. The fisherman would be happy because he knows that when a species is finished, it's finished for everybody. Part of the problem is the E.E.C. fishing policy which is a mess; before too long there will be French trawlers scraping shellfish from our beaches. They must be stopped."

Nonetheless he was quite optimistic about the future: "Things are looking good at the moment and the early Esso spill at the oil terminal found out the loopholes in the system that should have been put right by now. The problem is that the oil companies have set up committees which make you feel important, using the best public relations brains available. But the threat of a major disaster is always hanging over us like Damocles' sword – another Torrey Canyon, a pipe line ripped open, or a taxi-driver captaining a Greek tanker with the help of his school atlas. If it happens in the summer it will be the end."

The physical end of Shetland is Unst, the most northerly island in Britain, about 260 miles from Aberdeen and 650 miles from London, but less than 200 miles from Norway. Further north than Leningrad and Labrador, it lies on the same latitude as Cape Farewell in Greenland and the Kenai Peninsula in Alaska. It covers forty-seven square miles with a population of just over 1,000; its highest hill rises to nearly 1,000 feet, and it claims the unofficial British wind speed record at 177 m.p.h.* The name of "Unst" is of interest in itself, for it could have derived from "ern's isle" (eagle isle), as "erne" is an alternative name for sea eagle.

At Uyeasound I stopped for petrol at a solitary pump outside the village shop. Ironically Shetland petrol is the most expensive in the country, for although millions of gallons of oil are pumped to the islands each year, it is all crude and unrefined.

By a dilapidated castle a crofter with a wind-burnt face and a woolly hat was working his sheep dogs, and again, im-

*Another claim for Unst is 202 m.p.h.

mediately friendly like so many of the islanders, he invited us in to drink tea and to talk. The bungalow was sparsely furnished, with lino on the floor, but warm, heated by a peat-fuelled stove: "We've got sixty acres of sheep, ponies and potatoes and I do a little long-line fishing as well. We've got two sons but there's not enough money for them. One has become a joiner; the other wanted to fish but he couldn't make a living so he joined the merchant navy. It's the purse nets that finished the fishing, not the seals; they prefer conger eels and fish like that."

His wife brought out her knitting, traditional Shetland patterns on jumpers, jerseys and shawls. She knitted with three needles, sticking one into a leather belt containing a pouch with holes: "One visitor who watched me expected the wool to come out of the holes," she said. "The pouches were made from quill feathers in the old days and you could stick the needle in just the same. The young ones don't do as much knitting as we used to. At one time, too, many Shetland girls became nurses; now they get more money putting gravy on a plate. The oil has given them more money but people aren't happier."

Bill fetched some peats for the fire: "I cut them myself; they come out just like butter. We still use seaweed as fertiliser on the land and the ponies go down to the shore to eat it. A lot of the ponies are sent to England and Scotland, because they gradually increase in size with the better conditions down there, and so the English like to fall back on proper island stock. We improve the grazing by putting artificial fertiliser on the heather, which kills it; then it's so wet and warm we just sprinkle grass seed on the surface and it grows." When the two spoke together their dialect became so broad that it was impossible to understand; they called it "Shetlandic".

They were content with island life: "It's quiet and peaceful, and if we get ill we often treat ourselves, even though we've got a really good doctor. Oatmeal, cream of tartar, and ginger mixed with hot water can be taken for 'flu, and whisky, hot water and sugar – 'a toddy', for colds."

Not only did an elderly neighbour knit, but she also spun her own wool using her mother's spinning wheel: "It's nearly a hundred years old and I always use local wool which comes from Shetland sheep crossed with Cheviots." She spun quickly and expertly, with sensitive hands, to produce a wool so fine that it looked like cotton, but it was much softer to the touch. Her knitting was even more remarkable; using three steel needles and a knitting belt she produced a knitted lace, so fine that it looked like crochet or tatting and a finished shawl passed easily through her wedding ring. I had expected these skills to have been long lost, and was reassured to see such patience linked to a love of beautiful things.

Along the track in a croft by the sea an old man was working in his garden. His trousers were hitched up and rolled over at the top, in the absence of a belt. He was unshaven and puffing, but proud of his work: "I'm over eighty and have you ever seen a garden with rows so straight?" He pointed to a cabbage-like plant: "That's Shetland kale; some fill out with a heart, but I like the outside leaves, they are nearest the sun. I've got the most fertile garden on the island because I use plenty of good muck from the byre [cow shed]."

He had been born in the croft. His father had been in the navy, earning £3 to £4 a month, before becoming a fisherman: "He went in the old herring boats, six to a boat; it was hard and many were drowned and injured. But the fish have gone; it's foreign boats that have done it. It's not the seals. When I was a boy there were far more seals, because that was before they were hunted for skins. They take a lot of blame unfairly, like the whitrits."

"What's a whitrit?" I asked.

He was as confused as I was: "Why, a whitrit's a whitrit. We've always called them whitrits." Later I was told that a whitrit was a stoat, introduced to Shetland in the seventeenth century, and found mostly on Mainland. The word whitrit probably comes from "white rat", as northern stoats get an ermine coat during the winter.

He had a wealth of memories recalling an island way of life that had almost disappeared: "At one time there was a fiddle in virtually every house and fifty years ago you could get a shawl for £3.10sh. There were twelve pairs of Clydesdales [cart horses] on the island then; they could do everything except talk to you. The Shetland ponies were used for taking home the peats and for harrowing and things like that. We worked Highland Garrons, too – they were a strong little pony.

"But times change. My nephew now works at Sullom Voe on a tug, looking after tankers. That's where I was in the navy during the war, looking after ships and Sunderland flying boats. We were often attacked by German planes; if they couldn't find any ships they bombed Sullom Voe. Oil's been good for Shetland, it's provided jobs, but too many have gone to people from the south and too many people have been taken away from the soil. We need the oil, but we don't need home rule. We are just rocks in the middle of the North Sea and there's not enough to keep the place going."

He was satisfied with his lot, and from his garden and croft he looked over a wide bay, with rocks, a pebble-littered beach and a deep azure sea. As I left, he hitched up his trousers, giving them another twist around the waist, and moved with his hoe from his rows of Shetland kale to the equally straight rows of potatoes.

It seemed almost an idyllic life, and, for me, with warmer weather and trees the situation would have been perfect. The people all seemed remarkably content, friendly and healthy. I wondered if their way of life was reflected in the absence of ulcers and illnesses caused by stress, so I telephoned the island's doctor. I received a shock, for the most northern doctor in the British Isles had the broadest possible Pakistani accent. A pleasant and friendly man, he invited me to visit his house.

Croft

By his front door was a notice: "T.N.T. – The New Testa-
ment is dangerous – read it." He appeared smiling, and
ushered me inside. His three small children were playing
various games and his wife fetched the inevitable pot of tea and
home-made cakes. His arrival on Unst had been unplanned:
"My background is atheist and Mohammedan. I studied
medicine at Cardiff and I decided that I wanted to serve my
own people and went to work in a hospital in Pakistan. But life
was too cheap. I performed 10,000 eye operations; they got
better and paid their money without even saying thank you,
which would have been the best payment. One offered to pay
me by shooting anybody I did not like. In Britain it's so
different, everybody is respected, not just the British but
everybody." Love intervened in Pakistan, where his wife, a
Cameron, was working as a sister for a missionary society in
the hospital where he was the medical superintendent. They
married six years ago, and after coming to Britain for a holiday
they stayed on: "It's been marvellous on Unst; people have
accepted us as if we had lived here always: we've fitted in like
drops of water in the sea. When I first came over on the ferry I
paid my fare. Then they found out who I was and insisted that
I took my money back. It's so peaceful here, there's no crime,
no mugging and I never lock my car or my house; the only
thing I lock is the medicine cupboard. Everybody just walks
in. A man down the road left his shears on the verge. They
stayed there for days, nobody took them, then he remembered
where he left them. It's a real community with everybody
helping everybody else. Last year at Christmas when my wife
asked if there were any lonely people, she was told, 'There are
no lonely people on Unst'."

Not only does he like the inhabitants, but he finds the island
beautiful: "I have driven off the road three or four times
watching the sun set, and have had to be pulled back on to the
road. But the surprising thing is, the islanders are not insular,
they are very knowledgeable. With their televisions and radios
they know what is going on in England and the world. But
how many people on mainland Britain have heard of Unst, yet
alone know what is going on here? In the winter we have
evening classes, including the fiddle and keep-fit. We have

discussions, too and the people are widely read and articulate. In the summer we can start playing tennis at twelve-fifteen at night, and when there is a wedding the shops and schools close early. It's wonderful."

The door opened and a nurse with a broad Yorkshire accent walked in. She had been up all night. The doctor had been called out in the early hours and she had accompanied the expectant mother to Lerwick hospital, where she gave birth within forty minutes of arrival. The journey from Unst to the hospital had taken two hours, most of it by air ambulance, with a former Red Arrows pilot at the controls.

The doctor was a fine man and confirmed that there were few ulcers and signs of stress on the island. He took me down into the village of Baltasound to see an old fisherman whose son had got the only full-time fishing boat on Unst. The old man, wearing glasses and a beret, was making a murderous rat-trap, with weights and exposed nails. Again he talked of over-fishing changing island life: "Why, I've seen Baltasound with so many boats that you could have walked from one side to the other over the decks. If herring used to get up a gully the locals would even get the nets off their little haystacks to scoop out the fish. Two nights ago some lads with long lines got several boxes of herring, the first for a long time, but the next day they had been frightened off by a 'herring whale' – we often see whales go by. Lobsters and crabs have gone too."

Around his walls were several fiddles; he took one down and played a number of old Shetland tunes expertly: "Some of the local youngsters don't like the traditional music. They prefer pop music and all that shite; but Shetland music's best."

With one son owning the only fishing trawler and another the hotel, the family seemed to be taking over the island. The hotel bar was full of personnel from an R.A.F. tracking station; smooth men with tinted glasses trying to impress, and heavily made-up wives sampling the most expensive cock-tails. I preferred the islanders.

In the north of the island, between moorland and a large loch, we set up camp next to a small stream, with marsh marigolds and cuckoo flowers still as fresh as a southern spring. Six red-throated divers flew in with necks outstretched and fast wing-beats, calling at first like far off geese. They were graceful birds lying low in the water, looking as primitive as their surroundings. It was a long late dusk with bands of flamingo pink clouds colouring the water. Curlews bubbled in the fading light.

We woke to a bright sunny morning and walked northwards over moorland. A pair of curlews watched anxiously and great skuas with nests nearby dive-bombed half-heartedly. For such large, tyrannical birds their efforts seemed feeble and cowardly. Gradually we climbed through heather and peat to Hermaness, an astounding coastline of tumbling cliffs with ledges, sheer rock faces, grassy slopes and clumps of flowers, red campion, bird's foot trefoil and beds of thrift (sea pink). They overlooked circling gannets, fulmars and kittiwakes, gleaming white against the backcloth of the gently swelling sea, 600 feet below. Dark birds with "whirring" wings joined them, guillemots, razorbills and puffins; there were tens of thousands of birds and it seemed remarkable that none collided in mid-air. Suddenly, through the noise of surf and the cacophony of countless cries came the clear distinctive song of a solitary skylark. Skuas drifted in air currents at cliff-top level and sheep grazed close to the edge, some on grassy banks surrounded by seemingly inaccessible rocks.

Westwards the cliffs fell away to platforms and skerries of bare granite, while ahead the sea stretched out in endless blue, uninterrupted until arctic ice.

Roger was well acquainted with the area: "Well, you had better get your 'tick', hadn't you? If you want to see the albatross you have to look over the edge of that rock jutting out over there." I crawled warily on to the small, grass-covered overhang, with a drop of several hundred feet on three sides: "Go on, look over the edge."

All I could see were gannets and their fluffy young: "I can't see an albatross."

"Hardly surprising," he replied. "I was just seeing if you had really grown into a 'twitcher'. The albatross is down there," he said, pointing to a more easily viewed part of the cliff.

Razorbill

He enjoyed his joke, and I crawled back with weak knees to a safer spot and looked down. There a solitary, black-browed albatross sat on an eggless nest, in the wrong hemisphere, surrounded by gannets. It was preening and looked at ease, for it had spent several summers at Hermaness; yet it should have been in antarctic latitudes, nesting during our winter.

The whole coast was spectacular. A sheep walk took us zig-zagging down through rocks and pink-flowering thrift, using ledges and footholds that looked almost sheer as soon as they were above us. The path must have been centuries old and

worn by generations of sheep; in places it was several inches
deep with wool caught on the sides. Puffins watched from a
few yards, with little fear, some with their beaks full of sand
eels for their underground young. We climbed down to a
grassy bank where a great pyramid of rock jutted into the sea;
the air was pungent with the smell of stale bird droppings. On
one side was sheer rock with horizontal ledges crowded with
guillemots and their young, downy, vulnerable and trusting.
Some of the adults were "bridled", with a peculiar white line
around the eyes as if they were wearing spectacles. On other
ledges gannets were crowded, with nests of weed and torn fish
nets; large, noisy and white, they lived up to their name of
"solan goose". Two shags with vivid emerald eyes perched on
a rock, and another gannet landed with a beak full of vegetation. Across the small bay was an island, a natural arch of
rock, and that too was white with gannets. Two-thirds of the
world's gannet population breed around Britain's coast, and,
with the fulmar, it is one of the few birds experiencing a rise in
numbers.

Away from the gannets and guillemots great slabs of rock
fell with a gentler slope into the sea. As I clambered over
lichen-covered boulders I passed too close to an incubating
fulmar; it spat a white, oily substance at me, but missed. I sat in
the hot sun at the water's edge, watching strands of weed
trailing and waving in the clear, sighing sea; then without
warning gannets began diving after fish just off the shore.
Wheeling effortlessly on long, black-tipped wings they suddenly plunged headlong after underwater movement.

I walked back along the coast, past the offshore *Muckle
Flugga* lighthouse built by Robert Louis Stevenson's family
firm. At a headland, an arctic tern dive-bombed me more
aggressively than the skuas, until a fulmar cruising by, veered
from its path to drive it away. It resumed its course along the
clifftops almost as if it had not liked such disturbance on a
peaceful day.

There is no doubt that Hermaness ranks among the great
wildlife areas of the world; the presence of oil and the fishing
for sand eels make it also one of the most threatened.

Returning from Unst to Yell and then to Mainland, Sullom Voe looked insignificant, just a few storage tanks and pipes. On driving along the Voe Road, however, the full impact of oil became clear. It was a huge terminal covering 1,000 acres of land, in addition to jetties for tankers in a wide "voe" (viking for loch). It was at Sullom Voe that the tanker *Esso Bernica* crashed into a jetty on December 30th, 1978, losing nearly 1,200 tons of oil and giving Britain its first oiled otters. Sheep, too, were oiled as they fed on the shore.

The figures for the site give an indication of its size, complexity and importance. It takes oil ashore from the Brent and Ninian pipelines which in turn take oil from seven North Sea fields. The two pipelines each have a nominal daily capacity of 1,000,000 barrels, the pipes being just thirty-six inches in diameter, with one-inch thick walls and surrounded by two inches of concrete. There are sixteen storage tanks with each one capable of holding 21,000,000 gallons of oil, enough to get the average family car to and from the moon twelve times. 1,000,000 tonnes of materials were transported to the site simply for construction. The aim of the terminal is to make crude oil safe, by the removal of gases, to store it, and then to dispatch it in tankers for refining and processing elsewhere. When in full production it will take up to 800 tankers a year and the water is deep enough for vessels of up to 300,000 tons.

Arriving at the guarded gate I met with success at last, for a B.P. representative was there, as arranged. B.P. is one of about thirty oil companies involved at Sullom Voe. My guide was understandably proud of what had been created in such an isolated and desolate area: "We had over 7,000 workers here during construction and there was a real pioneer spirit and feeling of excitement. It was a modular construction like a giant Mecanno set. Now there are about 400 people working on site plus 180 involved with security. About forty per cent of them are Shetlanders. The islands do well out of it. The council owns the site and has a fifty per cent interest in the facilities such as the unloading jetties. It gets 2p a ton through the terminal and runs the ports and harbours, charging the tankers who use the facilities. The ratable value is £52 million per year. The rest of Shetland is £3 million. Over the next twenty years they will get at least £78 million, which is not bad for 23,000 people. Then of course it gives Britain £5 million a day benefit to the balance of payments.

"There are problems and there are bound to be some spills, but we think we have things under control. We can shut the whole place down in eight seconds. Part of the difficulties with the tankers is the weather. When the *Esso Bernica* broke loose the wind changed 180° and increased eighty-five knots in twenty minutes. Then the pipelines being trawled up is another possible danger, but that could be controlled quite quickly."

A company Range Rover took us round the site, a conglomeration of tanks, chimneys of up to 350 feet and a general complexity of pipes. A huge 200,000 ton Shell tanker, made in Japan, was loading at the jetty. "We are very strict and fifty to sixty items are checked on every tanker from the time the pilot gets on board. If anything was wrong they would not be allowed near the terminal." The water looked clear and clean; in fact it looked better than the average holiday beach.

In exactly the same way that natural phenomena induce feelings of awe, man's creations can also inspire; the problems arise when they cannot be controlled, or divorced from the motives of greed and power.

The Range Rover sped off towards Lerwick and we went for lunch at a farmhouse converted into a pub. The lounge resembled a northern drinking hall – basic, with plain chairs and tables engulfed in cigarette smoke. The room was full of overweight Scottish labourers drinking beer and whisky. They talked in broad Scottish accents, with foul words outnumbering normal words two or three to one; if such sentences were analysed they would be obscene, impossible and totally meaningless.

The public bar was less crowded, with a juke box, a one-armed-bandit, and pool – a game for dull minds and one of the most boring ever invented. Chips came with everything on the menu, served mechanically by a pale barmaid without a smile. Also having lunch was a man from Dumbarton who worked on security and oil leaks: "Working four days on and four days off." He arrived initially for the money: "I was building my own house back home. Now, because of unemployment down there I can't get a job so I'm stuck. I live in a council house here with three other blokes. My wife and little girl were here too, but they've gone back as the wife's expecting again. It means I've got to commute backwards and forwards. I'll have to get shares in P&O and travel at half price. The trouble up here is the weather. My daughter couldn't understand why it was always cold and raining and would cry because she wanted to play outside. Then there's nothing for the women to do apart from walk a mile and a half to the shop. Some of the blokes are getting over £300 a week and a few of the women are making £130 a week cleaning. It's all right for them, but so few women can work."

Back at Lerwick it was cold and wet. In the early evening gull-trailing trawlers were returning with their catches of sand eels. The two buskers were pleased, for they had been asked to perform later, in a local pub. They played to people eating scampi and chips and drinking lager; it was respectable and quiet, and after each number came a smattering of light applause.

The young barman was not dismayed: "As soon as we call 'time' we'll do better for them." He led us through the centre of town to a large back-room bar. It was warm, with bodies, smoke and the smell of beer, crammed with Norwegian fishermen, oilmen and locals. The buskers soon started to play and alcohol encouraged clapping and cheering: "This is better," the barman smiled. "Shetland's good for parties and dope. This is one of the major routes for dope going to mainland Britain." At the end of a late evening, a woolly Shetland hat was passed around and the buskers made several pounds.

My last day in the islands was windy with broken cloud. The M.V. *St. Clair* had docked and already a large lorry containing live sheep had parked nearby; a sad way for Britain and Europe to receive its mutton. We decided to visit the small 700-acre island of Noss, close to Lerwick, and a National Nature Reserve. In the narrow sound separating Noss from the island of Bressay, eight trawlers were ploughing their furrows through the spray-topped waves. The water was clear, deep blue and edged with jagged moving turquoise.

The boatman – a graduate working for the summer – arrived with his inflatable dinghy. It was an island of moods and changes; first moorland with great and arctic skuas diving. The smaller, more streamlined arctic skuas attacked with much greater speed and accuracy, causing me to duck on several occasions. Then, low vertical cliffs topped with crumbling rock; oystercatchers flew as their young sought refuge and ringed plovers ran quickly on clockwork legs. Around narrow inlets fulmars nested among sea pinks and on rocks were a few black guillemots – tysties – velvet black with white wings; striped guillemot would have made a more appropriate name. They were beautiful birds made more attractive by their crimson beaks and legs. Two, in an act of affection, stretched up and opened their beaks to reveal equally crimson throats.

Gannet fishing

The furthest and highest point of the island was the Noup of Noss, with a vertical drop of nearly 600 feet. It was like a giant fortress against the sea, with weathered sandstone creating ledges and corrugations where thousands of gannets and auks nested; the air was alive with parent birds flying to feed themselves and their young. Great skuas wheeled high above, and then for the first time I saw their piracy. From clifftop level a bird began to fall, diving and accelerating as it fell, veering right and left to follow its selected victim. It plunged hundreds of feet to make a guillemot disgorge its food as it took evasive action. One guillemot plunged into the sea to avoid pursuit.

The dives were spectacular and even puffins were chosen. I felt an irrational surge of anger. Not far away were the plucked, downy feathers of an eaten eider. Nature is neither humane nor cruel; in the main it has no feeling. It is a matter of blind survival with no respect or quarter given. Death is a meal and life means responding to sun, rain, hunger and thirst.

In the sound the fishermen continued to fish for sand eels and a helicopter from an oil rig flew by. Man needs food, but to survive with meaning he needs far more than fish meal made from sand eels, oil, the grind of routine and the grasping for material possessions. He needs an awareness of his position, an understanding of his achievements and an appreciation of the beauty around him, and which depends on him; only then can he gain contentment and purpose.

I had been travelling for several weeks; on the farm, harvest would be ready and I would be needed. I turned towards the harbour.

Reflections

My journeys showed that although Britain is a grossly over-crowded collection of islands, it is still possible to visit remote places and to find solitude and beauty. I hope that by writing this book others too will be attracted to share some of the experiences that I enjoyed. Such a wish is not a contradiction, as it is possible for more people to interest themselves in the countryside without disturbing its wildlife or destroying its beauty. However it does mean that if areas such as the Peak National Park, as well as some of our islands and bird reserves, wish to retain their character and wealth, access will have to be controlled. It has become fashionable over recent years to advocate the opening up of the countryside, with unrestricted access, but such an approach could lead to disasters as great as those inflicted by development and pollution.

Controlled access and the use of permits would be required; a system that worked extremely well at Minsmere, when I first visited the reserve many years ago. It would encourage people to become "travellers" rather than "tourists", requiring them to plan, observe, understand and exercise patience. The tourist simply pays and demands, to get entertainment rather than fulfilment; he or she could be catered for adequately at resorts, zoos, and wildlife parks.

Pressure from people will increase anyway, when it is realised that the main reward from the technological revolution is, for the first time in the history of man, freedom from work. It is an exciting prospect and should not be feared, but prepared for, even in our schools, to be used and enjoyed. Pack, an old countryman who corresponded with me over several years, had the answer: "It is time to start teaching people how to be unemployed. Establish unemployment schools, parallel and opposite to technical schools, with 'O' levels in qualified loafing about. How to watch birds. How to consider the lily. How to stare at the ever busy bee having a hearty suck. I deplore never attending a school to teach me these time-consuming subjects. I had to learn how to be idle the hard way, by assiduous practice; fortunately I had a natural gift."

There are dangers of course in more people wandering about the country for, as in all things, there will be those who want to abuse it or exploit it for money. Indeed, because of the threat from egg collectors and falconers I have not been able to give the exact locations of the kites, the Lake District golden eagles, and the area on Rhum where I saw the wild sea eagles. It is a sad reflection on both people and the inadequate laws that protect much of our wildlife.

Since visiting Rhum, another sea eagle has been found dead – poisoned. Yet recommendations were made years ago banning the use of poison (allegedly against moles). There are safe ways of killing moles, as shown by the Universities Federation for Animal Welfare (8 Hamilton Close, Potters Bar, Herts.). In any case the threat to birds of prey could be alleviated simply by making mole control the responsibility of the Ministry of Agriculture and fining any landowner with poisoned carcasses on his land. Such a solution, it seems, is much too simple.

In fact sensible conservation is simple, made difficult only by the lack of vision and knowledge of our politicians. Swans could be protected by banning barbed hooks and lead weights, without denying anglers their sport; instead we have committees and ineffective voluntary recommendations. Our areas of wetland and ancient forests could be protected with simple planning restrictions, without causing hardship to farmers, but again it has been a story of committees, complicated legislation and voluntary agreements, while valuable areas of importance are still being lost. There could even be a proper government department for conservation and wildlife. The politicians say that such an establishment would be too expensive, but with the Nature Conservancy Council, the Countryside Commission, Forestry Commission rangers, and some sections of the Ministry of Agriculture already in existence, the basis for such a body is already there.

The best thing about a series of journeys, however, is that they never really end, for during my wanderings I heard of other things that have aroused my interest and which will take me to new places in the future. I was attracted by the seals I saw, and want to find out more about them, and the apparent scarcity of salmon also concerned me. I was told of farmers still using horses in their fields and of craftsmen in wood and silver. More excitingly, I heard a whisper that the large blue butterfly may still survive after all; it is going to be another busy and fascinating summer.

Useful Information

For those wanting to visit some of the places mentioned, or help in the work of safeguarding our remaining wild places, the following information should be helpful.

1. *Castles and Coalfields*

The Red House Inn, Knipton, Leics.
Belvoir Castle is open on Wednesdays and Thursdays, as well as Saturday and Sunday afternoons, during the summer.
Mine visits can be arranged through the National Coal Board, Midland Region, Eastwood Hall, Eastwood, Nottingham.
Long Clawson Dairy Ltd., Long Clawson, Melton Mowbray.
Details of the Cottesmore Lurcher Show can be obtained from the Cottesmore Hunt.

2. *Cornfield Casualties*

Alisdair Dunn (potter), Kingscross, Isle of Arran.
Isle of Arran Tourist Organisation, Brodick, Arran.
Arran Nature Centre, Cladach, Brodick, Arran.

3. *Plagues, Puddings and Peaks*

Bakewell Puddings can be purchased from Bloomer's Bakery and the Bakewell Pudding Shop, Bakewell.
John Brocklehurst, The Countryman's Outfitter, Bakewell.
Information about activities in the Peak National Park from National Park Office, Aldern House, Baslow Road, Bakewell, Derbyshire.
Information about all National Parks can be obtained from Countryside Commission, John Dower House, Crescent Place, Cheltenham.

4. *Butterflies and Bustards*

The Chequered Skipper (pub), Ashton, Nr. Oundle.

Worldwide Butterflies, Compton House, Nr. Sherborne, Dorset.

The Great Bustard Trust, c/o The Tryon Gallery, 41–42 Dover St., London.

The Butterfly Conservation Society, Tudor House, Quorn, Leics.

5. *Otters and Immigrants*

The Otter Haven Project, The Vincent Wildlife Trust, Baltic Exchange Buildings, 21 Bury Street, London.

The Southern Tourist Board, Old Town Hall, Leigh Road, Eastleigh, Hampshire.

6. *Beer and Badgers*

Hall and Woodhouse Ltd., The Brewery, Blandford Forum.

The Silent Woman Inn, Coldharbour, Wareham, Dorset.

Poems from the Piddle Valley Parsonage, etc., from The Vicarage, Piddletrenthide, Dorset.

Otterton Mill, Fore Street, Otterton, Nr. Exeter.

Inch's Cider Factory, Winkleigh, Devon.

The King's Arms, Winkleigh, Devon.

The Wildlife Research Centre (deer farming), Middle Garland, Chulmleigh, Devon.

The Ashley Countryside Collection (T. R. Blackford), Ashley House, Wembworthy, Chulmleigh, Devon.

Castle Drogo (owned by the National Trust), Drewsteignton, Devon.

7. *Carvings and Kites*

The Welsh Folk Museum (part of the National Museum of Wales), St. Fagans, Cardiff.

Cors Tregaron (Tregaron Bog), National Nature Reserve; permits from the Nature Conservancy Council, Plas Gogerddan, Aberystwyth, Dyfed.

Kites: I also saw kites at the R.S.P.B. Gwenffrwd and Dinas Reserve, Llandovery, Dyfed.

Information on accommodation and craftsmen in Wales from the Welsh Tourist Board, 2 Fitzalan Road, Cardiff.

8. *Harbours and Havens*

Details of visits to Skomer from The Secretary, West Wales Naturalists' Trust, 7 Market Street, Haverfordwest, Pembrokeshire, Dyfed.

The Redgate Bird Sanctuary, Exmouth, Devon.

R.S.P.C.A. Wildlife Field Unit, Little Creech, Taunton, Somerset.

9. *Marshes and Madness*

Norfolk Naturalists' Trust, 72 Cathedral Close, Norwich.

Hickling Broad National Nature Reserve (closed Tuesdays), Warden's Office, Stubb Road, Hickling, Norwich.

The Swan Rescue Service, Sparham, Norfolk.

The Otter Trust, Earsham, Nr. Bungay, Suffolk.

Emily Mayer (taxidermist), Stockman's Cottage, Dickleburgh, Diss, Norfolk.

Ottignons (wood reproductions), Langmere Hall, Langmere Green, Nr. Dickleburgh.

Minsmere: details of all R.S.P.B. reserves from The R.S.P.B., The Lodge, Sandy, Beds.

10. *Horses and Harness*

The Tufton Arms Hotel, Appleby, Cumbria.

The Fairlight Restaurant, Glenridding, Ullswater.

Cumbria Tourist Board, Ellerthwaite, Windermere.

11. *Fish, Firewater, Forests and Fur*

Scottish Tourist Board, 23, Ravelston Terrace, Edinburgh.

R.S.P.B. Reserve at Loch Garten; R.S.P.B. Scottish Office, 17 Regent Terrace, Edinburgh.

The Highland Wildlife Park, Kincraig, Kingussie.

N.C.C. (Scottish Headquarters), 12 Hope Terrace, Edinburgh.

The Keeper, Reindeer Company Ltd., Aviemore, Inverness-shire.

12. *Eagles and Eyries*

The Chief Warden, White House, Kinloch, Isle of Rhum.

Bookings for Kinloch Castle can be made through Hebridean Holidays Ltd., 91 Rose Street, Edinburgh.

13. *Islands and Oil*

The Shetland Tourist Organisation, Lerwick, Shetland.

Acknowledgments

While on my "journeys" I received valuable help from many people and organisations. It will also be clear from the text that I cannot thank all of them by name; some would not want their privacy disturbed still further and others would wish to preserve their anonymity for obvious reasons. However I am very grateful to all of them.

I would particularly like to thank my family; brother John, my parents, sister, and sister-in-law, all had to do my work on the farm while I was away. Also to Philippa Scoones, Gordon Stuart and Roger Tidman, who made good travelling companions for some of the trips. Thanks are due to Teresa and Christine Brown for typing the final draft and to Fiona Silver for the fine illustrations.

The organisations that helped me were The Royal Society for the Protection of Birds, the Friends of the Earth, the Nature Conservancy Council, the Forestry Commission, the Ministry of Agriculture, the Vale of Belvoir Protection Group, the National Coal Board, the Universities Federation for Animal Welfare, the Royal Society for the Prevention of Cruelty to Animals, Texaco Ltd., B.P. Ltd., Hall and Woodhouse Ltd., the Central Electricity Generating Board, the British Trust for Ornithology, British Nuclear Fuels Ltd., the Orielton Field Centre, the Milford Haven Conservancy Board, the West Wales Naturalists' Trust and the Norfolk Naturalists' Trust.

In the Vale of Belvoir I received valuable help from Mr. A. C. Thompson, Mike Nicholas, Allenby Stephenson, Mr. A. G. Wyman, and John and Pussy Hawkesworth. James Cadbury of the R.S.P.B. advised on corncrakes, Alisdair Dunn and Howard Walker helped on Arran. In the Peak District assistance was received from Clarence Daniel, John Brocklehurst, Mr. Eric Bloomer, Dr. A. C. Warne of the N.C.C. and Dr. D. Yalden of Manchester University. My sister and brother-in-law, Mary and Brian West, gave me a roof over my head.

Miriam Rothschild, Gordon Beningfield and Robert Goodden revealed the beautiful world of butterflies, and the idiosyncrasies of the great bustard were explained by the Hon. Aylmer Tryon, Dr. Nigel Collar and Paul Goriup. The Hon. Vincent Weir, Philip Wayre, Angela King and Ian Linn of Exeter University told me much about otters. Further help in the south and west came from Les and May Drake, John Harbour, Mr. and Mrs. Charlie Hawke, Dennis Hawkes, Muriel Pike, Rev. and Mrs. D. Parry, Dr. John Henshaw, Mr. and Mrs. R. Blackford, David and Ruth Murray, John Hughes and Mrs. B. Massault.

My journeys through Wales were made easier by Gwyndaf Breese, Mr. and Mrs. Peter Brown, Peter Davies, Arthur Lewis, Tony Pickup, Roger Lovegrove, Michael Alexander and Dr. Chris Perrins. In East Anglia Clare and Roger Tidman were generous with their time and hospitality, as were Nancy Gull and Ethel, Stewart Linsell, Len and Sheila Baker, Michael Bignold, Emily Mayer, Jeremy Sorenson, Mr. D. Gledhill, and Sir Laurens van der Post.

Help in the Lake District arrived from Ian Armstrong and his R.S.P.B. wardens, Mr. and Mrs. Dennis Kitching, Mandy Stamper, Alan and Mrs. Wear, Scott and Kathie Naylor, Fritz and Clare Fuchs, Harold Thompson and Jake Kelly. Scottish and Shetland aid came from Bill Anderson, Sheila Stuart, Dr. Ted Needham, Dr. Derek Mills, Alistair Scott, Strawn Stewart, Willie Forsythe, James MacKenzie, Eddie Orbell, Stuart Taylor, George Massey, Isabel MacDonald, Alan Smith, Tilley Dansie, Dr. Ethel Lindgren, George Thompson, Janet Chisholm, John Love, Colin Browne, Peter Duncan and Wyn and John MacIver. Shetlanders included Jim Tate, Mr. and Mrs. Peterson, Bobby Tulloch, Dr. Karam, Gibbie Gray and Mr. and Mrs. Kenny Hughson.

John Parslow of the R.S.P.B. and Jean Ross of the N.C.C. gave me much valuable general help.

I am also grateful to William Deedes and Morrison Halcrow

of the *Daily Telegraph*, Michael Clayton of *Horse and Hound* and Tony Jackson of the *Shooting Times* and *Country Magazine* for wanting articles from some of the journeys. Finally thanks are due to Ion Trewin and Morag Robinson of Hodder and Stoughton for their patience and guidance.

Index

~~Hobby~~
{ Carluke area   I. Poppy
{ Eagle owls.

Chon

Chough.

M.M Prush
Buds.

Bl.. Redstart

Dottrel (Cym)

Ptarmigan
all nts (2/r)